LANCASTER
THE BIOGRAPHY

SQUADRON LEADER TONY IVESON, DFC
FORMER PILOT, 617 SQUADRON ('THE DAMBUSTERS')
AND BRIAN MILTON

ANDRE
DEUTSCH

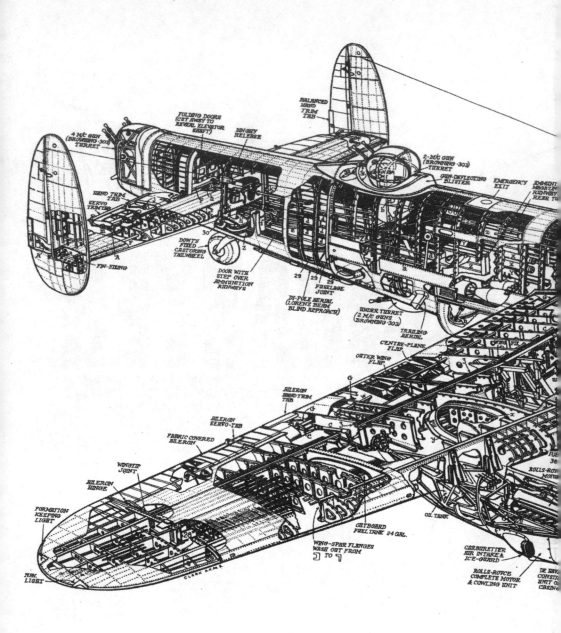

4 M/C GUN
(BROWNING ·303)
TURRET

FOLDING DOORS
(CUT AWAY TO
REVEAL ELEVATOR
SHAFT)

DINGHY
RELEASE

BALANCED
HAND
TRIM
TAB

2-M/C GUN
(BROWNING ·303)
TURRET

GUN-DEFLECTING
BLISTER

EMERGENCY
EXIT

AMMUNI
MAGAZIN
RUNNING
REAR TU

HAND TRIM
TAB

SERVO
TRIM-TAB

FIN-FILLING

DOWTY
FIXED
CASTORING
TAILWHEEL

DOOR WITH
STEP OVER
AMMUNITION
RUNWAYS

29   25   25
28
FUSELAGE
JOINT

DI-POLE AERIAL
(LORENZ BEAM
BLIND APPROACH)

UNDER TURRET
2 M/C GUNS
(BROWNING ·303)

TRAILING
AERIAL

CENTRE-PLANE
FLAP

OUTER WING
FLAP

GUN FIL

3

AILERON
HAND TRIM
TAB

FUE
36

AILERON
SERVO-TAB

ROLLS-ROY
MOTOR

FABRIC COVERED
AILERON

WINGTIP
JOINT

AILERON
HINGE

FORMATION
KEEPING
LIGHT

OIL TANK

OUTBOARD
FUEL TANK 114 GAL.

WING-SPAR FLANGES
WASH OUT FROM
⅃ TO ⅂

CARBURETTER
AIR INTAKE &
ICE-GUARD

DE HAVIL
CONSTA
UNIT OI
CASING

NAV.
LIGHT

CLARK AERO.

ROLLS-ROYCE
COMPLETE MOTOR
& COWLING UNIT

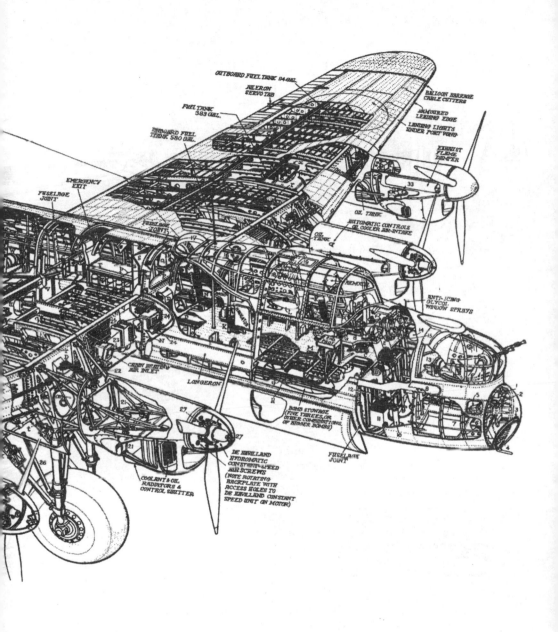

OUTBOARD FUEL TANK 114 GAL.

AILERON SERVO TAB

FUEL TANK 383 GAL.

INBOARD FUEL TANK 580 GAL.

BALLOON BARRAGE CABLE CUTTERS

ARMOURED LEADING EDGE

LANDING LIGHTS UNDER PORT WING

EXHAUST FLAME DAMPER

EMERGENCY EXIT

FUSELAGE JOINT

OIL TANK.

AUTOMATIC CONTROLS OIL COOLER AIR-INTAKE

FRONT SPAR JOINT

OIL TANK

ANTI-ICING GLYCOL WINDOW SPRAYS

CABIN HEATING AIR INLET

LONGERON

CARRY HEATING AIR INLET

BOMB STOWAGE (FIVE THREES, OR OTHER COMBINATIONS OF BIGGER BOMBS)

FUSELAGE JOINT

COOLANT & OIL RADIATORS & CONTROL SHUTTER.

DE HAVILLAND HYDROMATIC CONSTANT-SPEED AIR SCREWS (NOTE ROTATING BACKPLATE WITH ACCESS HOLES TO DE HAVILLAND CONSTANT SPEED UNIT ON MOTOR)

Published in 2009 by André Deutsch
An imprint of the Carlton Publishing Group
20 Mortimer Street
London W1T 3JW

10 9 8 7 6 5 4 3 2 1

ISBN 978 0 233 00270 5

Printed in and bound in the UK by CPI Mackays, Chatham ME5 8TD

ACKNOWLEDGEMENTS

The verses from 'Friends Ain't Supposed to Die When They're Young'
from Billy Bishop Goes to War are reproduced by kind permission of
John Maclachlan Gray and Eric Peterson.

Lie in the Dark and Listen is reproduced by kind permission of the
Noël Coward Estate.

We had a great deal of help from the following people and
organisations, without whose insight, kindness and attention we would
not have been able to write this book. We hope they come to feel that it
was worth the effort:
Nigel Baldwin, Reg Barker, Alex Beetham, Sir Michael Beetham,
John Bell, David Birch, Philip Birtles, Stan Bradford, Don Briggs,
Jim Brookman, Eric Brown, Tony Butler, Charles Clarke, Geoffrey
Claridge, Peter Clegg, Peter Collins, Dennis Cooper, Gerald Coulson,
Seb Cox, Colin Cruddas, Lettice Curtis, Sir John Curtiss, Jim Dooley,
Patrick Dorehill, Rolf Ebhardt, Peter Elliot, David Fellowes, Michael
Fopp, Benny Goodman, Gerald Coulson, Ray Grayston, George
Hart, Michael Hedgeland, Julian Hellebrand, Jim Heyworth, Henry
Horscroft, Robert Horsley, Colin Hudson, Fred Hulance, George
Johnson, John Langston, Rosemary Lapham, Michael Leckie, Stephen
Lewis, the Lincolnshire Lancaster Society, Grant McDonald, Robert
Mason, John Maynard, Les Munro, Jim Norris, Rupert Noye, Heinz
Orlowski, Rob Owen, Fred & Harold Panton, Harold Penrose, Al
Pinner, Dennis Potter, the Press Association, Douglas Radcliffe, RAF
Club, RAF News, Andrew Renwick, Clive Richards, Kurt Schulze,
Vincent Stanley, Fred 'Doc' Sutherland, Michael Turner, Eric Verdon-
Roe, Rob Wiffen, Jinny Wootton.

CONTENTS

Foreword

This is the story of the few men left alive, the 'last witnesses', and the superb aircraft in which they flew in World War Two, the Avro Lancaster.

I am proud to have been one of them.

Though many of us are aged over 80 and a few have even passed their 90th year, it is a young man's story. We were the cutting edge of the 'Shining Sword' that 'Bomber' Harris dubbed the Lancaster, and survivors of the Bomber Offensive in which 55,573 young men who lost their lives as we endeavoured to stop Hitler ruling the world.

I joined the RAF straight from school in 1941, trained as a pilot in America and entered Bomber Command to fly Lancasters in the Autumn of 1943. I loved the Lancaster. It was a friendly aircraft in lay-out, it felt right, it handled beautifully and was a delight to fly. If it was heavier on the controls than we now consider proper in a modern aircraft, back then this weight gave a young pilot confidence, and you got used to it.

By the end of the war, more Lancasters were produced than any other heavy bomber, and it was generally acknowledged to be the finest heavy bomber of any nation. I went on to complete over 2,000 hours on them.

Having spent over 40 years on the active list and flown a wide variety of aircraft in the Royal Air Force inventory, including the Canberra and all three V-bombers, I have often been asked which is my favourite aircraft?

I always reply, the Lancaster. It was my first love at the age of 20 in 1943 and has remained my favourite throughout my flying career.

The Lancaster, with its four beautiful Merlin engines that saw so many of us through our tours, was almost the perfect aircraft.

There are not many of us left now, with experience of flying it.

In another few years, inevitably, none will be left, and historians will be able to throw their opinions around with the insouciant knowledge that those of us who were actually there will not be able to contradict them

Tony Iveson is right to dub us – a generation seventy years older than the young men alive today – the 'last witnesses'.

To those of us who shared the unique experience of flying and fighting in Lancasters, we have a common bond.

We commend the values of that bond to the younger generations that follow us.

Sir Michael Beetham GCB CBE DFC AFC
Marshal of the Royal Air Force

'In this land of hours a same people has lived for generation to generation up till now. They, by their courage and their virtues, have handed it on to us, a country that is free. They certainly deserve our praise, for it was not without blood and toil that they handed it down to us of the present generation. We are capable of taking risks and of estimating them beforehand. The man who can most truly be accounted brave is he who knows best the meaning of what is sweet in life, and then goes out undeterred to meet what is to come. In the fight, they thought it more honourable to suffer death than to save themselves. Remember, posterity can only be for the free, and that freedom is the sure possession of those alone who have the courage to defend it.'

Pericles, Greek statesman

As Admiral of the Athenian fleet in 430BC, Pericles gave a funeral oration for the young Athenians who had fallen in action during the first era of the Peloponnesian Wars.

'When I look around to see how we can win the war I see that there is only one sure path. We have no continental army which can defeat the German military power. The blockade is broken and Hitler has Asia, and probably Africa to draw from. Should he be repulsed here or not try invasion, he will recoil eastward, and we have nothing to stop him. But there is one thing that will bring him back and bring him down, and that is an absolutely devastating, exterminating attack by very heavy bombers from this country upon all of the Nazi homeland.'

Winston Churchill

Churchill wrote this on 8 July 1940, and it is quoted by his biographer Martin Gilbert in *Finest Hour* (William Heineman Ltd, 1983). In 1982, Sir Arthur Harris commented to Gilbert: 'It was the origin of the idea of bombing the enemy out of the war. I should have been proud of it. But it originated with Winston.'

Prologue

It was day 16 of the ninetieth year of my life.

Sixty-three years after I had last captained one, I was going to get my hands on the controls of a Lancaster bomber again.

It was foggy on the dawn of that Saturday – 27 September 2008. I had stayed overnight at the Petwood Hotel in Woodhall Spa, Lincolnshire, which was once the wartime Officer's Mess of 617 'Dambuster' Squadron, a squadron in which I had served.

We set out early for the drive to nearby RAF Coningsby, home of the Battle of Britain Memorial Flight – which includes a Spitfire, a Hurricane and the greatest of all the wartime bombers, an Avro Lancaster.

I was to fly a Lancaster again from the 'dicky' seat. Lancasters normally did not have a second pilot's seat, this one does.

But am I still a capable pilot?

This time, preparing to fly was very different.

I dressed up in long socks, boots, and a sweater, over all of which I put on an overall. I had to be fitted for a 'bone-dome', or flight helmet, measured front and back, and ear to ear. It wasn't very comfortable.

As we approached the Lancaster on the runway, I described to *Daily Telegraph* Chief Reporter Gordon Rayner what went on in the aircraft when we used it for bombing – what the mid-upper gunner, the wireless operator and the rear gunner all did. I was there as Chairman of the Bomber Command Association to launch our £2 million campaign for a permanent memorial. Bomber Command lost 55,573 airmen during the Second World War yet there has never been a permanent memorial to those brave souls. The *Daily Telegraph* was supporting the campaign and Gordon was there to cover my flight in the Lancaster.

I explained the Lancaster's controls to Gordon – as much as I could remember of them, anyway. I recalled a reasonable amount because, compared with today's aircraft, they were very simple. If there are four dials, they are the boost gauges; four more dials are the rev-counters and if there are four levers they are the throttles. Four more levers, pitch control. The trimmers and the stick were straightforward, and the blind-flying panel was common to all RAF and American aircraft. That was easy.

When we are ready to fly, I am asked to sit in the wireless operator's position. This is a desk on the port side of the aircraft, behind the navigator and right beside the main spar, a huge piece of metal that runs right across the body of the plane from one wing to the other. Without that spar the aircraft would fall apart, but its presence makes for a very cramped interior.

To my left is the window that looks out on to the port engine. The propeller is a little further forward of the wireless operator's position but the noise is still very loud.

In front of me are a couple of radio sets, along with two or three pieces of communications equipment, about 3ft (90 cm) square, which, with today's technology, could now be made small enough to fit in your pocket.

I remain in this seat for 20 minutes, for take-off, and the first fly-by we perform past Lincoln Cathedral. Inevitably, I start to think back to my operational flying days, how the wireless operator got in here, plugged himself in, fixed up his oxygen, and that's where he stayed – on the *Tirpitz* trip, for example – for $12^1/2$ hours! He may have got up occasionally to stretch his legs, but this would have been his position for most of that time, as he listened for any possible messages.

I suddenly wish that, in my operational time in the squadron, I had sat in the wireless operator's cubbyhole – I would have been so much more sympathetic to the poor bugger. He was the one who controlled the heat, and the rest of us were always complaining about not getting enough heat, while he sat there and roasted.

I also realise why, back in 1945, my own wireless operator had moved so quickly to the back of the aircraft when I said, 'Stand by to abandon aircraft', over Bergen, in northern Norway. The engine that had been set on fire was right *there*, outside his window, the flames shooting by… no wonder he got up and went to the rear.

My thoughts are interrupted when the Lancaster pilot, Flight Lieutenant Mike Leckey, asks me to come forward.

The Lancaster is an aircraft where the flight engineer always had a little seat – the 'dicky' seat – which could be clipped on to a bar. On this Lancaster, with dual controls, I am to fly the aircraft from the dicky seat.

I feel overwhelmed by the fact that there is so little room in the cockpit. With the stick between your knees and your feet on the rudder bar, you have very little room for manoeuvre. The flight deck, if you could call it that, is nothing like as spacious as I remember. It is very cramped indeed.

I am also conscious, looking around me, that the Lancaster was a war machine. That's what it was built for, and that's what it was. There was hardly any spare space anywhere. It was all utilised for two purposes, to bring the heaviest weight of bombs to the enemy and to defend itself while doing so.

I sit in the right-hand seat with a cushion back, and the rudder bar at my feet.

Mike asks, 'Would you like to fly it?'

I say yes and take control.

I am lined up on the DR (Direct Reading) compass and gradually the nose starts to swing. I try to correct it, and it doesn't take any bloody notice!

'Let's do a turn-around,' Mike says, and I am amazed at how heavy it is.

Did I really control this damned thing for hour after hour?

I know we had 'George', the automatic pilot and I had used George whenever possible on operations, but a lot of the time I would be flying manually. On this trip, I could have trimmed it differently. Mike had already set the trim so I wasn't about to disturb it, but it shakes me, the force I need to apply to make it go where I want.

We have three display jobs to do. After making four passes around Lincoln Cathedral with me in the wireless operator's position, we fly on to Winthorpe in Newark, a heavy conversion airfield when I flew Stirlings in 1943, now an exhibition ground where 619 Squadron are re-dedicating their memorial.

We complete a couple of passes, dive and pull up. Then we turn back towards the coast and Mike spots a Dakota and manoeuvres into formation with it, flying number three to the left of it. The Dak's door is open, because they keep it open. It is from Coningsby and part of the Battle of Britain Memorial Flight. We are number three and he decides to go through and fly the number two position, to the Dakota's starboard side. Then we fly line-astern, looking up at the Dak's tail-wheel rocking above me. It is a wonderful sensation to be back in an RAF aircraft, formating on another.

We pull off, flying in the direction of Cleethorpes where the promenade is full of cars and people who have come to see the Lancaster. We pull out to sea, where Mike performs a steep turn, the ocean speeding past, around 600ft (182m) below us.

'Okay,' Mike says, 'take it back.'

'I'd like to try some turns,' I reply.

But I'm not in control of the damn thing!

I really grip the wheel and fly it for a while. I feel some of my old skills coming back…

Don't be bloody silly, you haven't touched controls like these for 60 years. You haven't touched any aeroplane for donkey's years. How can you expect to slot straight back into it?

If I'd started again with Wellingtons, and built back up to Lancasters, I might have been able to cope. It was just a case of practice…

But I don't want to land it, so I give it back to Mike.

We landed. I really had the strangest feelings when I got out. I thought, 'I cannot believe I flew these things over a period of months, on operations, day and night.'

I could not do it now. I could not *possibly* do it now.

I stood on the tarmac and looked at the Lancaster, and felt emotional for the number of Lancasters – nearly 4,000 – that we had lost, and the number of young men we had lost with them.

I looked at it and thought, 'How would you get out if the thing was on fire?' If you were the wireless operator, you would have to duck under the mid-upper gunner. You would be very lucky to get to the back door. I imagined an NCO crew, just through their training, having been posted straight into a squadron with no extra flying hours, on their first trip, somewhere deep in German territory on a nasty winter's night in late 1943.

I really felt emotional about it. My friend Mary came across to meet me. I had to hug her. I said to her, 'I am not suggesting I was a sort of superman in those days, I'm not being conceited about it, but I really don't know how we did it.'

In my present age and situation, I couldn't.

Maybe with training I could.

You might ask, why would I expect at the age of 89 to be able to fly the way I did when I was 24? I don't know whether that's what I really expected, but I was surprised that I couldn't do it. The bloody thing was so heavy and I felt it needed an awful lot of rudder, much more than I remembered.

If I had been on my own, of course, I might have sorted out the throttles, and I would have trimmed it slightly differently. Who knows? Yet I may have got it totally wrong.

The DR compass, I could not fly a straight line on that. And when I started flying on the directional gyro and that kept on wandering. That's normally the sign of a beginner pilot. *A sprog.* Me!

I don't know what Michael Leckey thought. He was too courteous to comment.

How the hell did we do it all those years ago?

CHAPTER ONE

The Bergen Incident

January 12, 1945

It did not help that morning that my Lancaster, F-Fox, had brake failure. We had started her up before dawn and were about to move off when we discovered our problem. To taxi halfway around the airfield with no brake pressure and a 12,000lbs Tallboy bomb on board, just wasn't on. It was not possible to fix it immediately. We shut down.

F-Fox was a Mark I Lancaster which my crew flew regularly, first off the line in the fourth production batch of 250 ordered back in 1942. Despite being an Avro Lancaster, she was built by Metropolitan Vickers in Moseley Road, Manchester. AJ-F-Fox, number ME554, was delivered in November 1943 straight to 617 'Dambuster' Squadron six months after the famous Dams Raid. I did not join the squadron until 14 months after the raid, eight months after F-Fox turned up. She came to me and my crew third-hand but in good condition, even though she had been to exotic places and done difficult things. Bomber Command's ground crews were famous for the long, freezing hours they put into servicing 'their' aircraft and keeping them in top condition.

Before I arrived, F-Fox had taken part in the Toulouse Raid in early April 1944, and the attack on the Juvisy rail yards 13 days later. She had also bombed Munich on the 25 April raid, all attacks led by Leonard Cheshire VC. The aircraft had accommodated an extended crew – 13 in all instead of the usual 7 – on the night before D-Day, 5/6 June, when 617 Squadron fooled the Germans with *Operation Taxable*. They confused the German raider, making the enemy think that the invasion fleet was approaching Calais and not Normandy. Three of the extra men on board spent hours chucking 'Window' – thousands of small metallic strips – out of the door at four-second intervals, in a rotating timetable with straight-line flights of 35 seconds, then reversing for 32 seconds, and then back again for 35 seconds, hour after hour. It had to be *absolutely* exact to give the German radar the impression that an invasion fleet was approaching and that is why the most elite bomber squadron in the RAF was chosen to make it happen.

I had missed that, along with the last Cheshire-led operation conducted by the surviving Dambuster legends – New Zealander Les Munro, Australians Dave

Shannon and Mick Martin, and American Joe McCarthy. Cheshire was relieved of command (squadron commanders served a set period in this highly stressful position before being stood down) the day after he invited me to join the squadron, and was soon to receive a Victoria Cross. The new 617 commander, James Tait – always known as Willie – already had three DSOs and a DFC. He was taking over a hard-bitten squadron that naturally set out to test him. Like all the wartime 617 Squadron aircrew who were not 'originals', I was very conscious of the reputation they had established and the absolute necessity of maintaining those high standards. My crew was the first to join the Squadron without any previous bombing experience.

Perhaps it was to be expected that my astounded flight commander, the Australian veteran David Shannon, exploded: 'Sprogs like you – they'll have you for breakfast!' Though he was only 22 years old, he had a right to make that comment. Shannon had been one of the eight Dambuster Squadron pilots that followed Guy Gibson in the first wave to attack the Mohne Dam; by the time I joined 617 he had won four serious gongs, two DSO's and two DFC's.

My time on 617 in the second half of 1944 included all three Lancaster raids against 'The Beast', the giant German battleship *Tirpitz*. F-Fox had seen me and my crew safely through some difficult spots, including an extremely dangerous landing in a tiny Russian field. By now Tait had been posted out with a fourth DSO and a second DFC to his credit and we had a new squadron commander for our first raid of the new year. We were led on the operation that January day by a Canadian, Johnny Fauquier, in an attack against German U-Boat pens in the Norwegian port of Bergen. Fauquier had been in the Canadian 6 Group, first as commander of a Pathfinder Squadron, later a full group commander with the rank of Air Commodore. He chose to drop down to Group Captain rank – similar to the drop from Brigadier to full Colonel – to take over 617 after Tait.

I did not know much about Fauquier because I had been on leave over Christmas. When I came back, Fauquier had been there a few days, and we only had a few days more before the Bergen trip. It would be my first operational flight led by him. He chose to fly the Mosquito with which 617 Squadron was equipped, and which Cheshire had often used in his pioneering roles as a 'Master Bomber'.

It was typical winter weather at Woodhall Spa. There had been snow, and soldiers had come in to clear it off the runway. The day was clear, no low cloud, no rain, no mist. We had woken in darkness ready for a seven o'clock takeoff, and prepared for a round-trip flight of 900 miles.

All seven of us in F-Fox were pretty irritated at discovering the brake fault, but we were determined to make the raid anyway. Transport took us over to the reserve aircraft (M-Mike, NG-181) which had been flown on the second and third *Tirpitz* attacks. Bergen was to be its third operation. M-Mike was quite new, having been one of 400 Lancaster I's in the fourth production batch made by

Armstrong Whitworth in Coventry. They were still churning Lancasters out there at the rate of 14 per week as we climbed on board M-Mike. We went through the checks and taxied out, but by the time we got airborne the rest of the squadron had gone. I took M-Mike into a climb and set off after them, looking for a short cut. We were not to know that three of us would not return that evening.

Nor did we know that it would be my last operation with 617.

Heinz Orlowski, the Luftwaffe pilot responsible for three of my crew not making it home from that raid, was 21 years old at the time; four years younger than me. He was born on 28 September, 1923 in Loetzen in East Prussia, a small town of about 20,000 people, north of Warsaw, Poland. Loetzen was almost the furthest east one could go in the Germany that then existed. The son of a labourer, Orlowski was nine years old when Hitler came to power, and a teenager when the growing German Wehrmacht established the town as an Army area headquarters. The German army had held no attractions for Heinz Orlowski though, and on 1 December 1941, barely 18 years old, he volunteered for service in the Luftwaffe. This was six days before Pearl Harbour brought the United States into the conflict and made it truly a world war.

Orlowski trained as a non-commissioned officer, an Unteroffizier, over an 18 month period in various parts of Germany. He reached flying operational proficiency towards the end of 1944 and graduated to fly the best of Germany's wartime fighters, the Focke Wulf 190. At the age of 21 he was posted to one of the coldest places on earth, up near the Barents Sea west of Murmansk, the airfield of Petsamo in northern Finland. Later he was to say about the fighting conditions he encountered: 'It was not easier and not more difficult than the rest of the Russian Front, but fundamentally different.'

The aircraft he was allocated, the FW190 A-8 had a top speed of 408 miles an hour at 16,000ft (4,876m), able to climb at 2,500ft (762m) per minute with a ceiling of 37,000ft (11,277m) and a range of 500 miles. The FW190's Mark 108 30mm cannon were powerful enough to destroy most heavy bombers with just two or three hits. In the right hands, it was a deadly killer of Lancasters.

The New Year attack on Bergen was supposed to be one of the less dangerous raids by 617 Squadron, undertaken, as in the *Tirpitz* attacks, alongside 9 Squadron, the only other RAF Lancaster Squadron able to carry Tallboys. We were to be protected by 13 Mustang fighters, equipped with long range fuel tanks and said to be the best escort fighter in the world, flown by 315 Polish Squadron. We had a lot of faith in Polish pilots. The highest-scoring squadron in the Battle of Britain had been Polish. We also had two Mosquitoes with us from 100 Group, aside from Fauquier's. Their specific role was to jam enemy transmissions and harass German fighters. Altogether, there were 31 aircraft involved in the attack.

I knew my crew well, we had been through a lot together. We were all young. I may have been the oldest at 25, having started as a sergeant pilot at 20 and been made a squadron leader less than five years on. It was a foible of mine to be correctly dressed on bombing raids, shirt and tie both done up correctly. In the event of being shot down and involuntarily meeting a German officer, I did not want him to think that RAF officers were scruff-buckets.

My flight engineer, a young Welshman called Desmond 'Taffy' Phillips, was only 20. He had already saved our lives by his quick actions on a terrible power-affected take-off on the second *Tirpitz* raid, and was to perform similar life-saving feats over Bergen. Taffy was the last of my crew to join me at the Heavy Conversion Unit four weeks before we became part of 617; he had not needed the kind of initial training the rest of the crew went through. Taffy's job as a flight engineer meant he concentrated purely on the engine controls, nothing like the same training as navigators, wireless operators, bomb-aimers and gunners. But he knew his aeroplane.

My navigator, Jack Harrison, was a Yorkshireman from Sheffield, and my bomb-aimer Frank Chance, a Londoner. This was their first tour, a tour normally consisting of 30 operations, and we had got together in the usual Bomber Command way. At OTU – Operational Training Unit – we had been left, as was usual RAF practice, to mill around together in a hangar, each of us trying to make shrewd judgements about whom we wanted to risk our necks with. Jack Harrison told me later that he had managed to get a look at my log book and discovered I had a lot of flying hours. He said he thought it might be useful to have an experienced pilot, and was the first to come up to me. He then said he knew someone who might be a good bomb-aimer, and introduced Frank Chance, taciturn and mature beyond his years.

My wireless operator, Alan Tittle, was a quiet, self-contained individual from Staffordshire. He said very little and rarely joined us when we went out together to the pub. He was a restrained young man, just 21 years old.

Ted Wass, our rear gunner, came from Peterborough. Leslie Smith, mid-upper gunner, was the only one who had any kind of previous bomber experience prior to joining 617 Squadron, even if it was not on wartime operations. He had been in a Wellington crew up at Lossiemouth, on the bleak Scottish shores east of Inverness, in an OTU. His aircraft had crashed on a night training flight, and he was the only survivor. He did not appear to have been traumatised by this experience. He was a cheerful Cockney, or rather he spoke like a Cockney, although he came from Edmonton, not quite within the sound of Bow Bells. His party trick was to eat razor blades.

As we played catch-up in M-Mike, the rest of the squadron was flying up to Peterhead, in the northeast corner of Scotland, where they were going to pick up the Polish Mustangs. They then planned a dog-leg straight to Bergen across more than 300 miles of open sea. Because we were late, my navigator set a course straight across the North Sea direct to Bergen and we settled down to make a journey of 750 miles, estimating a rendezvous three hours away. Most of the flying was done by 'George', the automatic pilot, though each of us checked our various jobs. The navigator had given me a course to fly and I set 'George', with each of us checking the course from time to time. The navigation system, GEE, was a form of radar operated through a chain of stations on the east coast of Britain which the navigator could monitor. Jack Harrison tuned into these stations and took bearings from one, then another, even a third. Where the plots converged on the map, gave us our position. GEE was very accurate. Harrison could get a pretty good idea of the wind situation in the first hour or so because of GEE, to plot things accurately. At some stage German 'jamming' would have taken effect, but that point was quite a distance from our shores.

Leaving Lincolnshire flying out over the North Sea, there was nothing to look at aside from the odd ship. The gunners tested their guns, letting me know first before firing a burst or two. I did not have a mid-upper turret at the time; these had been removed for the *Tirpitz* raids and never put back. Leslie Smith came along for the ride, even though he had nothing to do, because each operation counted towards the total of 30 that added up to the end of a tour and a six-month relief from operations. Though 617 Squadron did not pay much attention to that 30-trip limit, Leslie was there as a kind of reserve.

Heinz Orlowski had flown south on 14 December 1944, heading for his new Staffel (Squadron) base at Herdla. They landed at Værnes, near Trondheim, before supposedly making the final leg of their journey to Herdla, 16 miles northwest of Bergen in Western Norway, but the dreadful weather so prevalent in December in Norway delayed the transfer. It was not until the new year, 10 January 1945, that Orlowski's Staffel could finally touch down at the small island airbase at Herdla, destined to become their permanent residence for the rest of the war. By now Orlowski had been allocated a genuine FW-190 A-8, call-sign White 11. It was in this aircraft that Orlowski was to have the chance to revenge the humiliation inflicted on him and his colleagues by their failure, through a series of bungles that had proved to be so lucky for us, to prevent the sinking of the *Tirpitz* two months earlier.

In M-Mike we observed radio silence throughout the long flight, and despite hundreds of miles over the sea without landmarks, we knew where the rest of the squadron would be at a certain time. We aimed to be there to make a rendezvous. Bergen, halfway up the Norwegian coast, is just above 60 degrees north, seven degrees south of the Arctic Circle. It was ranked second in importance only to Oslo as a Norwegian port. Its industries were ship-building, ship repairing and fitting, cod-liver oil refineries, gold and silver work. Chief exports were fish products and base metals. This was all before the war. Now, six years into it, the Germans had established a U-Boat base in Bergen to harass the vital convoys we were sending to Russia. We were after those submarine pens with our 12,000lb Tallboy bombs.

When I found my squadron I joined in with the very loose formation we termed a 'gaggle'. We did all the attacks in gaggle formation, nothing like as rigid as the American day-bombing formations of B-17 Flying Fortresses. Each Lancaster had been given a height to fly, and we checked that by having a common broadcast altimeter setting. We flew at 250ft intervals of altitude. After several trips one got accustomed to the idea of a Lancaster just ahead with its bomb doors open and the green Tallboy in sinister view, the same Barnes Wallis-designed special bomb that had sunk the *Tirpitz*. I still have a vivid memory over one target of a Lancaster sliding underneath me, or I slid over him, and the rear gunner signalling wildly, flinging his arms apart, obviously telling me to go somewhere else. It was not uncommon to be hit by 'friendly' bombs from above.

The sky was clear all the way to the target, but then we saw there was a ground haze and the Germans were pumping out smoke to make target identification difficult.

It had been an uneventful morning for Orlowski's 9 Staffel at Herdla, a beautiful clear sunny day, though very cold. As usual, some of the squadron were at cockpit readiness, and Orlowski was actually sitting down to lunch when the alarm went off. He raced to his aircraft, which had been made ready-to-scramble by his ground crew, and started up the engine at 12.49. He and a dozen others climbed furiously to 14,000ft (4,267m), getting there in less than six minutes, and soon found their British targets. The Polish Mustangs that were supposed to provide protection were nowhere to be seen, and the Focke Wulfs were able to close in without alarming the pilots of the two RAF bomber squadrons.

I steered M-Mike into the gaggle and headed towards the target. We were at 15,000ft (4,572m), all of us on oxygen. It was not particularly cold. I did not have an electrically heated suit – rear gunners always had them – because we had heat from the starboard side of the port inner engine. It came in by the wireless operator, he could control it, and always complained about 'frying, baking, roasting', whilst, further from the heat source, we kept asking him to turn it up. But it did not feel especially cold, even that close to the Arctic Circle. I remembered as we went in that on the *Tirpitz* attacks we had turned in much further north, at 65 degrees of latitude.

One of the early bombers let a bomb go down on the Bergen target in conditions of no wind. The Tallboy threw up a huge cloud of muck and dust that remained stationary over the target. Fauquier, as Master Bomber in the Mosquito, told us to orbit the target, so instead of arriving, bombing and getting away, our usual practice, we hung around waiting – fatally – for a clear view.

If we could not see the target, and with no wind there was no prospect of getting a clear view, what were we doing there? *Just messing about.*

Fauquier had a tremendous record throughout the war with the Canadians. He had been a bush pilot in the 1930s, a splendid flyer who had flown in all sorts of aeroplanes in the Canadian northern territories. He was really experienced – he had a DSO and bar and a DFC – and was regarded as a real warrior, but we should not have spent the time we did hanging around, because the inevitable happened. After a while my rear gunner, Ted Wass, said, 'Okay, skipper, we've now got the fighters.' He thought they were the Polish Mustangs, and so did I.

They were not. We learned very quickly that we had attracted a collection of some 20 Focke-Wulf 190's and Me109's. The next thing we knew there was lots of noise.

Orlowski had taken off from Herdla together with his friend, Unteroffizier Kirchner, but Kirchner's FW 190A-8, White 5, developed a gun stoppage during his first attack and he chose to return to Herdla to rectify it. As reports came in of low-flying enemy aircraft, probably the errant Polish Mustangs ground-straffing, Kirchner and a colleague, Feldwebel. Georg Lieber in FW-190A-2 - White 12 - took off again. Neither returned.

Lieber ran out of fuel and was forced to land in the freezing Arctic sea where he died of exposure. It normally took less than 90 seconds.

No one found out what happened to Kirchner, who was never seen again.

They were the only two German losses that day.

I remember there were sheets of white stuff going over the top of the canopy and the port inner engine suddenly burst into flames. At the same time, M-Mike tried to stand on its tail! A Focke-Wulf 190 had come in behind us and fired at us. He was, thankfully, not a very good shot. If he had been a yard or so to the right he would have been firing cannon shells right through the fuselage – tail to nose – and he would probably have killed us all. As it was, he hit the port fin and rudder, the port elevator and tail-plane, tearing great lumps out of them, knocking out the port inner engine and setting us on fire. Being on fire is normally fatal, especially when the seat of the blaze is close to the fuel tanks. I was a bit too busy to see that Focke-Wulf go by.

Our immediate problem was the engine blaze to my left, though I was personally struggling to stop the aircraft rearing up vertically. In the circumstances I gave the 'stand-by to abandon aircraft' order almost automatically, but I was in no position to do anything like that myself. My flight engineer, bomb-aimer and navigator were all up the front of the aircraft with me. They could see what was going on and we were struggling to control the aeroplane. If we had to bale out, our designated escape route was through a narrow forward hatch only 22 inches (56cm) wide – one of the reasons why Lancasters had the poorest record of British heavy bombers for bale-outs. The wireless operator and both gunners took their positions by the rear door.

We had frequently practiced stopping an engine fire. Having amassed 1,500 hours as an instructor, I was diligent about these matters. I often told my engineer on take-offs – when we were not operational – to cut any engine without warning. My reasoning was, do it on a nice day and get used to losing an engine, so that if it happened on operations the procedures will be routine. It worked out that way. Taffy feathered the engine immediately and stopped the prop. He cut off the fuel, running through the drills automatically. Then he fired the graviner switch, which sprayed the engine with carbon dioxide and put out the fire. We did it so fast that the fire really didn't get going. That was all down to our having practised these rapid routines. The main actor in this drama was the flight engineer, Desmond Phillips, *Taffy*.

The fire had produced a lot of flames and smoke and it must have looked to others in the squadron, and to the enemy fighters, that we were goners. We still had a Tallboy on board but I had pulled out of the squadron formation. I seemed to be on my own. I cannot remember other aircraft around, though I could hear Fauquier's instructions on the radio. At any moment my Lancaster threatened to rear up vertically, flip over and go into a fatal dive from 15,000ft (4,572m). What stopped it was my knees and my hands, pushing the control yoke forward. I stuck my knee in between the stick and my seat and was holding the heavy yoke forward with both hands.

We decided to jettison the bomb, Frank did whatever was necessary and it dropped into the sea. Aside from talking to my immediate crew, I was far too busy to talk to anyone else. I did see one Folke-Wulf climb up in front of me and do a half roll.

I remember thinking, you cheeky bugger!

Frank came up from the bomb-aimer's position and managed to find a piece of rope somewhere and tied it to the stick – with some difficulty – so he could pull it forward and get some of the strain off my arms. Taffy went back and discovered loose ends from the trimming wires to the elevator, which had been shot half to pieces. He started scrabbling with these control wires, managing to collect them and tie them on to something. Intercom communication with the rest of the crew was no longer possible, because the port inner engine provided the power for the intercom and that had been shot away. Taffy passed shouted messages through the navigator, Jack Harrison, to me, and kept asking, 'How's that?' I would reply, a little more, a little more, and eventually we got it to the point where I had some control. He tied up the trimming tabs. Then he went back and discovered three helmets on the step next to the door, and three parachutes missing!

In his combat report Orlowski said he attacked the Lancasters immediately from the front, but then rounded and made an attack on my aircraft from the rear.

'I succeeded in damaging one engine during my first attack on M-Mike from the rear. I tried to eliminate the defence and destroy the tail unit.' It looked convincing, with M-Mike trailing smoke, the inner port engine in flames and three parachutes floating away from the stricken aircraft.

The last thing my crew members in the rear part of the Lancaster – Ted Wass, Leslie Smith and Alan Tittle – had heard from me before their intercom went silent was 'prepare to abandon aircraft.' They heard nothing else, the aircraft was all over the sky and seemed to be doomed, so they baled out on their own initiative.

Convinced of one kill, Orlowski turned to chase after another Lancaster, 'Willing Willy', this one from 9 Squadron, piloted by Flight Lieutenant Ray Harris.

Harris wrote later: 'The four "Mustangs" were now getting closer when my mid-upper gunner, Mac Williams, shouted, "Christ, they're 190s, corkscrew starboard – Go!" ['The corkscrew was the standard evasive manoeuvre.] Seconds later Heinz Orlowski, flying his FW190, was on my tail and putting a salvo of cannon fire into my Lancaster which promptly put the hydraulics out of action. Four fighters made 15 separate attacks as I corkscrewed in every direction possible to evade the cannon shells. We were down to 4,000ft (1,220m) and still descending when the final attack came in.

'Then, there was silence. All four of the German machines had used up their ammunition. "Willing Winnie" was still airborne but we went down to only 1,000ft (305m) and were in very poor condition, all her turrets out of action.'

In the myths and legends formed around that day, Orlowski was said to have admired the skill and bravery of the English pilot so much that he flew along the port side of the stricken 9 Squadron aircraft, smiled, and then saluted. He thought it had been fatally injured and intended to claim it as a 'kill'. Ray Harris thought otherwise. Instead of saluting back, he drew his service revolver and shot at the fighter that had done so much to try and bring him and his aircraft down. A pistol fired against an armoured FW-190 had as much effect as a pea-shooter against a rhino. Orlowski did not seem to notice that he had been fired on with a puny pistol, and joined the other three German fighters heading back to Herdla, landing at 13.45. He had a damaged oil cooler, and claimed two Lancasters shot down. It had been the only time during his entire Luftwaffe career that Orlowski had seen a Lancaster.

'I was amazed by its huge dimensions,' he said.

As he did not have a witness for the second claim – Harris's 'Willing Willy' – and had not seen it go down, he was only awarded the first kill, us in M-Mike.

The anti-aircraft defences claimed 11 Lancasters destroyed. In fact only three were, two from 617 Squadron, one from 9 Squadron.

In M-Mike we continued our struggle, jinking all over the sky. At one stage I put the Lancaster back into the flak area, thinking that might deter the fighters from coming after us again. We did have another attack, but it didn't seem to add much to the confusion. Perhaps that was the aircraft, the 'cheeky bugger', that I saw doing an upward roll in front of me?

There were 30 Lancasters in the sky and Fauquier wanted us to continue to orbit the target until the smoke and dust cleared. By that time I was not interested in the target. My only option, flying a crippled aeroplane with a jettisoned bomb on three engines; with a fire-damaged wing and tail-plane shot to bits; lacking a rear gunner and with no top turret anyway, was to get the hell out of it.

Because of the yoke being roped forward and the tied-off trimming tabs, we seemed to have more stability. I said to Jack, 'I think I can get it back, where's the nearest airfield?'

'Sumburgh,' he said, 'right at the bottom of the main Shetland island.' He gave me a course, 224°. It was a 340-mile journey entirely over the sea.

We set off.

CHAPTER TWO

The Birth of Avro

Edwin Alliott Roe is credited as the first man in Britain to fly an aeroplane. He did it on 8 June 1908 at the age of 31 in a flying contraption he built himself, powered by a French engine, at the Brooklands Motor Racing Circuit where he was an unwelcome guest. The whole flight was measured in seconds, covering a distance of just 50 yards, and was unofficially witnessed by three men – a gate-keeper, a gardener and a friend.

Edwin Alliott Roe, born 26 April, 1877, was the fourth child of a family of seven – three girls and four boys – the son of a prosperous general practitioner, Dr Edwin Hodgson Roe and his wife, Sophia Verdon. From his schooldays Edwin was an inventor, and in his twenties he was attracted to the exciting area of aviation. This was a field of endeavour in which the French thought they led the world until the shocking news was finally confirmed that two American brothers, Wilbur and Orville Wright, were streets ahead of them.

The Wrights were staying airborne for more than an hour while the first heavier-than-air flight in Europe, all of 196ft (60m), was achieved by the Brazilian playboy Albert Santos Dumont, at the Bagatelle Park in Paris on 23 October, 1906.

In Britain there were a few hopeful aviators including Geoffrey de Havilland, Frederick Handley Page and Tommy Sopwith, with Edwin Alliott Roe among the more prominent of them.

Alliott – he used his second forename and added his mother's maiden name Verdon in 1928 to become officially A.V. Roe – had been unwelcome at Brook-lands that July day in 1908 because the racing track's management 'considered the sight of so vulgar an object as a flying machine would bring the track into disrepute.' He was soon asked to leave.

His achievement should be set against the five years of flying experience that the Wright brothers had accumulated by 1908. Wilbur was dazzling the French by accepting pretty women passengers at Le Mans, and had made a flight of 24 miles, while Orville demonstrated a full hour's flying to the US Army in Virginia.

Alliott had been in touch with the Wright brothers even before their successful flights at Kittyhawk on 17 December 1903. He was convinced he could repeat the Wright brothers' success, but he had his difficulties. The expulsion from Brook-lands was followed by a nasty letter from management:

'I shall be glad to know from you whether you intend selling your (home-built) aeroplane shed to us for £15 or will remove same by Saturday. A reply by same will oblige.'

Alliott wrote later: 'Aviation was looked on at this time as a rather fantastic form of suicide, and any would-be airman as a reckless adventurer.'

The following year, 1909, Alliott established himself in two railway arches in Lea Marshes in the East End of London, and soon pioneered – and patented – an acceptable flight control method involving a control column and rudders, a system still in use today. He and a tiny band of helpers built a triplane, and at 5 o'clock on summer mornings – to avoid turbulent thermals – they wheeled it from the arch to a suitable corner of the marshes, and there...'to the jeers of onlookers we tried to start the engine (which usually took 15 minutes). On average, we would work hard for two weeks, have a large hop, a crash, and another two weeks' work.'

On 13 July 1909, Alliott first flew 100ft (30.5m) in the triplane, a milestone because it was an all-British flying machine, including a British engine. The *Daily Mail* published photographs of it in flight. But Alliott had the same problem at Lea Marshes as he had had at Brooklands, and was threatened with prosecution, a bailiff snooping around with instructions to issue him a summons for flying over Common Land:

'Whenever the bailiff appeared I used to disappear into my hangar like a whelk into its shell, and fortunately we were always repairing the machine after a crash. At last he caught me flying it, but I was saved at the last moment from appearing in court, as Louis Bleriot had just flown the Channel in July, and they dropped the case to avoid embarrassment.'

Alliott was eventually driven out of Lea Marshes and found a site at Wembley Park in November 1909. By now known as A.V. Roe – to distinguish him from his brother Humphrey, known as H.V. Roe – A.V. was chronically short of money. Humphrey, an officer veteran of the Boer War, had already achieved some success making men's braces – 'Bullseye Braces!' – and with their mother's encouragement the two brothers went into the aviation business together. A.V. Roe & Company was formally founded on 1 January 1910. Humphrey ran the business and invested a total of £10,000 in it, while A.V. was the designer, builder and test pilot, enduring a number of early crashes learning how to control the flying machines he built.

The business survived despite him taking terrible risks. Demonstrating the very limited capabilities of the 'Roe II Triplane' in Manchester on 4 March 1910, for example, a wealthy motor body manufacturer, Walter Windham, came over and asked how much it cost. A.V. Roe plucked a figure out of the air.

'£550,' he said, 'and that includes tuition.'

'Done!' said Windham.

At the time there were no flying schools and hardly anyone – including A.V.

Roe – knew how to fly. As Windham's paid-for machine was being built, it was constantly being modified to cope with the experience of yet another crash.

A.V. Roe was not a great success at the then-important Blackpool Meet in 1910, except that he and the famous aviator and showman Claude Grahame-White were invited to cross the Atlantic to demonstrate flying in Boston, Massachusetts. They agreed to go, but first A.V. Roe married Miss Mildred Kirk, the 26-year-old daughter of a Nottingham lace manufacturer on 20 August 1910, in Blackpool. They had a rushed three-day honeymoon before he sailed for America without her, but with the hope of a handful of orders for aircraft.

Six weeks later A.V. demonstrated the newly-named 'Blackpool' Triplane in front of eager American crowds. What he demonstrated was three crashes, first on 6 September, then on 8 September, and the third time injuring himself – though not too badly – on 14 September. Claude Grahame-White went from strength to strength, winning considerable prize money as well as landing and taking off – by invitation – on Pennsylvania Avenue in Washington DC in front of the White House while visiting American President, William Taft.

A.V.'s reputation survived his mishaps, he established useful contacts in America and also met President Taft. Grahame-White stayed to tour the USA, while A.V. came home to his young bride and further design work. Over the next 14 years Mildred produced nine children, three of whom became pilots in the RAF.

On 26 July 1910, A.V. Roe qualified as the eighteenth licensed pilot in Britain. A year later he designed the first of the famous Avro 500 series of biplanes, at the same time as the War Office, concerned about the Dreadnaught Battleship race with an increasingly belligerent Germany, started issuing specifications for 'military aeroplanes'. A.V. Roe pitched for a contract, and the Army ordered three of his Avro 500 two-seaters, powered by French-designed Gnome engines. They proved so reliable that the War Office ordered four more, then two were ordered by the Admiralty, another five single-seaters were ordered by the War Office and there were three civilian orders. Seventeen orders! Avro was in business. The brothers could actually see a return on their investment, working out of premises they shared in Manchester, Brownsfield Mill, where the famous 'Bullseye Braces' were made. In 1912 they brought in a Tory MP, James Grimble Groves, from a wealthy brewing family, and were registered as a limited company with capital of £30,000 on 1 January 1913.

The most important aircraft built and designed by A.V. Roe was the famous Avro 504 series, 10,787 of which were built. The Avro 504K became the standard aeroplane in which RAF pilots first flew, and the company created a niche for building training aircraft. By this time, Avro had become the major champion of 'tractor' aircraft, with engines in the nose and the propeller pulling the aircraft through the air, rather than 'pusher' aircraft, with the engine behind the crew.

Two significant events occurred to the company before the First World War. In 1911 a young man called Roy Chadwick became A.V.'s design assistant, and went on in 1919 to become Chief Designer for Avro. Chadwick was destined to become the designer of the Lancaster. Three years after Chadwick was hired, a young man called Roy Dobson was taken on, another of the Lancaster's progenitors.

There was a change of management at Brooklands, the new man Major Lindsay Lloyd welcomed aviators, and a runway was built to become the site of the new Avro flying school. At the same time new premises were taken in Manchester and a separate building used as a drawing office block. A production site was acquired in Hamble, Southampton and between 1914 and 1918 thousands of Avro 504s were delivered to the RFC (Royal Flying Corps) and the RNAS (Royal Naval Air Service), progenitors of the RAF, which was eventually formed on 1 April 1918.

Avro aircraft were credited with one of the earliest British bombing missions against Germany, on 21 November 1914. Four Avro 504s had been smuggled in great secrecy from the factory in Manchester. They were transported in pieces by rail, cross-channel ferry and by road at night to a French airfield called Belfort, the four pilots from the RNAS being hidden in a dirigible shed to avoid exciting German spies in the town. Each Avro 504 was equipped with an extra fuel tank and four 20lb bombs, a load so heavy that an observer could not be carried.

Three machines got airborne before 10 o'clock in the morning – the fourth failed to lift-off and broke a tail-skid – and set off over 123 miles of enemy territory at 5,000ft (1,524m), following the Rhine River to Lake Constance. They were led by Commander E.F. Briggs with J.T. Babington and S.V. Sippe in support, arriving at Friedrichshafen at noon and heading for the Zeppelin factory north of the town. Eleven of the 12 bombs were dropped – Sippe had a bomb hang up – under heavy rifle and machine gun fire. They claimed the destruction of one shed with a Zeppelin inside, a claim later disproved. Briggs was wounded, brought down and taken prisoner. The other two pilots completed a four-hour flight to get home, averaging about 60mph. It was the fragile harbinger of things to come.

The war years were good for Avro, but immediately after it ended, production plummeted and there was consolidation inside the company. Workers were laid off and in May 1920 Avro was bought by Crossley Motors, which had made thousands of light trucks and cars for military use. A.V. Roe was company chairman, Chadwick produced the designs and Robson rose through the company ranks.

This was one of the mainstream aviation roots of the Lancaster. The other was the development of Rolls-Royce engines.

Two men, the Honourable Charles Rolls and Henry Royce, who were to become household names across the world, met in the Midland Hotel, Manchester on 4 May 1904. Charles Rolls, born in 1877 into a wealthy family and educated at Eton and Cambridge University, was an eccentric aristocratic motoring enthusiast, one of the few men in those days with a proper understanding of the motor car.

In sharp contrast, Henry Royce was a brilliant, hard-working engineer from a poor background. Born near Peterborough in 1863, his early experience with a railway engineering firm and then an electricity company enabled him to set up his own business in Manchester in 1904 to produce electric equipment. The two men discussed going into the motor trade and the meeting between them led to an agreement whereby Royce would produce the cars and Rolls would sell them. After the public floatation of Rolls Royce Ltd in 1906, the 'Silver Ghost' was so successful that a new factory was built at Derby in 1908 to produce 200 cars a year!

Charles Rolls' adventurous spirit led him into the new sport of aviation and he rapidly became one of England's pioneer pilots. He was the first to make a non-stop return flight across the English Channel in a Wright Flyer in 1910. Tragically, he was killed in the same machine later the same year when he crashed during an air display at Bournemouth. Henry Royce fell gravely ill soon afterwards. He left Derby to live on the south coast, continuing to play an active role in the company until his death in 1933.

With the outbreak of war in 1914, Royce soon realised it would be fought in the air as well as on land and sea, and Britain's aircraft would need a reliable engine. He designed the Falcon water-cooled aero-engine which developed into the 200hp Eagle, later to power the Vickers Vimy on the first non-stop trans-Atlantic flight in 1919. Rolls-Royce went on to build engines such as the reliable Kestrel, fitted to Hawker's Hart, Hind and Fury machines. But the culmination was the famous 'R' engine which would develop into a 60-degree V12 of 27 litres capacity, with a rating of 1,280hp at 3,000 rpm for take-off. This became the Merlin.

Avro concentrated its design work in Hamble appointing Captain 'Sam' Brown as chief test pilot in 1928. Along with Chadwick and Robson he would become vital to the development of the Lancaster. That same year Crossley struck a deal with the great industrialist Sir John Siddeley, later Lord Kenilworth, so that the Armstrong Siddeley Group bought out Avro. Most of Avro's production was returned to Manchester. A.V. Roe cut his personal ties with the company and went on to found Saunders Roe to develop flying boats. He had originally bought Hamble, next to the sea, because he wanted to produce seaplanes.

In the 1930s, Avro built a series of mail planes as well as trainers, the most significant of which was the Avro Tutor. From this, the Avro Anson was developed, the RAF's first monoplane bomber and another big seller. A twin-engine coastal patrol aircraft with a top turret and the capacity to carry 250lb bombs slung under the wings, more than 11,000 Ansons were built, becoming the standard runabout with a variety of air forces. Forty RAF squadrons were equipped with Ansons.

None of this seems really to be an adequate preparation for building what was to be the finest heavy bomber of the Second World War.

CHAPTER THREE

Last Witnesses, Two Avro Boys and Eleven Lancaster VCs

Look at the names on the statues,
Everywhere you go;
Someone was killed…
A long time ago;
I remember the faces,
I remember the time
Those are the names of friends of mine.

John Gray,
'Billy Bishop Goes to War'

There are well-recorded histories of the men who built the Lancaster, of their roots in Avro, the commercial competition they faced from rivals and the key role in the aircraft's evolution played by the company's chief designer, Roy Chadwick, as well as his tough Managing Director, Roy Dobson. They had been young men in the dawn of aviation in Britain before the Great War, when it was not always certain that however well designed, *any* new aircraft would actually fly.

By the time the Second World War started, a new generation of men were reaching flying age, all of them born in the crucial decade between 1915 and 1924. The Lancaster would come to dominate the lives of tens of thousands of this generation of young men. The oldest of these had been born into a world embroiled in the horrors of the First World War. The youngest were born in the middle of the Jazz era, three years before Charles Lindbergh's New York-Paris flight, yet they would still only be in their early twenties when the Second World War ended.

The average age of the Lancaster's pilots, those whom I have dubbed Last Witnesses as there are so few left who can relate their first-hand experiences of the great bomber, was 22 years old. The overwhelming majority of them were not full-time professional airmen but civilians in uniform, in the military for the duration. They were part of a force in RAF Bomber Command that took the war to Adolf Hitler from the first day to the last, and suffered far higher casualty rates than any other unit. It took some time for the best of the wartime bombers to arrive on the scene, and the carnage among aircrews in the first three years to 1942 was terrible. An average tour comprised 30 operations, to be compared against the average life expectancy of 21 operations. Any aircrew living beyond 21 operations was on borrowed time.

In following the development of the Lancaster, we must also follow the story of 38 of these men, including two Avro sons, 11 Lancaster VCs and the Last Witnesses, all of whom helped to create the aircraft's great reputation and all of whom were born into that crucial decade. These young airmen, some of them German – including Heinz Orlowski, who tried and only just failed to kill me – grew up with the gradual certainty that the Great War had been no war to end wars, as had been promised. They came to believe they were living in the half-time period of a longer war between Germany and much of the rest of the world.

1915

In August 1915, Alliot Verdon-Roe's first son, Eric, was born. He was brought up in Hamble House, his father's beautiful mansion on the 300 acre site purchased for Avro's development in 1914. Half of Eric's teenage years were spent in relative prosperity during the 1920s, the Great Depression following the 1929 Stock Market Crash having little effect on him. Eric made his first solo flight in one of his father's aircraft at Eastleigh in 1931 on his sixteenth birthday, and went into the RAF on a short service commission in 1934.

Just a month earlier, on 7 July, future Victoria Cross winner Edwin Swales had been born in Inanda in Natal in the Union of South Africa, one of four children fathered by Harry Swales, a farmer who was to die in the influenza epidemic of 1919. Edwin's mother, Olive, took her boys to Berea in Durban, and young Edwin grew up to be a notable rugby player – close to international level – and a keen Boy Scout. He worked for Barclays Bank before the outbreak of war in 1939.

1916

Three men who would go on to make their names in Lancasters were born in 1916. These were Last Witness George Hart in Norfolk, England on 28 May, future VC winner Andrew Charles Mynarski in Winnipeg, in Canada on 14 October and James 'Willie' Tait on 9 December in Manchester, England.

George Hart was born in his grandmother's house but moved to Essex where he grew up. He was struck down with meningitis when he was nine, leaving him with eyesight that would not be up to scratch for aircrew. As soon as he was old enough to leave school he joined Cornhill Insurance in the City of London.

'Andy' Mynarski was a first-generation Canadian, the son of Polish immigrants. He was educated at King Edward and Isaac Newton Elementary Schools in Winnipeg, later graduating from St. John's Technical School. His father died in 1930, and to help support his family Andy worked as a chamois cutter. In 1940, he joined the militia unit, the Royal Winnipeg Rifles but only served a short time before enlisting in the RCAF.

James Tait was educated at Wellingborough School, and decided at the age of 12 that he was going to be a pilot after seeing one of Sir Alan Cobham's air displays in 1928. He graduated as a Pilot Officer from RAF College Cranwell in August 1936, and joined 51 Squadron flying Whitley bombers.

1917

In 1917, two future Lancaster Victoria Cross holders were born, John Nettleton in Nongoma, Natal in South Africa on 28 June and Leonard Cheshire on 7 September in Chester, England.

John Nettleton went into the Merchant Marines for 18 months after he left school in the 1930s, and then decided he wanted to be a civil engineer. During his engineering apprenticeship, he worked in various parts of South Africa for three years, and joined the RNVR. He was described as a tough 'Botha Boy' and served as a naval cadet on the same sail training ship, *General Botha,* as his fellow South African and future Spitfire ace 'Sailor' Malan. Nettleton was commissioned into the RAF in 1938.

Leonard Cheshire was the son of Professor Geoffrey Cheshire, a barrister, academic and influential writer on English law. Leonard was brought up at his parents' home near Oxford, and educated at the Dragon School, Oxford, then Stowe School and Merton College, Oxford. While at Oxford, where he was a member of the University Air Squadron, he was bet half a pint of beer by a friend who said he could not reach Paris with just a few pennies in his pocket; Cheshire won his bet. While staying with German friends he witnessed a Hitler rally in Germany, causing great offence to his hosts by not giving the Nazi salute. He graduated in Jurisprudence in 1939.

1918

In 1918, the year the end of World War One was celebrated, two VCs and one Last Witness were born. The future VCs were Guy Gibson, born in Simla in India on 12 August, and Ian Willoughby Bazalgette on 19 October of English/Irish parents in Calgary, Alberta, Canada. The Last Witness was Ray Grayston in Dunsfold in Surrey on 13 October.

Guy Gibson's father, Alexander, was an official of the British Raj in India who moved his young family to Porthleven in Cornwall in 1921. Guy was sent to Folkestone in Kent at the age of eight to attend St George's Prep School, and went on to St Edward's School in Oxford. He had average grades in education but was good at sports. At the age of 19, with an eye to being a future test pilot for Vickers, he was commissioned into the RAF in 1937. From being a 'shy, quiet child' he had developed into a handsome young man who cut 'a glamorous film-star like figure.'

Ian Bazalgette, known within his family not as Ian but as 'Will' to distinguish him from his father Ian, had his early education at Toronto Balmy Beach School. His family returned to England in 1927, and he grew up in New Malden, suffering from poor health and diagnosed with tuberculosis as a teenager. He underwent lengthy treatment at the Royal Sea-Bathing Hospital in Margate.

Ray Grayston grew up and discovered he had technical skills, so when he volunteered for aircrew, intending to be a pilot, he was mustered as an engineer.

1919

1919 was the year three of the Last Witnesses were born, as well as one VC. The Last Witnesses were Eric Brown on 21 January at Leith in Scotland; Les Munro on 5 April in Gisborne on South Island, New Zealand; and my birthday was 11 September in York, England. The future VC was Norman Jackson, born on 8 April in Ealing, West London

Eric Brown's father had been a balloon observer in the RFC, one of the most dangerous of all aviation jobs. Eric was brought up in Edinburgh and as a schoolboy won a scholarship to the Royal High School. He excelled in languages – French and German – and in sports. Despite his small stature, that attracted the nickname 'Winkle', he played in the school's rugby First XV, and was the school's gymnastic champion.

Les Munro's father had emigrated to New Zealand in 1903 mainly for health reasons, after developing tuberculosis working in a woollen mill in Glasgow. Les was brought up on a sheep station in the Ormond District, where his father worked as a shepherd.

My family origins go back to the tiny village of Gayle in Wensleydale, North Yorkshire, at least to 1670; the family name has Viking roots. My father was a police inspector after four year's service in France with the Royal Fusiliers, where he was wounded three times, almost succumbing to severe chest wounds on 1 July 1916, the first day of the Battle of the Somme. I was the first of four sons and expected to become an architect when I left school.

Norman Jackson, an orphan, was adopted by the Gunter family as a small child and was educated at Archdeacon Cambridge and Twickenham Grammar School. Interested in engineering, he became a fitter and turner after he left school.

1920

This was the year one of the Last Witnesses was born and two of the VCs. The Last Witness was Laurence 'Benny' Goodman, born in London on 24 September.

The future VCs were Robert Palmer in Gillingham in Kent on 7 July, and George Thompson on 23 October at Trinity Gask in Perthshire, Scotland.

'Benny' Goodman's father had fought as a private on the Eastern Front in the First World War, facing Bulgars and Turks. In the 1920s he had made a success of his own advertising business and ran a Rolls Royce. Benny went to boarding school from the age of seven and, faced with leaving school, had the enviable choice of living in Paris to learn French while staying with his mother's French aunt, or going to university to study languages and history.

Palmer was the son of a World War One pilot in the RFC. He and his younger brother, Douglas, were brought up amid hundreds of hours of stories of life in an RFC Squadron on the Western Front. Robert was educated at Gravesend Grammar School and joined the RAFVR as soon as he could.

Thompson, son of a farmer, was educated at Portmoak Primary School and Kinross High School. He grew up with a love of tinkering with wireless sets, but became apprenticed to a grocer in Kinross, joining the Local Defence Volunteers in 1939. He was not accepted for aircrew until June 1943.

1921

Five Last Witnesses, a second Avro boy and one future VC were born in 1921, though one of the Last Witnesses was German and is included because of what *did not* happen one day to my squadron.

The Last Witnesses were Bob Horsley on 4 May in Upper Poppleton, west of York; Jim Norris on 21 June in Cardiff in South Wales; Patrick Dorehill in Fort Victoria, Rhodesia, on 4 July; Karl Schulze in Kassel on July 30; and Reg Barker in Luton, Bedfordshire on December 11. The Avro boy, the founder's seventh child, was Lighton Verdon-Roe, born in May at Hamble, Southampton. The future VC, William Reid, was born on 21 December in Baillieston, Glasgow.

Bob Horsley, whose father was a wool merchant, was the youngest of four brothers. He was educated at Haughton School in York, and excelled in maths, French and athletics, school champion in the school's two-mile race, 800 yards and 100 yard sprint.

Patrick Dorehill, an only child, was the great nephew of Sir Herbert Taylor, Chief Native Commissioner in Rhodesia. Patrick's father was also a native commissioner. At the age of eight, Patrick was sent to school in South Africa, with secondary education at Michaelhouse public school near Pietermaritzburg. He had finished school and completed a year's education at Witswatersrand University in Johannesburg, South Africa, before joining the RAF in June 1940.

Kurt Schulze was an only child, 11 years old when Hitler came to power, and graduated from High School in March, 1939. His birthplace, Kassel, was an industrial centre as well as a major railway junction where, in the nineteenth century, the Brothers Grimm collected and wrote most of their famous fairy tales. Schulze had been accepted as an airman cadet in 1938, despite suffering from hay fever, but a month after leaving school he was forced into the Labour Service for six months, a reluctant service which ended when war was declared.

Reg Barker spent his childhood in Wood Green, North London, and left school in July 1938 to work as an insurance clerk. He remained a civilian through the Battle of Britain, but joined the RAF in July 1941, before being sent to the United States to learn how to fly.

Lighton Verdon-Roe was the third son of the founder of Avro and, like his brother, Eric, Lighton had a privileged childhood, sheltered from the economic nightmare that affected so many others of his generation. He went straight into the RAFVR from school.

Jim Norris, the son of a seaman who became a docker, was one of eight children, four in front of him, three behind. All he wanted to be when he grew up was a businessman. Like his father, he favoured going to sea if there was a war on, but opted instead to be an airman.

William Reid, the son of a blacksmith, was educated at Swinton Primary School and Coatbridge Higher Grade School in Glasgow. He would later study metallurgy. He was 20 when he applied to join the RAFVR.

1922

This was, oddly, a sparse year for Last Witnesses, with none that we found, but there was a VC, Leslie Manser, born on 11 May in New Delhi in India. Manser was educated at Victoria School in Kurseong in the Darjeeling District of West Bengal. The school had been opened in 1879 for the children of lower-ranking British government officials. Kurseong, famous as one of the best tea plantations in India, was a hill station at an altitude close to 5,000ft (1,524m) and favoured as a site for sanatoriums where the British could escape the summer heat of the plains of India.

1923

In stark contrast to the previous year, 1923 saw the birth of nine of the Last Witnesses, all of whom knew nothing of any other life after school than as airmen. These included two Germans. One was Heinz Orlowski, the other was Rolf Ebhardt, born on 22 October in Koblenz in the Rhineland.

The other Last Witnesses were Rupert Noye, born 16 February in Middlesbrough; 'Doc' Sutherland on 26 February in Peace River, in northern Alberta, Canada; John Bell on 25 March in Wandsworth, London; Michael Beetham on 17 May in London; Tony Hiscock on 8 August at Hove in Sussex; Desmond Pelley on 28 August at Godstone in Surrey; and Stan Bradford, on 23 September at Leigh in Lancashire.

Rolf Ebhardt was the oldest son of a local government official in the German

Rhineland and came from a broken family. He was nine years old when Hitler came to power. In his teenage years he admired the Kondor Legion fighting in the Spanish Civil War. The Second World War broke out when he was 16, and he was upset that it would be over before he was in it. He thrilled to the Blitzkrieg in Poland, the Low Countries and France, and could not wait to join up.

Rupert Noye, son of a private hire car driver, was one of six children. He moved to Bournemouth when he was four and grew up hoping to be a mechanic. Noye left school at 16 and worked in a furnishing store until volunteering for the RAF in 1941, 10 days after his eighteenth birthday.

'Doc' Sutherland, who had two sisters, was the son of a country doctor and the grandson of a Scottish immigrant expelled during the Highland Clearances. His mother's family was Cree Indian and involved in the fur trade. 'Doc' grew up in Peace River, an isolated rural community of less than a thousand people. He had very little formal education.

John Bell left school in 1939 and went to work for a firm of chartered accountants in the City of London. As soon as he was 18 he volunteered for the RAF as aircrew.

Michael Beetham was educated at St Marylebone's Grammar School. His father had won an MC in the Great War as an Army major in the trenches. He wanted his son to go into the Army but, with his father stationed near Portsmouth, Michael spent the summer holidays of 1940 watching RAF fighters in the Battle of Britain tackling German bombers trying to destroy the local docks. He went straight into the RAF himself in 1941, at the age of 18.

Tony Hiscock was the third of five children of a petty officer in the Royal Navy, an instructor skilled at building model aircraft targets for Navy guns to shoot at. Tony was a keen fan of the 'Biggles' stories as a boy, but never thought he would qualify – for reasons of social class – as an RAF pilot. Hiscock wanted to be a boy entrant into the RAF and joined the ATC at school, so he was allowed to volunteer for aircrew when still not yet 18 years old.

Desmond Pelley went to one of England's top public schools, Charterhouse, and grew up wanting to be a racing driver. The school was a prime target for RAF recruiting boards and they recommended him for aircrew while he was still a schoolboy. He joined up on his eighteenth birthday.

Stan Bradford was a big young lad and wanted to follow his father into the sheet metal business in Lancashire, a 'reserved occupation' when war broke out. His firm repaired ambulances, police cars and buses, as well as assembling trucks sent from the USA and Canada before passing them on to the Army. He was driving a coach he had repaired, delivering it to Blackpool, and passed three recruiting offices, Army, Navy and Air Force. The Army said, 'Reserved occupation, no chance', the Royal Navy said the same, and the RAF said the only way they could take him was as aircrew. He said, 'No problem at all, put me down.'

1924

In 1924, four Last Witnesses were born, destined not to have reached the age of twenty-one when the war ended. They were Don Briggs, born on 7 May in West Hartlepool in County Durham; John Langston in Dawlish in Devon on 30 June; David Fellowes on 24 July in Hurstpierpoint in Sussex; and John Curtiss in London on 26 December.

As a boy, Don Briggs wanted to make a career in the RAF, starting as an aircraft apprentice at Halton. The war began as he arrived there, at 15 years and three months old, and he completed an apprenticeship as an aero engine fitter, also passing all the aptitude tests for a pilot. But the commandant at the selection board said towards the end of 1943 that by the time he trained overseas as a pilot, the war would be over: 'You're a corporal engine fitter and all you need is the Lancaster conversion and you can be in the fight within three months as a flight engineer.' That is what he did.

John Langston graduated from school and went to Wadham College, Oxford, before going to Canada in 1943 to train as a pilot. He passed his wings exam and was soon flying Oxford twin-engine trainers, finishing his elementary school with an above-average score. Then one day half his course was called into the Commanding Officer's office and told, 'Too many pilots, you can be navigators or bomb aimers.' He reluctantly decided on navigation.

David Fellowes was keen on aviation as a boy, made model aeroplanes and gliders and first flew in 1932 with Alan Cobham's flying circus on a five shilling flight (five shillings = 25p). When war was declared, his father's work as an engineer took his family to Annan, and David joined the local ATC. When an airfield was built nearby as a Hawker Hurricane OTU, David used to cadge rides in Lysanders. He left school aged 17½ and knew he was going straight into the war.

John Curtiss, whose father was an Australian and his mother a New Zealander, went to Radley College – a public school – but his family moved to New Zealand when war broke out. He had originally intended to join the Royal Navy, returning to England on his own when he was 17 years old in 1942. He joined the RAF in October of that year.

Of these 38 airmen, 10 did not live to see the end of the war, while 28 – virtually the Last Witnesses to the legend of the Lancaster bomber – survived through to the eighth year of the twenty-first century, and can still testify to the potency of this iconic aircraft.

All those who died had physically dreadful deaths, nine of the 10 in Lancasters, and they were rightly seen as an inspiration to the rest of us. The proportion, 10 to die and 28 to live, does not reflect the reality of serving on Lancasters in RAF Bomber Command. Individually, we were not expected to get past 21 operations, yet four of us survived in excess of 100 ops, defying odds of more than 100-to-1 against.

The survivors, we few, went on to varied careers after the war. Some went back to the jobs abandoned when the war rolled over us. Others had distinguished careers, inside and outside the RAF. Two were knighted, one went on to become Chief of the Air Staff, a Marshal of the Royal Air Force.

As their stories crop up throughout the course of this book, bear in mind that in our intense relationships with the Avro Lancaster, we were all young men. As the lyrics of John Gray's brilliant World War One musical, 'Billy Bishop Goes to War' put it:

> *The statues are old now,*
> *And they're fadin' fast;*
> *Something big must have happened,*
> *Way in the past;*
> *The names are so faded*
> *You can hardly see,*
> *But the faces are always young to me.*

John Gray, 'Billy Bishop
Goes To War'

CHAPTER FOUR

The RAF, Schneider Trophy and the Merlin Engine

The dominant force in the RAF until 1940 was the man acknowledged as its founder, Lord (Hugh) Trenchard. Born in 1873 and a veteran of the Boer War, he led the RFC in World War One with a policy of constant attack. Even during bleak periods when the Germans had a technical advantage over British pilots during the 'Fokker Scourge' in 1915 and the average life of a RFC airman dropped to just 21 days, Trenchard continued to espouse aggression. Almost all the legendary combats carried out on the Western Front were behind the German lines.

When the Royal Air Force was formed from the RFC and the RNAS on 1 April 1918, it was the start of a terrific battle for survival as a separate force. The older services, the Army and Royal Navy, demanded that all aircraft operations should be tailored to their needs and maintained that there was no requirement for a separate service at all. They wanted their aircraft and their personnel back.

These attacks increased in fervour after 1919, when the RAF was looking for a role to play, and found one keeping the peace in the Middle East, especially in Iraq – then known as Mesopotamia – 'Messpot' to the troops – using aircraft to control troublesome natives. An aircraft could go and bomb an uppity tribal chieftain at far less cost than a punitive Army column, and at less risk. These small colonial police actions were the source of a peculiar practice, the 'goolie chit', still in use today with RAF squadrons in the Middle East. If, by chance, the natives brought down an aircraft and the pilot was found alive, to prevent them removing the pilot from his reproductive equipment the pilot was expected to proffer a document promising a payment in gold for his return intact. Sometimes it worked.

Throughout the inter-war years until 1935, the RAF was run on a virtual shoe-string, flying biplane bombers, fighters and transport aircraft. After the 'War to End Wars', there was a real reluctance to spend money developing weapons. The British public, however, in common with people in other parts of the world, still flocked to see air displays like Alan Cobham's Flying Circus, and followed record-breakers as if they were pop stars. Yet the public did not want to know about warplanes, and politicians reflected this view. Until the rise of Germany and Italy in the 1930s, war planes seldom had to be tested against the best in the world. This was a situation that was to lead to the tragic early years of Bomber Command operations where we had to make do with what we had got – and suffered for it. In bombing terms, until the 4-engined 'heavies' (especially the Lancaster) arrived in 1942, what we had got was not very good. We lost the cream of our young pilots to learn this lesson.

One exception to the complacency in Britain to our military aviation capability was the Schneider Trophy. Begun in 1913, the competition was limited to seaplanes and was first won by France's Maurice Prevost in a Deperdussin Monocoque over the sea off Monaco at an average speed of just 45mph. In 1914, Howard Pixton turned up as the British entry at Monaco with Tommy Sopwith backing him. He won at 86.7mph flying a Sopwith Tabloid. In 1919, the Schneider Trophy was raced over a foggy course in Bournemouth in Southern England – winners staged the races the following year – with Italy winning as the only entry, although the pilot was disqualified for failing to find one of the official turn-points in the fog. The Italians were outraged and were, therefore, granted the honour of staging the 1920 Schneider Trophy Race. They won, and won again in 1921. Luigi Bologna took the 1920 title in a flying boat, a Savoia S12, at 107.16mph, while Giovanni de Briganti won the 1921 race in a Macchi M.7 at 117.8mph. Both races were held in the Venice Lido, and a third win would give Italians the prestigious trophy in perpetuity.

The 1922 race was held in Naples and might have been won by the Italians but for the sole foreigner, a British entry, Henry Biard in a Supermarine Sea Lion II, who achieved a narrow victory at 145.63mph. That British win resounded across the world of aviation and made the Schneider Trophy, as one commentator put it, 'the most sought-after trinket' in the race for speed in the air. It attracted the attention of the United States, and in the 1923 races at Cowes in the Isle of Wight, the US Navy fielded four entries against aircraft from Britain, Italy and France. Though this was considered slightly unsporting – the London *Times* commented 'British habits do not support the idea of entering a team organised by *the State* for a sporting event' – David Rittenhouse won for the USA in a Curtiss CR-3 at an average speed of 177.27mph.

From then on, winning the Schneider Trophy became a matter of national honour. The key to the 1923 American win was the Curtiss engine using what was called a wetsleeve monobloc concept. Two Curtiss engines were bought by the Italians and sent home for Fiat to copy, while the British Air Ministry quietly sent one to Rolls Royce and told the firm to better it. It was a 'quiet' request because had this news gone public there would have been grumbling in Parliament.

The Americans sportingly called off the 1924 race to give the Europeans time to build and test new aircraft.The 1925 race was held in waters off Baltimore, Maryland, with two Italian entries, Macchi M33 flying boats; two British entries, both floatplanes but neither powered by Rolls Royce engines; and three American entries, Curtiss R3C-2 Navy Racers. The British beat the Italians and two of the Americans, but the third American pilot, a brilliant US Army airman called Jimmy Doolittle, emerged the winner, averaging 232.57mph over the 217-mile course.

With a third win the following year on the cards, the United States then lost interest in the Schneider Trophy! The US Navy was committed to defending its title but no public money could be spent, and the same three Curtiss R3C-2s were entered for the 1926 races at Chesapeake Bay. In Rome, meanwhile, Mussolini had decreed that Italy must win the race. This meant that two designers, Italy's Mario Castoldi of Macchi and Britain's Reginald Mitchell from Supermarine Aviation, should have gone head to head. But Mitchell was unable to get his Supermarine floatplane ready on time and the Italians won with the Macchi M39, piloted by Mario de Bernardi, at 246.5mph.

It was a close race with the Americans, and afterwards de Bernardi sent a telegram to Mussolini: 'Your orders to win at all costs have been carried out.' What was significant about the win was that the seaplane speed record was approaching that achieved by landplanes, set by the French in 1924 at 278.47mph.

The 1927 Schneider Trophy Race was a straight competition at the Venice Lido between four Italian entries flying Macchi M52s, and two British entries, the Supermarine S.5 monoplane and a new Gloster biplane. There was huge anticipation about the result, but the engines on all four Italian aircraft blew up. Britain's Sydney Webster won on the S.5 at an average speed of 281.66mph.

Winning the Schneider Trophy was now indisputably the most distinguished feat in aviation, but the rules were changed to stage races every two years, to give time for radical new aircraft to be developed.

The 1929 races were held at Calshott Spit, out of an RAF flying boat station at the open end of Southampton Water and opposite Cowes on the Isle of Wight. The competition was a straight fight between Italy and Britain. The new Macchi M.67 – 'a wickedly beautiful aircraft' – were very fast but untried, and had already killed one pilot, Captain Guiseppe Motta, after reaching 362mph over Lake Garda before suddenly diving into the water. He was thought to have been fatally affected by engine fumes and smoke.

The Macchis were up against Britain's Supermarine S.6s in which designer Reg Mitchell had abandoned Napier Lion engines and gone to Sir Henry Royce himself at Rolls Royce for a new power plant. The story goes that Sir Henry, now an old man, rejected the Italian method of seeking extra power by adding more cylinders. With his walking stick on a beach near his home, he sketched the outline of the now-famous R-engine, with three Rolls Royce engineers watching, a design destined to lead to the Merlin which would one day make such a perfect combination with Avro's Lancaster. The new engine should, he said, remain a V-12, with none of the ultrahigh compression the Italians were seeking. It should improve on the Curtiss wetsleeve monobloc configuration, and extra speed should come from a supercharger, forcing more air/fuel mixture into the cylinders than atmospheric pressure would normally admit.

The Italians were aware that they were at the limits of design and tried to get the races postponed. When this was refused – the stakes in international prestige were enormous – they entered anyway in 'a gesture of chivalrous sportsman-ship'.

A million people turned up to watch the races over a 33-mile course.

One Macchi 67 achieved 284mph and then had to land with a smoke-hazed windscreen. A second pilot, Giovanni Monti, averaged 301.5mph on his first circuit but as he began his second a pipe in his cooling system burst, scalding his arms and legs and filling his cockpit with steam. He landed safely, nevertheless, and was rescued and rushed off to hospital. The Supermarine S.6s flew without drama, roaring around lap after lap, RAF Flight Lieutenant Henry Waghorn winning at 328.63mph.

The Italian Minister for Aviation, the very ambitious General Italo Balbo, promised a gloves-off competition from now on and Italy developed the MC72 which reached 375mph in trials. Yet it crashed soon afterwards and Giovanni Monti, who had recovered from his scalding, was killed.

The French were also developing an entry, but neither Italy nor France were ready by September 1931, when the races were scheduled to be held. They asked for a postponement. The Royal Aero Club turned them down. The Italians and French intimated that the British would race and win on a bluff, at no better speeds than the 1929 races were won. The British resolved to win handsomely.

At the same time, the Great Crash of 1929 had affected financing and the Labour Government and Air Ministry decided that they could not fund the latest Schneider Trophy campaign. Without official backing, there seemed to be no hope of developing the engine that would be required to win the race. At this point an extraordinary woman entered the pre-history of the Lancaster, earning the right to be dubbed 'the mad old bat who saved England.'

There is an argument that Britain would not have won the war without the Spitfire to defend us against the Germans and the Lancaster to strike back. We would not have had the Spitfire or Lancaster without the Merlin, and we would not have had the Merlin without the fabulous Lady Lucy Houston. One of the richest women in the world, she put £100,000 of her own money into backing the British team in the 1931 Schneider Trophy. This was a colossal sum of money in those days, when one could buy a terraced house in East London for £100. Nowadays, the kind of support Lady Houston supplied would be worth tens of millions.

That Lady Houston was able to provide the cash at all could be said to stem from a series of fortunate incidents. She need not have donated the money; indeed, it is amazing that she ever had it in the first place. She was the widow of ship-owner and alleged 'robber baron' Sir Robert Houston, who had started life as an office boy and made his huge fortune anticipating supplies for the Boer War; he was Lucy's third husband.

But how did she manage to snare one of the richest men in Britain in 1924, at the height of the 'flapper' era, when marrying rich men just for their money and being called a 'gold-digger' was an honourable ambition? Sir Robert was 71, and she was – allegedly – 67 years old, yet she won out against a million younger women who would have killed to take her place. He married her against all the advice of his friends. She must have held a terrific attraction for him.

Born Fanny Lucy Radmall in 1857 (newspapers discovered after her death that she was seven years older than she said she was) she claimed to have been a 'wild street arab' from a large family in the City of London. In the 1870s and early 80s she was a small-part actress. Her first husband was Theodore Brinckman, heir to a baronetcy, whom she married in 1883 when he was 21 and she claimed to be 26, but was really 33. That marriage last, 12 years.

Her second husband was the ninth Lord Byron whom she married in 1901 at the real age of 51. He died in 1917. Lucy was made a Dame of the British Empire, DBE, that same year for establishing a Home for Tired Nurses. During this period Lady Lucy was an ardent suffragette. To further the cause, she bought 615 parrots, one for every voting constituency in the country, and taught them all to screech 'Votes For Women!'

In 1921 she started an affair with Sir Robert Houston – *what a goer she must have been!* – married him in 1924 when she was 74, and when he died mysteriously two years later abourd his yacht *Liberty*, Lucy was said to be too ill to leave the yacht to attend his funeral.

Having survived that scandal, allegedly pocketing £5 million – a massive fortune in today's money – and domiciled in the tax haven of Jersey, she sat down and negotiated her 'voluntary' death duties face-to-face with Winston Churchill, then Chancellor of the Exchequer. She personally wrote a single cheque for £1,500,000 to get him off her back, and claimed he was delighted.

It still left her £3,500,000 to play with, and five years later she spent part of that fortune rescuing the RAF team desperate for a third, clinching, Schneider Trophy win. In photographs, surrounded by all those handsome and ardent young men, at the age of 81 Lady Lucy Houston looks the picture of charm and contentment.

A typical quote: 'I am proud to say that I have inherited the spirit of my forefathers. We are not worms to be trampled under the heel of Socialism, but true Britons with a heart for any fate.'

I remember being at school in York, two days after my twelfth birthday, when a friend rushed into the classroom and said Britain had won the Schneider Trophy forever – flying at speeds of more than 300mph! This was just 28 years after the Wright Brothers first flew. John Boothman clinched the Trophy with a world record 340mph in a Supermarine 6B. Later that month, on 29 September 1933, he twice set new world records in the S6B, the first aircraft to break the 400mph barrier with an average speed of 407.5mph.

Lady Lucy Houston died in 1937, two years before war broke out, allegedly of a broken heart at the abdication of King Edward VIII over his love for Wallis Simpson. She was said to be so depressed about the abdication crisis that she gave up eating and suffered a heart attack. Few remember Lucy Houston now, perhaps partly because she thought Mussolini was a good chap for getting the trains in Italy to run on time – yet she did not think much of Hitler – but through the Spitfire and the Merlin, she is an extraordinary component of the Lancaster's history.

Arthur Sidgreaves, Rolls Royce's Managing Director, said of the research done to win the 1931 Schneider Trophy, research funded by Lady Lucy Houston, that it 'compressed 10 years of research into two.'

In May 1929, the first model of the Rolls Royce R-engine produced 1,545 horsepower, but after 15 minutes continuous use started chewing itself up. By the summer of 1931, under pressure to get it right, Rolls Royce in Derby kept the city's inhabitants awake at night with constant engine testing – and failures – until the fourteenth model, when the R-engine ran for an hour and 40 minutes at 1,850 horsepower.

The Merlin itself was conceived in 1932, a direct descendant of the Schneider Trophy-winning powerplants and initially a private venture by Rolls Royce, with the Air Ministry providing funding in 1933. Throughout the early 1930s, the British Air Ministry tinkered and chopped with budgets to develop new aircraft to meet the perceived threat from Germany and Italy, although hardly anyone wanted to admit there even *was* a threat. Liberal hand-flutterers dismissed it as 'claptrap'.

Reginald Mitchell at Supermarine talked his fellow directors into developing an advanced fighter plane, also as a private venture. In 1935 he discovered that he had cancer, aged only 40, and on 5 March of that year the prototype Spitfire made its first flight in Southampton (it was the first of 22,890 Spitfires built). In November 1935, Mitchell chose the Merlin engine for the future production Spitfires and the Merlin would go on to power at least four other of World War II's most iconic aircraft, the Hawker Hurricane, de Havilland Mosquito, P-51 Mustang and the Avro Lancaster.

CHAPTER FIVE

The Locust Years to War

Adolf Hitler came to power in 1933. He promised Germany that it need no longer suffer the shame and humiliation that most Germans felt about the 1919 Versailles Treaty from which the Western Allies, and France especially, had extracted crippling reparations. I was 13 years old and in the Third Form at Archbishop Holgate's Grammar School in York when Hitler took over as German Chancellor. My father and his friends were soon telling me they thought there would be another war and that the only good German was a dead one.

Hitler set Germany to work again, and looked to take back the Saar and Alsace-Lorraine, lost to France in the defeat of 1918. He also started to re-build the German Army, the Luftwaffe, and the German Navy, as well as to rethink the whole concept of war, especially of the 'lightning war' – *Blitzkrieg*.

In Britain that same year, 1933, there was a famous debate at the Oxford Union in which undergraduates voted that they 'would not fight for King and Country.' The students were affected by a sophisticated interpretation of the phrase 'King and Country' echoing Wilfred Owen and his tragic war poem:

The old Lie: Dulce et decorum est,
Pro patria mori.
('It is sweet and right to die for one's country', a phrase from the Roman lyrical poet Horace much used in nineteenth century England.)

The Oxford Union vote was seen in Germany and elsewhere as an indication that the British had a fatal infirmity of purpose. Three million people, overwhelmingly men, were unemployed in Britain, and Winston Churchill continued throughout much of the 1930s to be seen as a dangerous warmonger.

The British Empire, with the momentum of its 'mandates' in the Middle East and Africa, reached its greatest physical size in 1933, but British armed forces were thinly spread. The Royal Navy, still employing many Great War battleships, was the largest navy in the world, on a par with the United States Navy. These two navies and that built by the Japanese, the latter not then seen as belligerents, were measured in the ratio 5:5:3. The British Army then still pined for a decent cavalry war, believing the tank to be unsporting, though useful under certain circumstances.

The cavalry remained the favoured branch of the armed forces for sons of famous British fighting families.

There were a few aristocrats in the RAF, which probably reached its nadir as a fighting service in 1932, but being a pilot was still considered a gentleman's work. There were few regular squadrons, some Auxiliary squadrons formed in universities or via prominent families where flying training was given to young men, mainly middle-class, in order to increase the pool of available pilots when it began to look like there would indeed be another war.

In the RAF proper, aircrew were highly professional with rigid barriers between commissioned and non-commissioned men. As late as June 1942, Kings Regulations and Air Council instructions precluded non-commissioned officers – sergeants – from being designated captains of aircraft. Faced with mixed crews, commissioned and non-commissioned officers, regulations put the senior officer in charge, even if he was a rear gunner. An indication of the strength of these barriers shows up in the memoirs of John Colville, personal secretary to Churchill when he became Prime Minister in May 1940. Colville wrote in *The Fringes of Power* that Churchill was worried after the Battle of Britain that the middle classes were doing most of the fighting in the RAF – and could win the war! What would the upper classes do then?

It was said of the RAF in the inter-war years that Auxiliaries were gentlemen trying to be officers, regulars were officers trying to be gentlemen, and the chaps I joined, RAF Volunteer Reserve (RAFVR), were neither trying to be both. But I am certain there have always been three classes of people in every strata of British society over the last thousand years about whom a variant of that comment has been made.

1935 was a key year in the Lancaster's pre-history. The RAF was split into four commands – Fighter, Bomber, Coastal and Transport – and those with experience of bombing wanted something heavier than the biplane aircraft they then had. Bombing was the main article of faith of Lord Trenchard, reflected in a group of young RAF officers who had made their fighting reputations in Iraq in the 1920s, including Arthur Harris, Charles Portal and the Honourable Sir Ralph Cochrane. In 1942 these were senior officers wielding real power, and they cherished the view that enough bombers and bombing could win any war.

On 10 March 1935, Hermann Goering, a First World War ace with 20 kills who had once commanded the Red Baron's Jagstaffel, was put in charge of the Luftwaffe. For a number of years before this appointment, young Germans were secretly learning flying skills by gliding, but they were soon able to slough off the secrecy and started to acquire serious warplanes. Goering led a debate on whether Germany should build fighter or bomber aircraft, and if bombers, light or heavy bombers?

The concept of Blitzkrieg determined that they opt for light bombers, with the German high command estimating that no war against such a lightning force would last more than three months.

Britain, meanwhile, was beginning to wake up from a very deep sleep and on 6 November 1935 the prototype Hawker Hurricane made its first flight. The Hurricane represented a radical improvement in the performance of RAF front-line fighters, all of which until then had been biplanes. The Hurricane was a monoplane aircraft carrying eight machine guns and capable of more than 300mph. It was, though, not as radical as the Supermarine Spitfire. Originally intended to fulfil the same Air Ministry requirement as the Hurricane, the first Spitfire flew on 5 March 1936.

On 12 May 1936, the Me110 first took to the air, eventually to become Germany's premiere night-fighter, involved in thousands of night-time battles with Lancasters. International conflict came one step nearer in July of that year when the Spanish Civil War erupted. The German Kondor Legion, consisting of fighter, bomber and reconnaissance aircraft, entered the fray to support the fascist General Franco, honing the skills of German aircrews and developing combat tactics in real fighting over the next three years. On 9 November, Madrid became the first major city in Europe to be subjected to sustained bombing over three days and nights, the Germans testing the theory that air bombardment could so demoralise a population that it would cause them to surrender.

The horror of air war, bombs dropping on civilians, was brought home to the world on 26 April 1937, when the Spanish town of Guernica was virtually destroyed in four hours of continuous bombing by the Luftwaffe's Kondor Legion. It was an undefended town, and more than 1,600 civilians were killed. Public reaction around the world led the Nazi propaganda chief, Josef Goebbels, to claim: 'No German bomber took part in this bombing.' It was, of course, a lie.

Hitler was said to have been curious to test the effect of saturation bombing on a civilian population. He was impressed.

On 11 November 1937, the Luftwaffe gave notice of the power and performance of its fighter aircraft when a Messerschmitt 109 set a new world speed record of 379mph over Augsberg, smashing a record set in 1935 by the American billionaire Howard Hughes. Three months later, on 10 February, there came a British effort to show that Fighter Command was capable of taking on other air forces when a Hawker Hurricane, assisted by a 50mph following wind, flew from Edinburgh to London at an average speed of 408mph.

On 4 August, 19 Squadron RAF, based at Duxford, was the first to be equipped with Spitfires, the RAF having ordered a total of 310. Yet there was still a desperate wish in Britain not to acknowledge that war was looming. Prime Minister Neville Chamberlain went to Munich at the end of September 1938, signing away the German-speaking Sudetenland in Czechoslovakia to Hitler who, with his troops already having staged a successful *coup d'etat* in Austria, gave assurances that he now harboured no more territorial ambitions in Europe. He would go on to occupy the rest of Czechoslovakia on 15 March 1939.

On 1 November 1938, the head of RAF Fighter Command, Sir Hugh 'Stuffy' Dowding, boosted Spitfire and Hurricane fighter aircraft production, winning priority for fighters over bombers despite bitter opposition from Lord Trenchard, a champion of total bombing. Trenchard openly deplored the 'continuing clamour for defensive weapons.'

Five weeks later, on 8 December, Germany launched its first aircraft carrier, the *Graf Zeppelin*. Britain had seven aircraft carriers, the USA six, Japan five and France one. Germany had agreed in 1935 to have a fleet one third as large as the Royal Navy, but was secretly building enough ships to achieve parity by the middle of the 1940s; the war simply came too early. On 28 March 1939, the Spanish Civil War ended after Madrid and Valencia surrendered to Franco. The Kondor Legion returned to Germany as heroes, having evolved methods of fighter attacks on bombers that would confound many of the established RAF tactics.

On a personal level, I noted that on 1 April 1939 the battleship *Tirpitz* was launched, sister ship to the *Bismarck* and intended to operate as a commerce raider in the North Atlantic. I remember sitting in a cinema in York watching black-and-white newsreel of the *Tirpitz* splashing into the sea, listening to the triumphant commentary, and yet never imagining that three times I would have the chance to view her personally, though never from closer than three miles high.

The first flight of what was to be the greatest German piston-engined fighter in the coming war, the Focke-Wulf 190, took place on 1 June. It was the first of twenty thousand, built to be able to cope with heavy armour and to carry four 20mm cannon as well as two machine guns.

On 25 July, less than six weeks before war was declared, the Avro Manchester, twin-engined precursor to the Lancaster, made its 17-minute maiden flight.

Hermann Goering uttered the famous boast on 9 August that was to haunt him for the rest of his life. Knowing, surely, that war was inevitable, he told the German people that the Ruhr, the centre of German manufacturing, 'will not be subjected to a single bomb. If an enemy bomber reaches the Ruhr, my name is not Hermann Goering: you can call me Meier!' ('I shall be called Meier if...' was a German vernacular way of saying that something is impossible. Meier was the second most common surname in Germany, but by the end of the war Berlin's air raid sirens were known to the city's famously cynical residents as "Meier's trumpets.")

On 1 September 1939, Germany attacked Poland, and all RAF squadrons were put at war readiness.

I was called that day into the RAFVR. We were mobilised by telegram. There was a tearful farewell from my mother, of course, on a Friday evening. My next brother, Richard, was called up, too. He was in the Yorkshire Hussars, a Yeomanry regiment. Aged 19, I went off in my uniform with a chap called Neville Solomon, having packed a little bag, leaving my mother full of tears.

My father said the usual stuff, good luck, he didn't break down, of course, fathers didn't do that. Neville Solomon was a trainee manager at Marks & Spencers, and he and I drove over together to the town centre in Hull. Our boss was a Rear Admiral called Benson, he was the commandant, a retired officer. We bunked down on the floor, they had no facilities for us whatsoever. That Sunday, 3 September, we all went along to the Station Hotel and got stuck into a few beers, and everybody heard Neville Chamberlain's doleful declaration of war at 11 o'clock.

We went on to have more beers and spent another night in a strange state of mind. On Monday they called us together and said, well, we have nothing for you, so you should all go back home. Give us a call in three days time. After three days they said, nothing new, stay where you are, try again on the following Saturday.

After that they said, don't call us, we'll call you.

CHAPTER SIX

Birth of the Manchester

The situation in Germany after Hitler's election as Reich Chancellor in 1933, had been alarming the Air Ministry throughout the thirties. Rolls Royce had exported a handful of their V12 'Kestrel' engines to Germany in 1935 in part exchange for a Heinkel engine testbed, but disturbing intelligence was emerging from Hitler's Reich. The Kestrels were used to power prototype German warplanes that included the Me 109 fighter and the Ju 87 'Stuka' divebomber.

The RAF was in desperate need of new, modern aircraft, especially bombers. Air Ministry specifications calling for new aircraft tended to take at least 15 months to germinate. The first specification for P.12/36, issued in July 1935, called for an aircraft with a crew of six, a bomb load of not less than 12,000lbs – or accommodation for 24 fully-armed troops – and a normal cruising speed of not less than 180mph at 12,000ft (3,657m). Two tenders were selected, one resulting in prototypes from Supermarine (which were destroyed in a German air raid in Southampton in 1940), the second producing the Short Stirling, the first 4-engined monoplane bomber in the RAF.

A second Air Ministry specification, P13/36, was issued on 6 September 1935 requesting designs for a large, twin-engined monoplane bomber, capable of carrying an 8,000lb bomb load. The requirements for P13/36 were for:

'A twin-engine landplane medium bomber with dive-bombing capacity.
Minimum crew of 4, 2 pilots, 1 wireless/telegraphy operator, 1 air gunner.
Additional crew for longer flights, 1 navigator, 2nd air gunner.
Armament of 2 powered turrets, one 2-gun forward, one 4-gun aft.
With a crew of 6, typical service load of 5,900lbs.
Maximum bomb load of 8,000lbs, including 4 x 2,000lbs, OR
2 x torpedoes of 18 inches (46cm) diameter, length 18ft 2.5 inches (5.5m).
Provision should be made for carrying troops if needed.'

The specification also demanded the capacity for catapult take-offs and 'arrested' landings. The thinking was that in a war, large runways would be targeted by the enemy bombers, preventing their use by aircraft that required long landing and take-off runs.

Two separate tenders were accepted for P.13/36, one from Avro, the other from Handley Page. There had to be a great deal of faith within the Air Ministry for them to give Avro a chance to compete with traditional 'big bomber' manufacturers like Handley Page and Vickers. Until the Manchester tender, Avro's only experience of 'large' aircraft was the Anson, and that was hardly a bomber type, although it later served as one with Coastal Command. Neither had Avro any experience of all-metal, stressed-skin construction, having been known until then as a wood-working firm.

Among the engines suggested to power this new aircraft was the Rolls-Royce Vulture, a radical design that incorporated two Kestrel engines into one, so what looked like a twin-engine aircraft was, in fact, one driven by four engines. The main designer at Avro, Roy Chadwick, was particularly taken with the Vulture's design, and the performance claimed for it. Its drawback was that one engine could not go wrong without affecting its 'twin'.

It was only six days after the issue of the specification, 8 September 1936, that Avro secured an order for two prototypes, but as more intelligence came in about German progress, requirements for P.13/36 changed. There were doubts, particularly at Handley Page, about the distribution of the heavy bomb load and the take-off requirements, especially the idea that a heavy bomber could genuinely make a short take-off and landing. George Volkert at Handley Page was given permission to go ahead with a 4-engine model, the HP57, which became the Halifax, while Roy Chadwick at Avro persisted with the Type 679 – known as the Manchester – with two Rolls Royce Vulture engines. At the time, the Air Ministry was still toying with the idea of launching heavy bombers by catapult assistance. Though the catapult facility was never used, just meeting this specification was to give the Lancaster the in-built strength that was later so apparent.

The key difference between the two rivals, the Halifax and the Manchester (the Manchester III was to become the Lancaster) was in the bomb loads. With the July specification P.12/36, there was no requirement to carry individual bombs heavier than 2,000lbs. With P.13/36, two months later, the aircraft had to accommodate two long torpedoes as an alternative to 2,000lb bombs, which meant a massive bomb bay. In the Manchester, all the bomb load was to be in the fuselage, and all the oil and fuel in the wings, with two 400-imperial gallon tanks in each wing. But it was the huge bomb-bay that was ultimately to give the Lancaster such a terrific advantage over its rivals from any air force until 1944.

Detailed design work on the new bomber continued throughout 1937, yet even at this stage an Air Ministry contract for 200 production aircraft was received by Avro on 1 July, and it was months yet before the first prototype would even fly! Someone was getting seriously nervous about Adolf Hitler, and the Air Ministry was thinking ahead, modifying its specification to achieve ease of quantity production. The design of the aircraft was split into modules, four sections to the fuselage: the bomb-bay, stretching under the cockpit section; the wing-root; the centre fuselage; and a fourth separate tail section. Building the aircraft in modules allowed construction to be dispersed to different sites. No one wanted all their eggs in one basket. That basket could be bombed.

At the same time, crew dispositions and the arrangement of the bomb loads were thrashed out with the Air Ministry. The design of the Manchester resulted in a big, mid-winged aircraft with twin fins and rudders. Both wing spars passed through the central fuselage, the two engines mounted as close to the body of the aircraft as the propeller size would allow – to assist asymmetric flight in case one engine unit was knocked out – and the landing gear fitted into the engine nacelles. The initial wing span was 80ft 2in (24.5m), so it could fit easily into existing hangars. Four of the crew of seven were housed forward of the wing, beneath a large transparent canopy.

Avro were also working flat-out on a big production order for the Anson in the period leading up to the war, the Anson requiring a great deal of wood-working, at which Avro staff were highly skilled. A production order for 1,000 Bristol Blenheims in 1937 gave Roy Chadwick and his design staff the necessary experience at stressed-skin construction vital to building the Manchester. Without this experience, which led directly to the all-metal bomber, they could not have competed directly with the Short Stirling and the Halifax. Roy Dobson took the initiative to adapt wood-working and metal-pressing machinery on a huge scale, designing innovative tools to cope with the ideas Chadwick was developing. They broke new ground in milling spar sections of the size required for the Manchester.

Avro opted for a flexible production line, so any changes that were required after testing could be quickly incorporated. There was a great sense of urgency, the production and design staff very much aware of the threat to Britain, and the paucity of the weapons the country had to strike back at any attacker. Flexibility was part of the culture of the company; Avro had made two major changes to the Anson's tail-plane and elevator during flight trials. It was also an indication of the way vital decisions were being made at that time in what looked like a panic-striken Air Ministry. Even though both Avro Manchester prototypes had serious problems to be resolved, orders for the aircraft were placed not only with Avro but also with Metropolitan-Vickers, who were contracted to build 100 Manchesters in mid-1939; Armstrong Whitworth received contracts for 400 Manchesters by the end of 1939; Fairey Aviation landed orders for 150, along with 450 from Avro itself in January 1940. This amounted to a total of 1,100 on order, and any change made at the design centre by Roy Chadwick had to be transmitted to at least four other factories.

The RAF planned to have 20 operational squadrons of Manchesters by March

1942, yet as early as February 1939, Chadwick was tinkering with plans for a four-engined version, known as the Type 683. Some of his ideas were committed to paper, which was just as well because there were growing doubts about the reliability of the Vulture engine.

After weeks of procrastination due to dreadful weather, the prototype Manchester first took to the air at Ringway in Manchester on 25 July 1939 for a 17-minute flight. There had been recurring problems with the hydraulics, and one evening of very bad temper all round when a hydraulic accumulator burst and the design crew were covered in oil. Flying it was Avro's Chief Test Pilot, 'Sam' Brown.

In his log book, Brown wrote that it went off 'fairly well.' Privately, the view was that the new aircraft was 'a bit of a handful.' In fact, the hydraulic pump shafts had broken.

The Manchester prototype was seriously lacking in lateral stability – it yawed left or right – and landings were tricky because of a tendency to yaw to port when the engine throttles were closed. In addition, Sam Brown found the controls to be heavy, which he thought meant they needed to be balanced. The Vulture engines behaved well, though they were reported to 'run hot.' The most serious problem was a huge take-off run, though the aircraft was lightly loaded.

This was just six weeks before the war began.

More bad weather intervened, and it was not until 1 August that a second flight was made in the prototype; again, there were hydraulic problems, with another breakage. A third flight on 14 August was at Woodford, and yet again, a quill shaft on the hydraulic pump broke. Three days later, after a flight of just over an hour with detailed trim and hydraulic tests in the air, one of the brakes failed on landing, the aircraft skidded violently, and yet again, another hydraulic breakage!

On 30 August, Sam Brown did 40 minutes of taxiing and handling tests, and reported that the aircraft was 'not at all satisfactory.' It still had a bad swing on take-off, and violent vibrations from the Rotol airscrews. After the flight, the hydraulics were found to be full of foreign matter, oil mixed with glycol.

On 1 September 1939, the day the Germans marched into Poland, Sam Brown taxied the Manchester but judged it to be in such a poor state that it was too bad to fly. He grumbled that the de Havilland 'expert' sent to monitor the performance of the propellers did 'not seem to know much about his job.'

On the day war was declared, 3 September, Brown had more trouble during an attempted take-off when the 'constant speed' propellers 'went into coarse pitch for no reason at all. I am fed up and will not attempt to fly the Manchester again until a thorough investigation has been carried out.'

Sam Brown filled the next three weeks continuing to be 'fed-up' and test-flying the stream of Ansons and Blenheims coming off the production lines prior to their delivery to RAF squadrons. A ninth flight of the prototype on 26 September was again unsatisfactory. Sam Brown had it in the air for 43 minutes, but reported 'the propellers badly adjusted and hydraulic pumps failed.' More frenzied work in the now camouflaged hangars, more assurances it should work, and on 11 October Sam Brown had another go. It was even more exciting on this flight than on previous ones. He was in the air for 45 minutes, but approaching Ringway the port Vulture engine blew up! The crankshaft fractured and disintegrating pistons and con-rods poked holes in the crankcase. Fortunately, the Graviner fire control system worked and doused the flames while Brown manfully balanced the controls to land the aircraft. The calm test pilot, prone to understatement, wrote later that day: 'I had rather a shaky time getting her down.'

New propellers were fitted for his test flight on 18 October, when he flew it for 55 minutes and came down to report 'very difficult to control.'

The first trouble-free flight was on 23 October 1939, when Brown took the prototype Manchester up to 17,000ft (5,181m) and the serious tests began. Other test pilots, John Grierson from Armstrong Siddeley, Bill Thorn and H.V. Worrall, flew in the huge new aircraft, as well as Professor Shaw of Rolls Royce, who conducted 'vibration' tests on 15 November. There was already a certain amount of uneasiness about the performance of the Vulture engines. Nevertheless, it was decided to hand the prototype over to the Air Ministry's Aeroplane and Armament Experimental Establishment evaluation unit at Boscombe Down to give RAF pilots the experience of flying it, and on 28 November Sam Brown took Bill Thorn as his co-pilot, setting off south from Manchester. Fifteen minutes later both engines stopped!

They had just passed Stoke on Trent, flying over woods and fields. Nothing the two expert pilots pulled or pushed could get the engines to start again. In a brilliant piece of flying, Sam Brown aimed the Manchester – like a glider with the sink rate of a brick – at a large, open park on a hill-top surrounded by trees, lowering the wheels in the hope that he could affect a genuine landing rather than going in belly-up, the latter being the less dangerous alternative. He succeeded, little damage was done, and then they found that the fuel cocks on both engines had been set to 'Reserve' rather than 'Main' tank. It took a lot of hints about the Official Secrets Act to persuade the owner of Charnes Hall – where Chadwick had landed – to cut down a number of mature trees so he could fly the aircraft back out again two days later. A centre-fin was almost immediately added to cope with yaw. Sam Brown finally delivered the Manchester to Boscombe Down on 10 December.

The A&AEE pilots found they were running into the same hydraulic problems that Brown had experienced, along with bomb doors that wouldn't open and, on 20 December, the prototype was attacked by RAF fighters in the mistaken belief that the Manchester was a German aircraft! The attacks petered out with some violent manoeuvring and quite a lot of bad language. Three days later, with an A&AEE crew on board performing a series of special take-off tests, the port Vulture engine failed and the aircraft force-landed in a cabbage field near Boscombe Down. No one was injured but the co-pilot was covered in a hail of mud and decaying cabbages that flew through the bomb-aimers broken cupola. Not surprisingly, all A&AEE tests were suspended.

On the bright side it was found that the damaged aircraft could be easily disman-tled and quickly taken back to Avro for repair. The A&AEE pilots also told Avro how impressed they were with the general design, particularly of the pilot's cockpit.

Bad weather then descended on the country, especially around Manchester. Frost and heavy snow put paid to any testing in the bleak month of January 1940, so much snow that on 3 February the roof of one of the production buildings collapsed. When the thaw set in, the airfield was flooded, compounding landing and take-off problems because there were, as yet, no hard runways at Woodford. The weather was so dreadful that the production of Ansons piled up, 19 of them being test-flown on March 6, and 17 the following day.

On the Manchester prototype, very little happened until the first week in April. The production line was fully geared up to start, but what were they going to build? The aircraft still had a poor take-off performance, and with its tendency to yaw, the Manchester simply was not good enough to go into production. The wing span was changed, with bigger ailerons for more authority. The elevators were re-made to provide more balance and try and reduce the heavy handling, and they were changed from welded steel to fabric-covered, a familiar process used on building Ansons. A second prototype, which was to make its maiden flight on 26 May 1940, incorporated all of the changes. The wingspan lengthened to 90ft 2in (27.4m), there were better aileron hinges, work was going ahead to balance the elevators, and the fins and rudders were deepened by 8in (20.3cm). Avro persisted in working with twin fins because they had 'always' been used on British bombers, like the Hamden, Whitley, Hendon, Bombay, Harrow, Heyford, even the Vimy bomber that had crossed the Atlantic with Alcock and Brown in 1919. These earlier aircraft had used twin fins to achieve the required fin area without going for a single oversized structure. Twin fins could be smaller, providing greater structural integrity and stiffness. By the late 1930s, more advanced construction techniques would allow for a larger, single fin to be strong and rigid enough to do the job, but Avro persisted with two, eventually also adding a third central fin on the Manchester.

It was not until May 1940 that the repaired and modified prototype, this one fitted with turrets, returned to the testers at Boscombe Down. The British Army began evacuating from Dunkirk towards the end of the month and fears of inva-sion were growing daily, putting real pressure on Avro. Its great rival, Handley

Page, with far more experience of building bombers, had cleared the decks for its four-engined Halifax. More importantly, it had secured delivery dates for the Rolls Royce Merlin engines that everyone now wanted, *yesterday* if possible. Roy Chadwick still favoured the whole idea of the Vulture engine and seemed willing to take a chance on it, even though Rolls Royce had gone full speed ahead on Merlin production.

It was around this time that Air Chief Marshall Sir Wilfred Freeman and Air Marshal Arthur Tedder (Tedder went on to be Eisenhower's deputy on D-Day in 1944) went to Avro to see Roy Dobson. The two senior airmen flew in the second Manchester prototype and were distinctly unenthusiastic. Dobson admitted to his important visitors that Ernest Hives – works manager at Rolls Royce, later Lord Hives – was increasingly unimpressed with the Vulture engine. More problems emerged when the Vulture engine on the first prototype was stripped down and there was unexpected wear and tear on the big ends. It was deduced that running the engine at high speed meant the oil lost its viscosity very quickly. As Vulture engines on other aircraft were also running at high temperatures, the suspicion grew that what was wrong with them went a great deal deeper than the oil filters.

In the wider world, when war had been declared in September 1939, the RAF had 536 bombers and 608 fighters. The Germans had 2,130 bombers and 1,215 fighters. In the opening few months, German forces moved with such lightning speed that they overwhelmed all opposition; first the Poles and then, when they turned their attention to the West, the same happened to Denmark, Norway, Holland and ultimately – a terrific shock at the time - to France, which had held out so doggedly over four years in the Great War.

RAF Bomber Command's main role in the fighting was to send out twin-engine aircraft to mine the seas and river-mouths of Germany, also dropping leaflets telling the Germans they should get rid of that nasty man, Hitler. Any German capital ship was fair game, but the fear of being thought guilty of war crimes severely constrained British bombing operations if there were civilians in the target area. On 18 December 1939, for example, a force of 24 RAF Wellingtons from 149 and 9 Squadrons had set out on a daylight attack to bomb the German Baltic port of Wilhelmshaven. They were harassed by German fighters, guided to intercept them, unknown to the British, by radar; there was a mistaken belief during that 'phoney war' period that the 'Hun' did not actually have radar. The Wellingtons arrived over Wilhelmshaven, bomb doors open, with a battleship and a cruiser in their sights, but… nothing was dropped.

Why?

Because if they had missed the ships they might have hurt or killed German civilians, and could have faced a court-martial. They set off home, flying out of the barrage of flak and into deadly danger as German fighters fell upon them. Half of the 24 RAF aircraft were lost to enemy action, three others crashed-landed at home.

Until this raid showed the power of fighter aircraft, it was believed in the RAF that well-armed bombers would *always get through*. But the 60 per cent loss rate was too high, and British bombing operations were changed from day to night, despite the paucity of experience in Bomber Command of night flying. All through that winter British aircraft were used to drop leaflets rather than bombs. Arthur Harris, not yet in control of bombing operations, complained that the RAF was supplying the Germans with a year's supply of toilet paper. Such bombs as were dropped, compared to later years, were very light indeed, 250-pounders. Barnes Wallis, the boffin who changed all that thinking, said 'most RAF officers preferred eight 250lb bombs to one bomb of 2,000lbs because they had more chance of hitting something.'

Only when the Luftwaffe pulverised the Dutch city of Rotterdam in May 1940 did the RAF feel that they could risk killing German civilians. With Hitler apparently threatening to invade England, most of the summer months were spent in attacks on shipping and the collections of barges in French ports rather than raids on Germany. The invasion scare only diminished after the end of the Battle of Britain in October.

It was during this fraught period for the nation that the nascent Lancaster faced the very real prospect of never being brought into existence. The 'phoney war' had ended on 10 May 1940 with the German Blitzkrieg on France. Churchill became Prime Minister that evening and appointed Lord Beaverbrook as Minister of Aircraft Production four days later. Beaverbrook found that no less than *37 different types of aircraft* were being produced in Britain at that time, many of them absolutely no match at all for modern German warplanes. Beaverbrook stopped production on 32 aircraft to concentrate on five types – Spitfire, Hurricane, Blenheim, Wellington and Whitley.

A prudent Roy Chadwick, however enamoured of the Vulture, had already discussed a 4-engined Manchester with the Air Ministry. The fact that he had drawings, performance estimates, outline production schedules and, more importantly, that he had *shared* this knowledge, must have weighed deeply in the vital bun-fight that followed. Chadwick had said he could build a bomber based on the Manchester – to be called a Manchester III – but with four Merlin engines. The Air Ministry had been polite but a bit distant. They knew that the demand for Merlin engines was absolutely huge – even their 3,300 useless Fairey Battles were powered by Merlins – and having another manufacturer with his hand out looking to use these brilliant engines was just another supply problem.

Avro Managing Director Roy Dobson, able to see what might happen, had appointed a man called Stuart Davies on 1 April 1940, to progress design work on the Manchester III – called a Type 683 – with a minimum change of technique from building the twin-engined Type 679 Manchester I. The increase in size in the tail-plane span being mooted for prototype Manchesters, along with the increased wing-span, would work just as well with four engines.

Rolls Royce kept Roy Chadwick informed about their installation of a Merlin engine into a Bristol Beaufighter so that, without modification, the complete Beaufighter power unit could be fitted into the outer main-plane of the Manchester III. Davies was convinced that, should the change be necessary, there would be minimal delay in building the new bombers.

One of the pressures on the Air Ministry was that aircrew were coming in from abroad, from the Empire Air Training Scheme, fully trained and needing decent aircraft to carry the war to the Germans. In a brutal series of moves the Luftwaffe was showing how misguided the whole British policy of aircraft procurement had been in the years leading up to the war. There turned out to be just enough Spitfires and Hurricanes, especially after Lord Beaverbrook cracked the whip, to equip Fighter Command. But there were also thousands of existing bombers in which the lives of trained, brave, experienced crews were thrown away.

When the Battle of France had begun on 10 May, Fairey Battles were called upon to perform unescorted, low-level tactical bombing attacks against the advancing German Army. They were at risk of attack from Luftwaffe fighters and within easy range of the German Army's light anti-aircraft guns. In the first of two sorties carried out by Battles that day, 3 out of 8 aircraft were lost. In a second sortie, 13 out of 32 Battles went down, with the remainder suffering damage. Despite bombing from as low as 250ft (76m), their attacks had little impact on the German columns.

The following day, 15 Battles of the Belgian Air Force attacked bridges over the Albert Canal on the River Meuse. They lost 10 aircraft. In a second RAF sortie that day only 1 out of 8 Battles survived. There were other missions that produced an almost 100 per cent casualty rate amongst Blenheims; one such operation was mounted on 13 August 1940 against a Luftwaffe airfield in Denmark by 12 Blenheims of 82 Squadron. One Blenheim returned early; the pilot was later charged to face a court martial by Air Vice Marshal Donald Stevenson, AOC 2 Group, but would avoid the disgrace by being safely killed on a subsequent operation. The other 11 Blenheims reached Denmark and were shot down, five by flak and six by Me 109s. It is a testament to the courage of the men in these units that they continued to operate throughout these months with virtually no respite and little of the publicity accorded to Fighter Command, taking much higher losses than the Fighter Boys.

A great many useless bombers were built throughout this confused period and brought into war service. So many aircrew perished in those totally unsuitable aircraft, but they were all we had at the time….

Taking the hard decision, Sir Wilfred Freeman asked Rolls Royce to stop producing Vultures, which left the Avro Manchester up the creek. Rolls Royce could not put any more time or money into the development of the Vulture.

Either Avro went immediately for the 4-engined concept, or they were doomed to building another company's aircraft, the Halifax. On 29 July, Sir Wilfred Freeman wrote to Sir Roy Dobson, telling him to stop all development work on the Manchester III! They were to turn their production lines over to building Halifaxes.

Dobson and Chadwick reacted the same way.

Oh, no we bloody well won't!

CHAPTER SEVEN

The Short Unhappy Life of the Manchester

Within the Air Ministry, as within any bureaucracy, there were camps favouring one manufacturer or another. To an outsider, these camps often appeared to follow departmental interests, showing lesser regard for the national interest. There were Handley-Page men within the Ministry, and Avro men, and Dobson and Chadwick had to gear up the Avro camp to fight their corner.

Naturally, the Handley-Page camp in the Ministry would see any danger to their own supply of Merlin engines as a threat to their own standing. There was, therefore, determined resistance to allowing Avro actually to get their hands on Merlin engines to test the performance of the 4-engined Manchester III. Dobson and Chadwick were fighting for the survival of their heavy bomber, but the calculation about whether or not to help them was about matters a lot more parochial than whether or not they were capable of building the finest heavy bomber in Britain. It came down to meaner ends and arguments, and a very British way to win through, the 'Old Pal's Act.'

Following a great many phone calls and an anxious journey to London from Manchester, Dobson and Chadwick parked in the office of Patrick Henessy of the Ministry of Aircraft Production. There they made a detailed presentation on the potential of the Mark III Manchester. Henessy was convinced and took up their cause. He navigated them through the corridors of power to an ex-naval aviator, Captain R.N. Liptrott, who also became very taken with the aircraft's potential.

Liptrott, in turn, sent out a memo to all the decision-makers, endorsing Avro's 4-engined ideas, effectively saving the Lancaster. 'There is no reason,' he wrote, 'why this aircraft with four Merlins should not have the same performance as the twin-engined Manchester.' This has been described as 'masterly understatement' but it did allow Avro to go ahead and complete two 4-engined prototypes by July 1941. Given the somewhat jaundiced view held by Arthur harris of Royal Navay officers, it is ironic that the Lancaster which he came to see as his 'shining sword' was rescued at a vital stage of its development by a Royal Navy officer.

To beat the moves within the Ministry and elsewhere to starve them of resources, Dobson and Chadwick went to one of the most powerful men in Rolls Royce, works manager E.W. Hives. It was very much a case of, 'Wonder if you could help, old boy?' Hives found them two second-hand Merlin engines which had not been thrashed, plus two new Merlins which had been destined to power Beaufighters. Rolls Royce had a Merlin test bed for the Beaufighter Mark II, and gave the powerplant from this test aeroplane to Avros.

Chadwick had the engines by September, at the height of the Battle of Britain, and Dobson told Avro's head of experimental development, Stuart Davies, to have a 4-engined prototype flying by May 1941. Davies prepared a plan to accelerate the whole process and have the new aircraft flying five months ahead of deadline, on 31 December of that year. By this time the 4-engined Avro was emerging on its 'clearance to fly' design certificate as the 'Lancaster.' The name had been selected by Roy Chadwick as a tribute to the capital town of Lancashire, but approved by Dobson, a Yorkshireman.

Meanwhile, early in August 1940, Air Chief Marshal Sir Charles Portal, then C-in-C Bomber Command, decreed that the Strategic Bomber Force would be made up of 4-engined aircraft, the first on line being Stirlings.

All Avro had to do to the 2-engined Manchesters to turn them into 4-engined Lancasters was change part of the wing and add an extra engine each side. The rest of the machine had been largely tried and tested, and the early hydraulics that had given so much trouble were in the process of being rectified. But while research was continuing into the 4-engined version of the Manchester III, the RAF was in dire need of heavy bombers. Production lines had already been completed at Metropolitan-Vickers in Manchester to start manufacturing Vulture-powered Manchesters. The Vulture engines, although no longer being produced, were stockpiled ready to fit to the aircraft as soon as they were needed.

The first production Avro-built Manchester was delivered for testing at Boscombe Down on 5 August 1940. Trials with the prototype Manchester – two days after the first production model rolled off the lines – showed that in a high speed dive with the rear turret on the beam (virtually at right angles to the fuselage) there was a violent buffeting. The recommended cure was to 'cowl' the fuselage, which changed the airflow around the turret. More tests in September showed a marked improvement in longitudinal stability. At an all-up weight of 52,000lbs, 5,000lbs below maximum, the Manchester was reported to be very pleasant to fly.

Rolls Royce was desperate to find out why the Vulture engines were seizing up, and continuing changes were made to the oil cooling and distribution systems. The hydraulic systems, described by one source as a 'nightmare of increasing proportions', added to the scares. There were four such systems, one for the general aircraft and one for each of the three separate turrets. This design was introduced to allow the Manchester to be built in sections and then assembled. All the couplings were made by a single supplier. According to Avro's Harry Holmes, one ground engineer left the following description about the combined problems:

'We used to listen to the Manchester taking off and if the whine of the propeller in fine pitch continued beyond 1,000ft (305m) and they had not changed to coarse pitch by then, sure enough there would be a bang as the unit went and the engine packed up. As for hydraulics, every time a Manchester started up there would be one or more bangs and oil would pour out of the pipe joints. Even when we had cleared a Manchester for flying, we could never guarantee that next time it started up there would not be the same problems. The oil coolers would burst regularly – one day I fitted six successive oil coolers to one Manchester, and they all burst!'

At the beginning of November 1940, even as these problems were being diagnosed and frantic steps were being taken to correct them, 207 Squadron RAF at Waddington in Lincolnshire was picking up the first delivery of Manchesters. Of the first five rolled off the line, only two actually arrived at the squadron. By the end of the year, 28 of this cobbled-together aircraft had been produced, and the extra-large fins, up from 8ft 10in (2.7m) to 12ft (3.65m), along with a 33ft (10.06m) tail-span, were not introduced until the eighty-sixth aircraft off the lines, the same model chosen to delete the central fin.

Most of those first 28 Manchesters seemed to spend their winter days standing idle around Woodford's peri-tracks, awaiting modifications to their engines, propellers or hydraulics – or all three. Morale among Avro workers was not high, and might have been exceedingly low among the aircrews destined to fly this turkey, except they were not fully informed about the Manchester's faults, having to survive while finding out for themselves!

Eventually the hydraulic couplings that kept popping were ordered from another manufacturer, and changed to the more reliable 'olive' type. De Havilland came through with some decent propellers. But the key change was replacing the two Vulture engines with four Merlins. In retrospect, the bombing of the Metrovick factory by the Luftwaffe on 22/23 December 1940 was something of a blessing. Metrovick's first completed Manchester, looking bright, sturdy and reliable (while, in fact, anything but), produced that very day, was destroyed in the raid, as were the next 12 Manchesters on the line. The destruction of many jigs and tools meant a delay of three months in the supply of Manchesters to RAF Squadrons. In the end, out of the first production order of 200, 157 Manchesters were completed, while the remaining 43 ended as Lancasters.

Why was the manifestly inferior Manchester ever delivered to my generation of young pilots to take into the heat of battle?

Why couldn't they have waited until the 'perfect bomber', the Lancaster, came on line?

The answer is, what alternative was there?

Short Stirlings were going into service, but with a service ceiling of 16,500ft (5,029m) they were soon to become easy meat for Luftwaffe pilots. The Halifax was in full production, but there were early indications that it had handling problems that could quite easily be fatal in the hands of anyone other than the most experienced pilots. The twin-engine Wellington, designed by the brilliant boffin Barnes Wallis, could take extraordinary amounts of punishment, but was soon discovered to be too slow. British bombers already in use – Hampdens, Whitleys, Blenheims – were stop-gaps, thrown into the fight to show willing as Britain lost battle after battle, first thrown out of Europe and then beaten around most of the Mediterranean.

When searching for the means to give hope to the British public, Churchill, more than all other leaders, looked to Bomber Command, which remained for years the only way of hitting back at the Germans. Hope was everything and Bomber Command was the repository of hope. However poor and unreliable the Manchester, it was one of the 'heavies' taking the war to the Germans, and had its job to do. The flow of newly-trained crews needed something to fly and, as happened throughout the war, young men who survived each operation were expected to improve the performance of an aircraft through their reports on how they managed to stay alive. Despite the growing losses, there were enough survivors for feedback.

In the first year of the war, up to September 1940, Bomber Command had lost 1,908 aircrew. In the second year, as the Lancaster was developed, the losses had more than doubled to 4,330 men. In 1942, the year when the Lancaster began to be introduced, it began to make a significant contribution to the war effort, Bomber Command losses nearly doubled again, to 8,018, and the butcher's bill was to grow more bloody still over the following two years.

The pilots assembled to fly the Manchester in 207 Squadron were among the best and the bravest, the first six crews between them having already won a DSO, six DFCs and seven DFMs. It is said that no other RAF Squadron ever suffered the prolonged agony of such a difficult and frustrating task. Because the result of their labours was to be the almost faultless Lancaster – technically a Manchester III – we should look at the Manchester's brief service career.

All the leading airmen of 97 Squadron, for example, also formed at Waddington and flying Manchesters, were killed or Missing in Action within 14 months. One of the finest bomber leaders in Britain, Guy Gibson, emerged from flying Manchesters at 106 Squadron. One other VC and two of our Last Witnesses also had a role to play in the Manchester's difficult and short career.

Last Witness Bob Horsley joined the RAFVR at the age of 19 and trained in

Britain as a W/Op Air Gunner flying in Hampdens with 50 Squadron, RAF. His pilot on a nearly-completed tour of 27 operations was Pilot Officer Dennis Miller, a New Zealander. Horsley went off to be commissioned as a Pilot Officer and when he returned in May 1942, just past his twenty-first birthday, Miller was tour-expired after 30 operations. To complete the last three ops of his own tour, Horsley was posted to fly with a new pilot, Leslie Manser, just 20 years old and converted to flying Manchester aircraft. They flew two ops together and prepared for Horsley's last operation before six months off ops. Bob Horsley:

'On 30 May we went over to Coningsby to pick up a clapped-out, flak-riddled Manchester, ZN-D-7301. It had patches all over the place from a raid on St Nazaire 11 days earlier, and we took it for a night flying test (NFT). Leslie complained about the aircraft's climbing ability, but my radio was okay and the four other crew members also had no complaints.

'Unlike Lancasters, the Manchester had a co-pilot, Sgt Leslie Baveystock, with Navigator Richard Barnes, a second W/Op Sgt Stanley King, and two gunners, Sgt Alan Mills at the front turret and Sgt Ben Naylor at the rear. They were all inexperienced except for Barnes and myself, and all older than me except for Manser. It was scheduled to be my thirtieth operation that night when I would be tour-expired.

'Yet I had some apprehensions about flying Manchesters. I had done a dozen flights in them, and had walked away from three crashes, each of which had been totally burnt-out.

'Landing back at our base in Skellingthorpe after the NFT, I said to Leslie, "I pity the crew who are going on ops in this machine to-night."

'"Don't worry, Bob, it'll most likely be us," Les laughed.

'It was us.

'I went back to my room to rest before briefing and then had the strongest premonition that we would be shot down. I destroyed all the letters from my girlfriends and packed my kit. Whatever happened, being posted missing or completing the tour, I would leave the station. I took my spare escape kit, escape rations and foreign money, all of which I had neglected to return after my previous op, and stowed them away in my battledress. I took one last look around before going off to briefing.

'Though I worried about being shot down, I was also convinced I would not be killed. If the Germans did not meet me with fixed bayonets, well, I had been a good boy scout, had learned woodcraft, could live off the land and had been a champion school runner, so I felt sure I would get away.

'There was great excitement at briefing when it was revealed that the target was Cologne, the first of the thousand bomber raids in which Bomber Harris scraped together crews and aircraft from every part of the RAF available to him. We were told that as our aiming point would already be burning, we should aim at the nearest point not on fire. My personal feeling was that it was about time we took the gloves off and hit the Jerries hard to repay them for the destruction in London, Coventry and other cities. This looked like the beginning of real warfare.

'Back at the Mess for our aircrew supper, lovely bacon and eggs, the room hummed with excitement. A thousand bombers was awesome, and all of us being over the target at the same time hardly sunk in.

'On our Manchester the mid-upper turret had been removed, which I thought a good thing. We were to carry a full load of bombs and fuel, and not having the drag of the turret would help to compensate for the poor climbing power that Leslie Manser had complained about.

'It got dark about nine o'clock in the evening and we went out to our aircraft in the crew coach. I saw a great friend, Johnnie Tytherleigh and told him: "I won't be back tonight, Johnnie. I am taking my three-month end-of-tour leave in Europe."

'He laughed: "See you at the de-briefing in the morning." (He was killed 18 months later flying on operations with 617 Squadron.)

'We lined up on the runway at 22.50 hours. Les opened the throttles to give the engines full power and we roared off into the dark. It was not long before he reported that the engines were over-heating and they lacked power. He slowly eased the Manchester higher, but our climb rate was well below normal. It was a cloudless night and the full moon came up, and after we staggered up to 7,000ft (2,133m) Leslie decided the over-heating was alarming enough for him to level out. I checked my radio and all seemed well. I had the comfort of the heating system directly into my little space, so I could fly quite comfortably in my battledress and harness.

'We purred towards the Dutch coast with a perfect night, a bomber's moon, cloudless sky and light winds. Not a shot was fired as we headed inland, though at 7,000ft we were sitting ducks for the light flak batteries. The navigator, Barnes, soon warned us we were approaching the searchlight and flak belt the Germans had established across our flight path to all major targets in Germany. Still, surprisingly, no ack-ack appeared nor searchlight roamed the sky. I glanced out of the window and saw the Rhine reflected in the moonlight. I had been to Cologne a number of times before, everything seemed to be in the right place at the right time. He was not called 'Bang-on Barnes' for nothing, so why no flak?

'We were still wobbling through the sky at a mere 7,000ft, well below our briefed height and certainly a great deal lower than the Main Force aircraft. There was no danger of a collision but a great danger that someone would accidentally drop their bombs on us, never mind being sitting ducks for the German anti-aircraft batteries.

'As we neared the target, the city was clearly visible in the full moon. We saw the exploding blockbusters – 4,000lb "cookies" – of the early arrivals, and soon Cologne was lit up with burning incendiaries. I saw a Wellington aircraft, not much higher than ourselves, being coned by searchlights and shot at by light flak. Now it was our turn on the bombing run. Barnes had moved forward to the bomb-aimer's position in the nose and soon called "Target Sighted", "Bomb Doors Open", "Bombs fused", then the mantra, "left-left... steady... right...steady... bombs gone!"

'The Manchester seemed to give a sigh of relief as the bombs left it, and we gained more than 100ft (30.48m) in height.

'Barnes called, "Hold for the photograph... steady!"

'As if the last command had been a signal for the Germans, searchlights coned us and flak burst all around with deafening thuds, and sounds of light flak hitting us. The smell of cordite filled the aircraft. Manser immediately dived steeply to port and down to roof top level to get us out of trouble. As we neared the ground the searchlights switched off and the flak ceased. Manser levelled the aircraft and brought it under control. The rear gunner, Naylor, reported that he had been hit by flak. I reported smoke coming out of the port air vent. A few moments later the port engine burst into flames. Manser quickly feathered the engine and extinguished the flames. He asked the navigator for a course to the nearest Master Diversion Airfield – Manston in Kent – and ordered the crew to jettison everything possible.

'The tail of the Manchester had been so badly damaged that it made asymmetric flight on one engine extremely difficult. The elevators also seemed to have been damaged which made pitch control hard.

'I told the second W/Op, Stanley King, to go and get Naylor out of the rear turret and dress his wounds, but the poor chap was paralysed with shock. I thought he might have been wounded, but looked at him closely and there was no sign of physical injury. I asked him instead to take over my radio and send a hit-report back to base, and I headed to the back of the aircraft to try and get Naylor out of his turret, dress his wounds, and ensure he would be able to bail-out if we were so ordered.

'I switched on the internal lights of the aircraft and, after centralising the turret, pulled Naylor from the damaged area. I laid him on the floor near the rear door – there seemed to be blood everywhere. He had been hit on the bridge of his nose, his left shoulder and left foot. I gave him a shot of morphine to dull the pain, and tore away clothing around the shoulder wound to put on a shell-dressing, making sure the bandages went under his parachute harness in case he had to bail out. At the same time I plugged him into the intercom and kept shouting at Stanley King to send the hit-report.

'Meanwhile, Baveystock, Barnes and Mills were throwing everything they could out of the aircraft to lighten it. I suspected our bomb-doors were still open and had been damaged, and passed this news on. I finished dressing Naylor's wounds and plugged myself into the intercom to tell Manser I was going to jettison stuff myself.

'Manser, in a very cool and calm voice – as if it was a practice drill – said "Crew from Skipper, put on parachutes."

'I acknowledged and handed Naylor and King their chutes and saw them safely clipped in place. Then Manser said, "I can't hold this aircraft any longer. Good Luck! Jump! Jump! Jump!"

'I ordered Naylor and King out, but they appeared not to believe me and insisted that I go first. The rear door had been jettisoned and although the crew drill stated I should dive through the doorway, I thought this dangerous because of the low set of the tail-plane. I sat on the step of the door and rolled out. There was no counting to 10, I could see we were only 1,000ft (305m) over the ground so as soon as the tail-plane passed over my head I pulled the rip-cord.

'There was a sudden jerk as the canopy opened and slowed my fall. I talked to myself, "ankles together, knees slightly bent," and it seemed only a matter of seconds before I hit the ground with a splash! I had landed in a wet marshy area. A few moments later I heard the aircraft crash...'

There were no Germans with fixed bayonets in the marsh where Horsley landed, so he set out to escape by finding friendly locals – he had landed near Bree, just inside Belgium. He soon discovered that Les Baveystock, Stanley King, Alan Mills and the wounded Ben Taylor were also alive and free. Richard Barnes, the sixth member of the crew, did contact a Belgian, but this particular Belgian handed him over to the Germans and Barnes spent the rest of the war as a PoW.

In less than a month and after some incredible incidents – including eye-flirting with two beautiful Luftwaffe girls on the Paris Metro, to the sheer horror of his French Resistance guides – the irrepressible Bob Horsley and the rest of Manser's crew made it to Gibraltar and freedom

But 20-year-old Manser did not make it. His citation for his posthumous Victoria Cross tells a spare tale:

'Leslie Thomas Manser, Flying Officer, 50 Squadron, RAFVR.

'On 30/31 May, 1942 Flying Officer Manser was captain and first pilot of a Manchester aircraft which took part in the mass raid on Cologne.

'As the aircraft was approaching the objective it was subject to intense and accurate anti-aircraft fire. Manser held on to his dangerous course and bombed the target success-fully from a height of 7,000ft (2,133m). Then he set course for base, the Manchester damaged and still under heavy fire. Manser took violent evasive action, turning and descending to under 1,000ft (305m). It was of no avail. The searchlights and flak followed him until the outskirts of the city were passed. The aircraft was hit repeatedly and the rear gunner was wounded. The front cabin was filled with smoke; the port engine was overheating badly...

'Despite all the efforts of pilot and crew, the Manchester began to lose height.

'At this critical moment Manser distained the alternative of parachuting to safety with his crew. Instead, with grim determination, he set a new course for the nearest base in England, accepting for himself the prospect of almost certain death in a firm resolve to carry on to the end.

'Soon the aircraft became extremely difficult to handle and, when a crash was inevita-ble, Flying Officer Manser ordered the crew to bail out. A sergeant handed him a parachute but he waved it away, telling the non-commissioned officer to jump at once because he could only hold the aircraft steady for a few seconds more. While the crew descended to safety they saw the aircraft, still carrying their gallant captain, plunge to earth and burst into flames...'

Another one of the Last Witnesses, George Hart, had to deal with Manchesters before graduating to Lancasters. Hart had wanted to join the Royal Navy when war broke out but he was turned down, unless he wanted to be a stoker or a cook. 'Blow that,' he said, and joined the RAF, although he was rejected for aircrew because of his eyesight. After six months training as an engine fitter he was posted to Scampton in October 1940 to work on the Pegasus engines of the Hampden:

> 'Then for a few months we had Manchesters. We only had those temporarily, and they were horrible. The engines were called Vultures, twin engines working together, two engines in one as it were. With the Manchesters every time they went up, something happened. The air coolers used to go every time on the leading edges of the main-plane, and we used to have to change them. When we got the first lot of Lancasters, it was like working on a Singer sewing machine. They were beautiful. To learn how to service the Merlins we went up to Rolls Royce, for about a week. There was no comparison with the Vultures, which were not reliable at all.'

The Manchester played a vital role in the development of the Lancaster but was an unlucky and often fatal aircraft for the RAF squadrons issued with it – 207 and 97 Squadrons as full-on testers, plus 49, 50, 61, 83 and 106 squadrons. All these five Group squadrons were moved on to Lancasters for the great bombing missions of 1943. It is hardly likely that any of the aircrew or ground crew on Manchesters looked back with any joy at those experiences. Yet it was a necessary step for Avro to take in the huge and ambitious move from building the homely Anson to creating the legendary Lancaster.

CHAPTER EIGHT

Oh Boy, Oh Boy — What an Aircraft!

The first Lancaster was BT308, a Manchester airframe taken from the production line at the end of November 1940, authorised for conversion by an Avro board of directors acutely aware of the Air Ministry's intention that the firm should build Halifaxes instead of the ill-fated Manchester. The initial staving off of the threat was just that, the threat still hung over Dobson and Chadwick; the four-engine Avro bomber *had* to work…or else.

The Manchester airframe chosen had a central tail-fin, and also the 22-foot (6.7m) tail-plane and smaller fins that had not really given the Manchester stability, and boded the same for the newly-named Lancaster. Design work had been completed, and units tooled up, for a tail-plane with a span of 39ft (11.9m), along with much bigger twin fins and rudders, but these were not fitted to BT308. Speed was vital. Avro could not risk making too many changes too quickly. It was imperative to get a 4-engine aircraft in the air, demonstrate its performance and have that performance assessed by Boscombe Down.

The engines were Merlin X's, not the best possible, just the best available, and there were still difficult days ahead before authorisation to use them was to come from the Ministry of Aircraft Production.

The prototype was signed off to fly on 5 January 1941, but foggy weather set in and it was not until the afternoon of 9 January that Avro chief test pilot Sam Brown took the Lancaster up for its 15-minute maiden flight. He reported it 'trouble-free', in sharp contrast to his early experiences on Manchesters, although the half-expected 'directional stability' doubts were there. The aircraft left the ground quickly, and the swing to port on take-off – with which all future Lancaster pilots would become familiar – could be countered by leading with the port throttles. Elevator control and aileron sensitivity were better than the Manchester, and the landing technique simple.

Dobson, watching the maiden flight, was quoted as saying, 'Oh boy, oh boy, what an aircraft!'

Over the next fortnight, nine flights were made by Avro before the Boscombe Down testers took over, and every report tended to confirm Dobson's judgement. Following initial approval at Boscombe Down, BT308 went back to Manchester to have the larger tail-plane assembly fitted, and the central fin removed. The Ministry of Aircraft Production released four new Merlin XX engines which were fitted, and at the end of February the modified prototype went back to Boscombe Down for more assessment and speed trials. Everyone was delighted, though surprised, when the performance figures came through, indicating 310mph T.A.S. (True Air Speed) at 21,000ft (6,400m), and 301mph T.A.S. at 18,000ft (5,486m). This was almost 10 per cent above expectations, a significant improvement.

Politically, as far as Avro was concerned, this assessment saved the company's bacon. The production order, originally for 1,200 Manchesters, was changed – 200 Manchesters would be completed, 156 at Avro and 44 by Metrovick. After that, all production lines would be devoted to Lancasters, with 1,070 on initial order. The maximum bomb-load capable of being carried was raised to 14,000lbs, to cater for the arrival of the 4,000lb 'cookie' then coming into production.

BT308 went four times to Boscombe Down in the spring and summer of 1941. The changes introduced made handling much easier, the swing to the port containable with the bigger rudders alone, still leading with the port throttle and no use of brake pressure. Its asymmetric flight trials showed it could cope with two engines on one wing stopped and feathered and still maintain height, flying at around 180mph T.A.S., the yaw being held by full rudder down to 160 mph. These characteristics were to save the lives of so many airmen throughout the following three years of bitter fighting.

The last visit to Boscombe Down with BT308 brought heavy criticism of the heating system. The Wireless/Operator position, where hot air was fed in near his feet from a heat exchanger in the wing, could suffer 70° centigrade above the ambient temperature, the pilot and navigator at 60° above it, while the rear gunner froze his socks off. There were also confused plans for just a six-man crew, and there was still a second pilot. How could three gun turrets be manned in such circumstances, when a pilot, navigator, wireless operator and bomb aimer were also essential?

When Lancasters started to fly operationally, the idea of a second pilot was dropped; he was replaced by a flight engineer. It was an economy forced on us by war. Nevertheless, with the Lancaster we had to have a good bit of teamwork between the flight engineer and the pilot, especially on take-off when full throttle was needed. The pilot starts the throttles off, then the flight engineer takes over.

The second prototype, DG595, had its maiden flight on 13 May 1941, stressed for an all-up weight of 60,000lbs. Congestion at Boscombe Down was so heavy that there were not enough qualified pilots to make official reports for three months. This brought an unexpected benefit. Roy Chadwick used the delay to fly DG595 to Woodford and take 60 of his draughtsmen around every aspect of the new Lancaster, nit-picking mercilessly. Chadwick threw out all unnecessary parts and lightened everything he could find in order to maximise the war load. He also tidied up the hydraulics and, given the way the aircraft was assembled in sections, improved the ease of maintenance. The value of these changes was to be proved that winter as ground crew on wet, windy, freezing airfields struggled to cope with flak-damaged bombers.

Meanwhile, one of the Avro boys had died. Eric Verdon-Roe, eldest son of the Avro founder, who had joined the RAF on a Short Service Commission in 1934, completed a tour of 30 operations early in the war. Three trips into his second tour, by now a squadron leader with 102 Squadron flying Whitleys out of Topcliffe in Yorkshire, he and his crew of four were shot down leaving the Dutch coast for home on the night of 25/26 July 1941. Two other Verdon-Roe sons were destined for the RAF before the war ended.

In August 1941, Boscombe Down testers took the Avro Prototype DG595 into dives at 360mph to check, successfully, that there was no serious airflow turbulence when the front and rear turrets were rotated. A mid-upper turret was fitted – the new F.N.50A model from Nash and Thompson – and also a small ventral turret, unfortunately later dropped from production Lancasters. It had covered the one blind spot on a Lancaster that the Luftwaffe were to discover in 1943, with dire results for thousands of RAF aircrew.

A third prototype, DT810, was flown on 26 November 1941, powered by four Bristol Hercules VI radial engines, to become the Mark II Lancaster prototype. This engine change was a form of insurance policy. Virtually all the modern aircraft serving with the RAF now had Merlin engines and there were concerns over continuity of supply, especially should deliveries from Packard in the USA (licensed to manufacture Merlins) be disrupted after America went to war following the Japanese attack on Pearl Harbour on 7 December 1941. Fortunately, there was always a safe supply of Merlins.

The first production Lancaster – L7527 – was flown by Sam Brown on 1 October, 1941, making extensive use of Manchester components. As with the prototypes, it had four wing tanks and, still making changes on the hoof, it was then decided the Lancaster should have six wing tanks and a strengthened set of wing ribs. The aircraft was stressed for an all-up take-off weight of 65,000lbs, and it was recommended that it should never be landed weighing more. When I got to fly my own Lancaster in 1944, largely unchanged from the first production models, we regularly reached 68,000lbs as we set off down the runway with one of Barnes Wallis's Tallboys on board. Later, the all-up weight went to 72,000lbs carrying the Grand Slam bomb.

RAF squadrons, struggling all the way through 1941 with inadequate bombing aircraft, breathed a sigh of relief when the first three operational Lancasters were delivered to 44 Squadron at Waddington on Christmas Eve, 1941. Aircrew had lived with the rumours, and now had reality. The prototype BT308 had, in fact, been seen in September of that year, to provide some limited crew experience. Having seven Lancasters for 44 Squadron to take into 1942 was a real bonus.

The Squadron's commanding officer at the time was Wing Commander Roderick Learoyd, a regular RAF pre-war officer who had won a Victoria Cross bringing back a badly damaged Hampden from a low-level attack on the Dortmund-Ems Canal the previous year. But Learoyd left before the beginning of 1942 and the man responsible for bringing 44 Squadron up to scratch was a South African, Squadron Leader John Nettleton. He was charged with setting up a training programme that involved long flights along the Scottish coast, 'wasting' time on mining sorties. In fact, the squadron was training to attack and destroy the *Tirpitz*, a goal that haunted Bomber Command as well as the Royal Navy throughout the war. Nettleton's co-pilot (the second pilot wasn't actually replaced by a flight engineer until later in 1942) was to be one of our Last Witnesses, Pat Dorehill.

A second Lancaster unit, 97 Squadron at RAF Coningsby, struggling with Manchesters, received their first Lancaster aircraft on 14 January, and a quick rivalry grew up between 44 and 97 Squadrons. Both squadrons had been badly damaged by flying the unreliable Manchesters, with a high proportion of technical failures; 97 had lost its C.O. Denys Balsdon, just a week before Christmas.

The RAF compensated for making its young airmen fly the Manchester by giving priority to replacing them with Lancasters as they came rolling off the production lines. Number 207 Squadron was third to be re-equipped with Lancasters, then 83, 106, 50, 61, and 49 squadrons.

Number 9 Squadron was the first to make a conversion direct from twin-engined Wellingtons to Lancasters. This was the remnants of the 9 Squadron that had been unable to drop its bombs on German warships in Wilhelmshaven in the early weeks of the war because of fears of hitting civilians, and had lost half its aircraft and crews to German fighters. Three years later, now equipped with a much more formidable weapon and in a war in which the Germans had taken the gloves off first, there was to be no such compunction.

Production of Lancasters at Avro's plant in Manchester soon rose to 10 a week, with delivery starting in February 1942. Original Lancasters surviving into 1943 had their Merlin XX engines replaced by Merlin XXII's. It was a Lancaster from this batch, R5508 KM-B, flown by the CO of 44 Squadron, John Nettleton, that was to lead a raid as daring as the more famous Dambuster Raid the following year and with even greater sacrifice, because his was the only 44 Squadron aircraft to survive. It is almost forgotten now.

The establishment of Lancaster squadrons seemed to have caused a rush of blood to the heads of Bomber Command leaders and the War Cabinet. Heavy losses among aircrew caused by RAF daylight raids without fighter protection in the early months of the war were forgotten. 'Now we've got a big, well-armed bomber,' they seemed to say, 'let's send it into deepest Germany in daylight with no fighter escorts at all. And if we fly in formation at low level, they can protect each other, so it will be okay, won't it?'

So that is what they did.

Squadron Leader John Nettleton, 24, set out at the head of six 44 Squadron Lancasters, accompanied by six 97 Squadron Lancasters, on 17 May 1942, on a daylight raid against the M.A.N. factory in Augsburg, 30 miles south of Munich. The factory made diesel engines for U-Boats. The Lancasters were each armed with four 1,000lb bombs, and ordered to make the thousand-mile round trip daylight flight at low level, around 60ft (18.3m), to confound German radar. A diversionary raid by 24 Boston light bombers 10 minutes before the Lancasters crossed the French coast was intended to draw away German fighters. But the Boston raid happened half an hour earlier, 20 minutes ahead of schedule, and the effect was exactly the opposite.

Luftwaffe fighters returning to base with plenty of fuel and ammunition left over from chasing the Bostons missed the six 97 Squadron aircraft three miles to one side, but spotted Nettleton's 44 Squadron Lancasters and attacked. Although the Lancasters had eight machine guns, only six of which could be brought to bear, they were no match for the cannon of the Luftwaffe fighters, a mixture of Me109s and FW190s. One Lancaster, piloted by Warrant Officer J.F. Beckett DFM was shot down in flames with no survivors.

A second Lancaster, piloted by Warrant Officer H.V. Crum DFM, was set on fire and two crew were wounded, but Crum jettisoned his bombs and crash-landed safely in a field; the whole crew escaped but were eventually handed over to the Germans by the French police to become PoWs.

A third Lancaster, piloted by Flight Lieutenant R.R. Sandford DFC had all four engines set on fire and ploughed into the ground in a great sheet of flame. Again, no survivors.

Now Nettleton's section of three Lancasters came under attack, and the aircraft piloted by Sergeant G.T. Rhodes, hit at point-blank range, reared up on fire and threatened to fall on Nettleton's aircraft. It then stalled and crashed in flames. All seven crew died.

The German fighter pilots, low on fuel, broke off their attack, leaving two of Nettleton's original six Lancasters to press on to the target. The pilots of 97 Squadron, led by Squadron Leader J.S. Sherwood DFC just a few miles away, were unaware of the carnage wreaked on Nettleton's men.

The two 44 Squadron aircraft reached the target at virtually tree-top height, opened their bomb doors, and all their bombs – each with an 11-second delay – fell on factory buildings. But the Lancaster of Nettleton's colleague, Flying Officer

A.J. Garwell DFM, was hit by flak, set on fire, the cockpit filled with smoke, and Garwell ploughed into the ground at 80mph. Four of his crew, including Garwell himself, scrambled free, while the wireless operator and two gunners died in the blazing wreck.

Three Lancasters from 97 Squadron, led by Sherwood, now attacked in line astern, and as they pulled away Sherwood's aircraft was hit. Flames were seen on one wing, spread to the fuselage, and apparently out of control, it crashed and exploded. By a miracle, Sherwood was thrown free through the cockpit canopy in his armoured seat and into trees, surviving virtually uninjured to become a PoW. His fellow crew members were all killed.

The two other Lancasters in the section, piloted by Flying Officer Hallows and Flying Officer Rodley bombed and then set a shaky course for home. That left the last three Lancasters, led by Flight Lieutenant W.M. Penman DFC, who had orbited once 10 miles short of the target to ensure they could see it clearly, and then attacked. By then the German gunners were ready and sighted.

As the three Lancasters swept in they were all heavily hit. Two of them, one piloted by Warrant Officer T.J. Mycock DFM, the other by Flying Officer Deverill, were set on fire. Mycock's aircraft, fire raging in the port wing, was seen to drop its bombs and then blow up. Penman, convinced he was the only survivor, set off for home and was astonished to see Deverill formate alongside him, one engine stopped but the fire extinguished.

All four 97 Squadron Lancasters, and Nettleton's sole surviving 44 Squadron aircraft, made it back to base in the early evening and night. Deverill's aircraft was immediately declared a total write-off.

Patrick Dorehill, Nettleton's 20-year-old co-pilot in KM-B, wrote a first-hand survivor's account:

'There was certainly some surprise on entering the briefing room to see the pink tape leading all the way into the heart of Germany. I can't say I felt anxious. I had an extraordinary faith in the power of the Lancaster to defend itself. And then flying at low level seemed to me to be the perfect way to outwit the enemy. I thought the only danger might be over the target and, even there, believed we would be in and away before there was much response.

'Basically, those tactics were sound and it was only sheer bad luck that we flew past an enemy airfield to which their fighters were returning from the diversionary raids our fighters and Boston bombers had laid on to the North. 'Up they came and I shall never forget those terrible moments. I do not think there were as many fighters as our gunners reported, it was just that each made several attacks which made it seem like more. Being on the jump seat I stood up and saw quite a bit of the action. Maybe there were a dozen.

'At any rate I looked back through the astro dome to see Nick Sandford's plane in flames. He always wore his pyjamas on ops under his uniform. He thought it would bring him good luck.

'This was followed by Dusty Rhodes' plane on our starboard catching fire. The rest went down except Garwell on our port side. There was nothing for it really but to press on. A passing thought was given to turning south and then out to the Bay of Biscay but we reckoned that as we had come so far we might as well see it through.

'By this time I can tell you I didn't give much for our chances. On we went and I marvelled at the peaceful countryside, sheep, cattle, fields of daisies or buttercups. Along came the Alps on our right, wonderful sight, Lake Constance looking peaceful. We had climbed up a bit by then, it being pretty hilly, and then down we came again getting close to the target. My recollection may be faulty but I thought we approached Augsburg from the south, following a canal or railway. Factory chimneys appeared on the low horizon and then we came to the town. Large sheds were right in our path, Des Sands, the navigator and McClure the bomb-aimer had done a pretty good job of map reading.

'Bombs away at about a hundred feet.'

'The flak zipped past and as we crossed the town to begin a left turn for home a small fire was apparent, gradually gaining strength, in Garwell's plane. Our gunners saw it make a crash landing, which seemed to go relatively well.

'The trip home was uneventful, thank goodness. . . Nettleton did a brisk circuit and down we came to be almost out of fuel.

'Golly, I can tell you I was glad to feel those wheels touch the grass.'

The *London Gazette* of 28 April 1942 announced a group citation of one DSO, five DFCs and 10 DFMs which were – rightly – liberally distributed.
Patrick Dorehill was awarded a DFC. John Nettleton won a Victoria Cross.

'John Deering Nettleton, A/Sqdn Ldr, 44 (Rhodesia) Squadron, RAF.

'17 April 1942: Nettleton was the leader of one of two formations of six Lancaster heavy bombers detailed to deliver a low-level daylight attack on the diesel engine factory at Augsburg in southern Germany. The engines were destined for U-Boats. It was the first use of Lancasters in a daylight raid, and the identity of the aircraft was still a secret, being portrayed as Manchesters.

'The enterprise was daring, the target of high military importance. To reach it and get back, some 1,000 miles had to be flown over hostile territory. Soon after crossing into enemy territory his formation was engaged by 25-30 fighters. A running fight ensued. Nettleton's rear guns were put out of action. One by one the aircraft in his command were shot down until in the end only his and one other remained. The fighters were shaken off but the target was still far distant, and there was formidable resistance still to be faced. With great spirit, and almost defenceless, he held his two remaining aircraft on

their perilous course and after a long and arduous flight, mostly at only 50ft (15.2m)
above the ground, he brought them to Augsburg. Here anti-aircraft fire of great inten-
sity and accuracy was encountered. The two aircraft came low over the rooftops, and
though fired at from point-blank range, they stayed the course to drop their bombs true
on the target. The second aircraft, hit by flak, burst into flames and crash-landed. The
leading aircraft, though riddled with holes, flew safety back to base. Of the 12 aircraft
in two formations that made the raid, seven failed to return, five from Nettleton's flight.
Subsequent photographs showed great damage to the target.'

While 17 bombs had struck the target, only 12 had exploded, and there was
disruption only for some weeks. This astonishing feat of tenacity, courage and skill
was over-shadowed by more famous raids the following year, but Nettleton's VC
was gazetted just 11 days later. The press called him 'The Roof-top VC'.

Arthur Harris, quite newly appointed to lead Bomber Command, had been under
pressure from the Admiralty to attack Augsburg as part of the campaign against the
U-Boats, then at the height of their powers in the Atlantic. But Harris felt that a loss
of seven out of 12 aircraft was unsupportable, however celebrated the surviving crews
were. He grew more resolute in his view that he would not be diverted by Admiralty
and Army demands for help, and set out to mould Bomber Command into a single
strategic weapon.

Despite the huge losses, the Lancasters proved themselves, on this and subsequent
missions, and their reputations as fighting aircraft grew. Crews who flew both types
of aircraft, Halifaxes and Lancasters, said that getting into the Lancaster was like
getting into a sports car after driving a very good saloon.

The introduction of the Merlin to the Lancaster airframe was almost perfect.
Avro used Hercules engines on Mark II Lancasters, for example, but even though
the Hercules engine was much more powerful than the Merlin – an extra 250 hp
per engine – the Lancaster II did not have the performance of a Merlin-powered
Lancaster I. For one reason or another, the combination of the Merlin and Lancaster was aviation perfection for the time. There were no major changes in design once
it had been settled on. There were lots more electronic devices, but the basic aircraft
in 1945 was the same as the first production model in 1942. It showed how good the
aeroplane was.

Another of the Last Witnesses, Captain Eric 'Winkle' Brown, was, in fact, a Royal
Navy pilot and never served operationally on Lancasters, although during the war
he won renown as one of the greatest test pilots in the world. His record of testing 487 aircraft during and after the war, including German, Italian and Japanese
aircraft, has never been surpassed.

'Winkle' Brown had already had an exciting war before entering the dangerous profession of testing aircraft to their limits. Before the age of 23 he had shot down two 4-engined Condors using a style of head-on attacks that he pioneered. He had won a DSC, and spent three hours in the sea on 21 December 1941 when his aircraft carrier HMS *Audacity* was sunk by torpedo. Twenty men were gathered in the water around him awaiting rescue; he was one of only two to survive the cold.

He married almost immediately afterwards and soon started his career as a test pilot. Eric Brown:

'The thing about the Lancaster was, it was viceless from an aerodynamic point of view. It had very docile stalling characteristics, and good harmony of control. For a pilot, harmony of control is what makes a pilot happy. By harmony of control, I mean you need light ailerons, moderately light elevators and a moderately heavy rudder. If you have these three things as a pilot, you feel it's right.

'If you have too light a rudder, it can be misused and produce a lot of skidding around the sky, especially flying at night. This was not a fault with the Lancaster at all.

'The only real problem we had with Lancasters was with one particular model, Lancaster X's built in Canada. We were getting a lot of reports of rogue aircraft, and they were all Lanc X's. They were rogues because pilots had trouble with the controls, mainly the ailerons. They could be heavy, or they could be over-balanced. We had to go to Canada to find the source of the problem at the place of manufacture.

'It turned out that they did not have the skilled labour to manufacture Lancaster X's to the tolerances required. They were being made slightly out of kilter, it was just enough to make the aircraft rogues. It meant we had to send all those working on that part of the aircraft back into training until they got the tolerances right. Getting problems like this, especially on operations against the enemy, is a very serious business. Pilots have got to have faith in their aircraft.

'I did a lot of tests on the early Lancaster because of the problems 4-engined bombers were having cork-screwing. If an engine coughed or failed in a cork-screw in a Halifax, it was in great trouble. It could easily be fatal if the pilot was not sharp enough to catch it. Engine failure would probably put it into a spin. They had another problem in the early Halifaxes. When you are cork-screwing you need a lot of rudder to control it, but the Halifax had rudder over-balance. That means you're pushing the rudder, and as you push it the force gets heavier and heavier. Suddenly the rudder will go straight over, but it's locked there. This is very nasty indeed, and we had to modify the shape of the rudders.

'The Lancaster learned a lot from the problems we had with the Halifax, and had its rudders modified earlier in its life.'

So Lancaster production went into high volume to prepare for the gigantic battles ahead.

CHAPTER NINE

The Wider War

By the beginning of 1942 the Germans were almost totally triumphant. With the exception of neutral nations like Sweden, Spain, Switzerland and Eire, Hitler's forces occupied the whole of Europe and his armies had raced east to pound on the gates of Moscow. In the Middle East, British forces had been driven from Greece and Crete, while Erwin Rommel was building forces to drive towards Cairo and sieze the Suez Canal. Japan had entered the war and was thrashing American and British forces wherever it met them in the Philippines, Malaya, Singapore and the Dutch East Indies, heading for Burma and India.

The public mood in Britain had hardened because of the Blitz, the sustained bombing by Germany of cities all over Britain that had lasted from 7 September 1940 until May 1941. The Blitz started with an accident, but given Nazi Germany's bullying behaviour it was always going to be that way. On 24 August 1940, some German aircraft, tasked with attacking Fighter Command stations, strayed over East London and dropped bombs on Bethnal Green, Hackney, Islington, Tottenham and Finchley. Churchill, pugnacious as always, retaliated by ordering British bombers to attack Berlin the following night, a pin-prick raid undertaken more to demonstrate our defiance than anything else, but it did kill 10 people. Hitler was outraged; British cartoonists portrayed him chewing a carpet. The bomber war had begun in earnest. Winston Churchill told his War Cabinet on 3 September:

> 'The Navy can lose us the war but only the Air Force can win it. Our supreme effort must be to gain mastery in the air. The Fighters are our salvation, but the Bombers alone provide the means of victory. We must therefore develop the power to carry an ever-increasing volume of explosives to Germany, so as to pulverize the entire industry and scientific structure on which the war effort and economic life of the enemy depend, while holding him at arm's length from our island...'

On 7 September the Port of London was attacked late in the afternoon by a force of 364 German bombers escorted by 515 fighters, causing severe damage. That night London was attacked again by 133 German bombers. Many of the bombs aimed at the docks fell on neighbouring residential areas; 436 Londoners were killed, 1,666 were injured. Hitler's intention was simple, to destroy the morale of the British population. If destroying huge swathes of a city worked in Guernica, Warsaw and Rotterdam, why not London? The British capital went on to suffer 57 nights of bombing.

Between 100 and 200 German bombers attacked London every night except one between mid-September and mid-November. Birmingham and Bristol were attacked on 15 October, and the heaviest attack of the war so far – by 400 bombers and lasting six hours – hit London. The RAF only shot down one bomber that night. By mid-November, the Luftwaffe had dropped more than 13,000 tons of high explosive and a million fire bombs on Britain. Their losses were negligible, less than 1 per cent. Other cities – Belfast, Birmingham, Bristol, Cardiff, Clydebank, Coventry, Sheffield, Swansea, Liverpool, Hull, Manchester, Portsmouth, Plymouth, Nottingham and Southampton – also suffered heavy air raids and high numbers of casualties.

Probably the most devastating raid occurred on the evening of 29 December 1940 when German aircraft attacked the City of London itself, using incendiaries and high-explosive bombs, causing what has been called the Second Great Fire of London. A famous photograph showed St Paul's Cathedral surrounded by fire and shrouded in smoke. The future leader of Bomber Command, Arthur Harris, was witness to this raid, and used the words of the Biblical prophet Hosea:

'They are sowing the wind, they will reap the whirlwind.'

By the end of May 1941, over 43,000 civilians had been killed in Britain by bombing, half of them in London, and more than a million houses had been destroyed or damaged in London alone. As a result, there was not a great deal of sympathy thereafter for the Germans when the tide of war changed.

The only way Britain could physically hurt Germany itself between 1940 and 1944 was through Bomber Command. There was a simple and savage sentiment throughout the country. It was reflected in letters to newspapers, in comments in Parliament, in cartoons, in pub talk, and by people cowering in the London Underground as bombs rained down above: Germany, and Germans, *needed* to be hurt.

Churchill was continuously aware of the morale boost that people in Britain felt, every night, knowing that hundreds of young airmen set off to take the war to German-occupied France and Germany itself, each time sacrificing some of the finest RAF aircrew. This feeling was articulated by Noel Coward:

'Lie in the dark and listen.
It's clear tonight so they're flying high,
Hundreds of them, thousands perhaps,
Riding the icy, moonlit sky.

Men, machinery, bombs and maps,
Altimeters, guns and charts,
Coffee, sandwiches, fleece-lined boots,
Bones and muscles and minds and hearts,
English saplings with English roots
Deep in the earth they've left below.
Lie in the dark and let them go;
Lie in the dark and listen.'

Bomber Command had been led during the bleak 17 months from October 1940 until 22 February 1942 by Air Marshal Sir Richard Peirse.

When he took command, Pierse had 34 squadrons of twin-engined so-called 'heavy' bombers, comprising Hampdens, Wellingtons and Whitleys. When he left he had 48 squadrons, including three squadrons of Stirlings, three of Halifaxes and three Manchester squadrons, all fully operational and deserving of the 'heavy' title. Bombs had risen in size from 250lbs to 2,000lbs and then to the 4,000lb 'cookie', a huge programme of airfield construction and expansion was under way, and new navigation equipment was coming in.

Peirse could claim to be the man more responsible than anyone else in the RAF for ensuring the aircraft industry went flat-out building Lancasters. But by 1942, most of the original airmen that comprised his elite bombing force were either dead or PoWs. A new, young generation, including the Last Witnesses, was taking over, most of them civilians, in uniform only for the duration of the war.

That generation had to be trained to fly and fight mostly at night, a process that took about 18 months. The decision to set up the Empire Air Training Plan was made in December 1939. Instructors, sites and aircraft had to be found so the first graduates from the scheme would not appear until 1942.

A typical course of instruction included 10 days kitting-out, drill, aptitude tests, maths, general knowledge and yet more drill. Then there was 12 weeks at ITW – the Initial Training Wing – with ground work, PT, Morse code, drill, navigation, drill, meteorology, gunnery, aircraft recognition and more drill. Students were then sent to EFTS – Elementary Flight Training School – and if they had not gone solo by 12 hours, they were washed out. In any group of 100 volunteers classified as pilots 'under training' by selection boards, 25 would not make it to solo in the Elementary Flying Training Schools.

The Last Witnesses born in 1923/24 went through this system, scattered across the world in Canada, the United States, South Africa, Rhodesia and Australia. I was part of the system myself in 1941, but as an instructor. Having been thrown into the Battle of Britain as a Sergeant pilot in early September 1940 with just 10 hours on Spitfires, I survived a fight with a Ju88 only to be shot down while chasing it, ditching in the North Sea. It was just a few days after my twenty-first birthday. I was rescued by a passing convoy and somehow or other managed not to be killed during the rest of that year. Then I was sent on an instructor's course at Upavon, where I finally learned – in teaching – to become a decent enough pilot to have a reasonable chance in a fight.

It is a measure of the stern test the young aircrew faced that 5,000 of them were killed in training before they ever got near the enemy.

As the new bomber crews were coming on stream, they learned that the senior pilots who had been doing the fighting up to then had dropped most of their bombs a long, long way from where they intended. It cannot have helped Sir Richard Peirse's career as the AOC Bomber Command that it was on his watch that the officially-commissioned 1941 Butt Report revealed RAF bombing to be 'shockingly' inaccurate.

For the first two years of the war, RAF Bomber Command had no real means of determining the success of its operations. Crews would return with only their own word as to the amount of damage caused, or even that they had bombed the target at all. Uneasiness grew about these claims, fuelled by demands from the other two services, the Army and Navy, for the RAF to do more *tactical* bombing in their theatres of war rather than opt for strategic bombing.

The Air Ministry demanded that a reliable method of verifying the claims of bomber pilots must be developed, and cameras were mounted under bombers, triggered by the bomb release. This was automatic, not under a pilot's direction, and would show up crews who might have dropped their bombs early – like over the North Sea – to avoid German defences.

The Butt Report was initiated by Professor Frederick Lindemann, enobled as Lord Cherwell, a German-born scientist who hated Hitler and was a close adviser to Churchill. One of Cherwell's assistants, D.M. Butt, a civil servant in the War Cabinet Secretariat, was given the task of assessing 633 target photos and comparing them with crews' claims. The results, first circulated on 18 August 1941:

'Any examination of photographs taken during night bombing in June and July, 1941 points to the following conclusions.

Of those aircraft recorded as attacking their target, only one in three got within five miles.

Over the French ports, the proportion was two in three.

Over Germany as a whole, the proportion was one in four.

Over the Ruhr it was only one in ten.

In the full moon, the proportion was two in five.

In the new moon it was only one in 15.

All these figures relate only to aircraft recorded as attacking the target; the proportion of the total sorties which reached within five miles is less than one-third.

The conclusion seems to follow that only about one-third of RAF aircraft claiming to reach their target actually reached it.'

Churchill was furious at this revelation, saying 'this is a very serious paper and seems to require urgent attention.' Yet he concluded: 'The only plan is to persevere.' What other option did he have at that time to carry the war to Germany?

While the Butt Report was being compiled, RAF Bomber Command was ordered to hone its attacks, to ensure the 'dislocation of the German transport system and destroy the morale of the civilian population.' The official justification of the bombing was, in effect, 'Gloves off!' Continuous debate in Whitehall about the tactics to be used in prosecuting the war led to the February 1942 Area Bombing Directive. Bomber Command was simply directed to use area bombardment. The initiative again came from Lord Cherwell, whose 'de-housing paper' strongly advocated the bombing of German cities, leading to the thousand-bomber raids and the destruction of German cities in 1945.

The turning point for Bomber Command certainly came in 1942 with the arrival of new four-engined bombers like the Lancaster, along with more advanced navigational aids and a new commander. Air Marshal Sir Arthur Harris had a reputation as a blunt, unapproachable man that belied his true character. He was also a true disciple of the RAF's founder, Lord Trenchard, believing strongly that the war could be largely won by the bomber, with the Army coming along to pick up the pieces afterwards. 'Bomber' Harris was to pursue this course single-mindedly, against every ambush and argument by the other two fighting services. It was a policy that left him isolated with few supporters when sentiment turned, *except among the young airmen he led.*

The official directive issued to RAF Bomber Command ordered the specific targeting of 58 major German industrial cities. The primary objective was now described as destroying 'the morale of the enemy civil population and in particular, of the industrial workers'. Churchill endorsed this policy, but it was argued by Lord Cherwell, in a paper circulated among decision-makers on 30 March 1942, that the houses of the German war factory workers were a legitimate target. If they had nowhere to live, Cherwell wrote, they could not go to work.

'The De- Housing Paper:

The following seems a simple method of estimating what we could do by bombing Germany.

'Careful analysis of the effects of raids on Birmingham, Hull and elsewhere have shown that, on the average, one ton of bombs dropped on a built-up area demolishes 20–40 dwellings and turns 100–200 people out of house and home.

'We know from our experience that we can count on nearly 14 operational sorties per bomber produced. The average lift of the bombers we are going to produce over the next

15 months will be about 3 tons. It follows that each of these bombers will in its life-time drop about 40 tons of bombs. If these are dropped on built-up areas they will make 4,000–8,000 people homeless.

'In 1938, over 22 million Germans lived in 58 towns of over 100,000 inhabitants, which, with modern equipment, should be easy to find and hit. Our forecast output of heavy bombers (including Wellingtons) between now and the middle of 1943 is about 10,000. If even half the total load of 10,000 bombers were dropped on the built-up areas of these 58 German towns the great majority of their inhabitants (about one-third of the German population) would be turned out of house and home.

'Investigation seems to show that having one's home demolished is most damaging to morale. People seem to mind it more than having their friends or even relatives killed. At Hull, signs of strain were evident, though only one-tenth of the houses were demolished. On the above figures we should be able to do ten times as much harm to each of the 58 principal German towns. There seems little doubt that this would break the spirit of the people.'

Cherwell's expectation that British heavy bombers would have a life-span of just 14 operations (paragraph 3) is actually seven raids fewer than what turned out to be the average 21 sortie life-span of RAF Bomber Command aircrew.

Arthur Harris had no involvement in formulating the new policy and did not personally believe in the strategy of targeting civilian morale. As he later put it, how could low morale force the German people to capitulate with 'the Gestapo standing by' and 'the concentration camp around the corner'? But Harris did believe in targeting Germany's war economy by destroying German industrial cities so that her ability to wage war would be compromised.

Still, with very few Lancasters on his hands and extremely aware of the inaccuracy of his young bomber crews, Harris chose an 'easy' target to test his weapons. Five weeks after taking command, on 28 March 1942, he ordered the bombing of Lubeck, which he considered a port and industrial town of 'moderate importance.' It was an 'easy' target in the sense it could be found and seen easily at night.

With a full moon and clear visibility, 234 Wellingtons and Stirlings dropped 400 tons of bombs and 25,000 incendiary devices. An estimated 63 per cent of the buildings in Lubeck were damaged or destroyed, and 15,000 people made homeless. Local police estimated 301 deaths. This was regarded as the first RAF raid to focus on the morale of the civilian population, defined politically by the War Cabinet as a legitimate target.

RAF losses amounted to 12 aircraft. Harris felt that a loss rate of 5.5 per cent had to be expected on a clear night, but it was not a loss rate Bomber Command could sustain for long.

The Germans retaliated with the so-called 'Baedeker Raids', named after the famous tourist guidebooks, between February and May 1942, targeting historic cities with no military or strategic importance. These included Bath, Canterbury, Exeter, Norwich and York. Major landmarks such as the Assembly Rooms in Bath and the Guildhall in York were completely destroyed. There were over 1,600 deaths.

It was an extremely bloody war, but the Germans were winning it. We had years of fighting ahead to overcome them. It fell to my young generation and the other Last Witnesses at the sharp end to take the war back to Germany, in what Harris came to see as his 'Shining Sword', the Lancaster bomber – but the attrition rate for us was high, and climbing.

In 1942, Bomber Command flew just over 35,000 sorties, the huge majority at night. During this period, 1,716 aircraft crashed or went missing, a loss rate of 4.89 per cent.

Some nights – such as the 24/25 August raid on Frankfurt – losses were higher, at 7.1 per cent. Harris had sent off 226 aircraft – 6 Lancasters, 5 Wellingtons, 4 Stirlings and 1 Halifax did not come back.

By the early months of 1943, with the Lancaster coming into operational service in increasing numbers, only 17 per cent of men could expect to finish a tour safely with 30 ops. Only 2.5 per cent would survive two tours unscathed. The life expectancy of a new aircraft on an airfield was only 40 hours flying time. A third production batch of 207 Lancasters was ordered from Avro, with delivery starting in July and ending in November, building at a rate of 13 per week, at an average estimated cost of £58,974 per aircraft.

Morale became a serious factor twice, first in the late summer and autumn of 1942, second in the winter of 1943/4. They both corresponded to major efforts against the Ruhr and Berlin. Bomber Command, as we have already noted, had lost 8,018 aircrew up to September 1942. In the next year to the same month in 1943, another 14,163 young airmen were killed.

1944 was to be even worse.

CHAPTER TEN

Pathfinders and Hamish Mahaddie, Bennett's 'Horse Thief'

Lie in the dark and listen.
They're going over in waves and waves
High above villages, hills and streams,
Country churches and little graves
And little citizen's worried dreams;
Very soon they'll have reached the sea
And far below them will lie the bays
And cliffs and sands where they used to be
Taken for summer holidays.
Lie in the dark and let them go;
Theirs is a world we'll never know.
Lie in the dark and listen.

Noel Coward

In the first three years of the war, hundreds of young RAF aircrew set out every night to try to cripple the German war effort. They were mostly seen by the German authorities as a damned nuisance. Even the attack on Berlin by 169 pre-Lancaster bombers on 7 November 1941, was a total failure. When attention switched to the industrial centres of Germany in the spring of 1942, it was still deemed ineffectual.

As the echoes of the Butt Report reverberated through the autumn of 1941, a young Group Captain, 33-year-old Sydney Bufton DFC, was appointed Deputy Director of bombing operations at the Air Ministry. He had come into the job under Peirse, but when he produced his ideas for change and accuracy, he had to face a new bombing chief in Arthur Harris, two ranks above him and soon to be four ranks above him. For the rest of the war, including when he was promoted to Air Commodore and became Director of Operations, Bufton became a cross that Harris used to rage against.

Initially, Bufton suggested that RAF Bomber Command needed a specific target finding force – TFF – separate from Main Force Squadrons, dedicated to finding and marking the vulnerable areas of German industry. The target finders would be experienced pilots, and immediately seen as a separate elite. Harris, taking up his position on 22 February 1942, strongly opposed Bufton's idea, and a bitter feud developed. Harris felt that individual squadrons would not like to see their best crews drained away, and that an elite would breed rivalry and jealousy. This would, he thought, have an adverse effect on morale, and he was probably honestly representing the views of his individual squadron commanders in saying this.

It should have been a simple equation, a Group Captain proposes, an Air Marshal says no, that is it, end of story. But Bufton had powerful friends who supported him, including Sir Charles Portal, the man who had hired Harris from a job in Washington and who had led Bomber Command at the beginning of the war. Harris was also opposed by Sir Henry Tizard, advisor to Churchill and one of the chief scientists supporting the war effort.

Tizard's view was coached in a typically English way: 'I do not think the formation of a first XV at rugby union makes little boys play any less enthusiastically.'

Harris could argue that he was getting on with the job in a much more energetic way than his predecessors, so why did he need a special target finding force? Lancasters were coming into squadron service in large numbers, and helping to forge Bomber Command into a strategic weapon. The Germans began to take a different, more fearful view of Britain's aerial power after his three 'thousand-bomber' raids May/June 1942, on Cologne, Essen and Bremen.

Yet while the thousand-bomber raids caused huge damage, RAF bombers had not yet been able to cause significant damage on other raids, largely because only about a quarter of the bomb loads were delivered 'on target', defined as within three *miles* of the aim point.

The raids had, however, proved (to the great satisfaction of the Allied leadership) that through Bomber Command's sacrifices 'it had been demonstrated to the enemy that nowhere or at any time were they secure from air attack.'

While in the throes of planning his strategic campaign, it is not difficult to imagine the short-tempered Harris's fury at Bufton's championship of specialist target finders. Eventually, Harris succumbed to Bufton's idea and a separate group, designated 8 Group, was formed in August 1942.

The irony was that in choosing instead to appoint a young Australian Group Captain, Don Bennett, to lead the new elite force, Harris had selected someone whose independence of mind was legendary – so much so that, despite brilliant leadership over the next three years with the Pathfinders, he was the only group commander not to be knighted after the war.

Bennett was born in 1910, the youngest son of a grazier in Queensland. He had joined the RAAF in 1930 and transferred to the RAF a year later, starting on flying boats and developing a passion for accurate flying and precise navigation. He specialised in long-distance flights, breaking a number of records and pioneering techniques which would later become commonplace, notably air-to-air refuelling. In July 1938 he flew the Atlantic in the experimental Mercury-Maia composite flying boat. In 1940 he set up a new aircraft 'ferry service', demonstrating that with suitable training even inexperienced pilots could safely deliver new aircraft across the North Atlantic.

In 1941 he was appointed as a Wing Commander to lead 77 Squadron at RAF Leeming, flying Whitleys for Coastal Command. In April 1942 he was given command of 10 Squadron, flying Halifaxes, and shortly afterwards led a raid on the *Tirpitz*. He was shot down, evaded capture, escaped to Sweden and returned to Britain. In 1943 he would become the youngest officer ever promoted to Air Vice Marshal, at the age of 33, also winning a DSO that year.

Bennett started the new Target Finding Force, soon to become the PFF – Pathfinder Force – with just four squadrons. The Pathfinders became one of the elite units in RAF Bomber Command, PFF aircrew wearing a much-coveted brass albatross below their RAF wings. As Harris had feared, PFF creamed off some of the best crews from existing Bomber Command squadrons, a tactic that understandably caused great resentment with the other Group and Squadron Commanders.

The PFF role was to locate and mark targets with flares, giving Main Force bombers an aiming point and increasing their accuracy. While the majority of Pathfinder squadrons and personnel were from the RAF, the group also included many from the air forces of Commonwealth countries. PFF initially had no better tools than the rest of Bomber Command, flying its fair share of Wellingtons, Stirlings, Halifaxes, and Lancasters. But when new aircraft such as the DH Mosquito became available, PFF got them first and made good use of them by equipping them with ever more sophisticated electronic equipment. The first PFF operation on 18/19 August 1942, against Flensburg, was deemed a failure. This was due to the primitive navigational aids and to the limited training the crews had received. Bennett lost no time in ensuring that his new force was properly equipped, starting with GEE, which had been used operationally since the massive Cologne raid of 30 May 1942. Ten days later, a second operation against Nuremburg by 159 bombers was deemed a success, despite the unacceptable loss rate of 23 aircraft, including 4 Lancasters.

The next system to be commissioned was OBOE (from 21 December 1942), a highly accurate radio navigation and bombing aid. Finally, in early 1943, came the H2S ground-mapping radar. The first Mosquito mission equipped with Oboe flew from RAF Wyton in December 1942 and the first H2S Pathfinder mission was a raid on Hamburg on 30 January 1943 (see Boffins War, Chapter 13).

Mosquitoes were particularly suited to this type of work because they could fly fast and low and then accurately drop flares on the targets for the following bomber squadrons, although Lancasters were used in the Pathfinder role as often as Mosquitoes. The bombing accuracy improved seven-fold once the new squadrons were fully trained during 1943.

PFF crews found themselves given increasingly sophisticated and complex jobs, tasks constantly modified and developed tactically during the bombing campaign from 1943 until the end of the war. Among more usual tasks were as:

Finders – 8 Group aircraft tasked with dropping sticks of illuminating flares at critical points along the bombing route to aid navigation and keep the bomber stream compact. They also marked the approximate target area. If conditions were cloudy then these were dropped 'blind' using H2S navigational radar.

Illuminators – PFF aircraft flying in front of the main force to drop markers or Target Indicators (TI's) on to the designated 'aiming point' already illuminated by the 'Finders.' Again, if conditions were cloudy, then H2S navigational radar was used. These TI's were designed to burn with a designated colour for that mission, preventing German defences lighting decoy fires. Various TI's were dubbed 'Pink Pansies', 'Red Spots', and 'Smoke Puffs.' 'Illuminators' could include Mosquitoes equipped with 'Oboe' if the target was within the range of this highly accurate bombing aid.

Markers – would drop incendiaries onto the TI's just prior to the Main Force arrival. Further 'Markers' called 'Backers-Up' or 'Supporters' would be distributed at points within the main bomber stream to re-mark or reinforce the original TI's as required.

The role of 'Master Bomber' was also developed, though the German defenders kept its original RAF name, 'Master of Ceremonies'. An experienced senior pilot would circle the target throughout the raid, instructing approaching bombers by radio which parts of the target to aim at, marked with coloured flares. This dangerous task was invaluable to allow Main Force to bomb accurately even when target and markers were obscured by smoke and flames, or when the Germans lit decoy flares away from the correct aiming point.

Together with advances in navigation technology, these techniques helped turn Bomber Command into a striking force of real power that the German High Command was forced to counter with defensive measures involving nearly a million men. On each raid, Bomber Command aircraft ran a gauntlet of flak and enemy fighters. In the darkness, an RAF bomber on a 500 or 600 aircraft raid might see no other bombers until it was too late. Collisions were an ever-present danger as the RAF developed its technique of swamping enemy defences with hundreds of aircraft, guided to the target by the Pathfinders.

Last Witness David Fellowes survived one of those collisions as a sergeant air-gunner who had completed 33 ops:

'I was rear gunner in Lancaster O-Oboe of 460 Squadron RAAF, sent to attack Munich with a second wave from 1 Group, following a 5 Group attack two hours earlier. We were one of 18 460 Squadron Lancasters caught in cloud at 13,000ft (3,962m) near the German border, and we elected to climb into clearer air above.

'In a few minutes we were in and out the tops of the clouds, seeing the stars in the sky and the dim shapes of other Lancasters who had climbed earlier.

'Then "Christ!" came the shout in the headphones together with a crash and the sound of metal tearing. O-Oboe rocked. "We've been hit!" said another voice. "Did you see that other Lancaster? It's falling away."

Our port wing dropped and we went into a spin. Our pilot, Art Whitmarsh, fought with all his strength to regain control and after what seemed like an eternity we were straight and level...'

The airmen made their bomb safe and jettisoned it, and thought they saw the flash of the other Lancaster crashing. It had been crewed by six Canadians from 103 Squadron. O-Oboe turned towards England, heading for the emergency airfield at Manston in Kent. They climbed to 20,000ft (6,096m) to assess the damage…

'...the trailing edge of the starboard wing was well chewed-up, the aileron and wing tip missing. The mid-upper gunner reported that the whole floor and the starboard side of the fuselage – from trailing edge to the entrance door – was missing, as was the H2S assembly, a section of about 10ft (3m). The gunner was assisted from his turret over a gap four miles above the earth, using an escape rope and help from the wireless operator on the flight deck...the tail of the aircraft was swinging with lots of vibration, and it was impossible for me in the rear turret to go forward. I was given the option of bailing out but I preferred to stay, and besides, the risk of the enemy was still present and they needed a rear gunner...'

Art Whitmarsh reduced power and O-Oboe limped back to England. There they discovered that the Canadian Lancaster that had collided with them was lost with all crew. Not only did their Lancaster survive the wheels-down landing, but it was rebuilt and they were given it back again for operational use.

The Lancaster was the finest aircraft there was. I am sure that it saved our lives when we had our mid-air collision, just by staying in one piece. We got that aeroplane back after they mended it, and we used it on our next trip to Lutzendorf. Mind you it was a fiasco, there were so many things on the aircraft that didn't work. No oxygen in the rear turret, for a start. If you sit quietly at 14,000ft (4,267m) you're all right. The trim was u/s – unserviceable – the whole trip was a nightmare. But we lived.'

The PFF crews found their way into the Force via varied routes; crews or individuals could volunteer at any time while serving with Main Force squadrons, while aircrew who showed promise in their training could also find themselves seconded into the force. Some crews in mid-tour could also be transferred into PFF when numbers were needed to be made up to establishment where required. Recruits were given a two week course in marking techniques at RAF Warboys before posting to a Squadron. Bennett addressed each intake personally and the crews came to have an intense sense of loyalty, pride and professionalism in their membership of 8 Group. Tony Hiscock:

'We started off by being "supporters" to the main Pathfinder, learning the ropes until we gained a bit of experience. The first Pathfinders used to go in and drop markers for the Main Force coming behind us, they would not go in on their own. We kept them company.

'We dropped bombs, of course, but we were also an alternative target for the Germans trying to shoot down the main Pathfinder. We felt we were finally doing something, after all the training. I had been in the RAF since 1 December 1941, and here we were, end of 1943, we were finally having a go, and getting back at the Germans for all they had done to us. When I saw what they had done to us in the Blitz I thought, you so-and-so's! That really made me angry.

'After that, after what they had done to Coventry, whatever we did back to them, well, I just didn't worry about it. I think that was a common attitude.'

The PFF crews were also granted a step up in rank, and an increase in pay, but had to do a 45-trip tour rather than the usual 30 trips, for as long as they were serving in PFF. The PFF badge that was allowed to be worn on their uniforms was genuinely a sought-after achievement.

No story about the birth and growth of RAF Pathfinders is complete without telling of 'Don Bennett's Horse Thief', Group Captain Hamish Mahaddie, who started his RAF life as a non-commissioned metal rigger at the age of 17. He ended the war as a 34-year-old Group Captain with a DSO, DFC and two AFCs.

Mahaddie, real name Thomas Gilbert Mahaddie, was from Leith in Scotland. In 1933 he was posted to the RAF base at Hinaidi, near Baghdad in Iraq. A year later he was accepted for aircrew training and earned his wings in Egypt, flying Avro 504Ns. Posted to 55 Squadron for two years, he bought a horse called 'Hamish', but his fellow aircrew claimed that there was no real difference in appearance between the horse and its owner, and Mahaddie acquired the nickname 'Hamish' for the rest of his life.

Returning to England in 1937, he was serving as a Sergeant pilot with 4 Group's 77 Squadron, flying Whitleys out of Driffield in Yorkshire when war broke out. His wartime operations included covering the Dunkirk evacuation, flying 23 operations against the advancing Germans and surviving this experience to receive his commission before being assigned as an instructor on Whitleys at Kinloss in Scotland. He rose to the rank of Squadron Leader within two years, a tribute to his enormous personality and leadership qualities. He won an Air Force Cross there – AFC – which he referred to as an 'Avoiding Flak Cross'. Mahaddie began a second tour of operations in August, 1942, flying Stirlings with 7 Squadron, joined Pathfinders in October, and by 3 December he had completed his fiftieth operation.

Then, over a period of only eight weeks and following his promotion to Wing Commander, he was awarded a second AFC, the Distinguished Service Order (DSO), the Distinguished Flying Cross (DFC), and the Czechoslovakian Military Cross. Various citations included phrases such as, 'consistently attacked heavily defended targets with coolness and determination, often in adverse weather,' 'powers of leadership of a very high order,' and, 'unflagging enthusiasm which has had an inspiring effect on his comrades.'

Hamish's closest call came on a raid to Cologne on the night of 1/2 February 1943. After releasing his target-marking flares, cloud cover that had provided some protection broke. Flak damaged the Stirling's intercom system and put the rear turret out of action. At the same time a Ju-88 night-fighter raked the fuselage with cannon fire from 80 yards. The mid-upper gunner, wireless operator, and bomb aimer were injured, all the compasses and navigational equipment were destroyed with the exception of the astro-compass, and the aileron controls were severed.

Somehow, second pilot Thompson was able to provide navigation bearings back to base while Flight Sergeant Stewart treated the wounds of the three injured crew members.

'Meanwhile,' according to Bob Pointer, the rear gunner, 'the skipper was fighting with the aircraft. Having had the aileron controls badly mangled by the cannon shells he could only fly the aircraft by varying the power of the engines. Jock, our engineer – clambering in the wing root with a torch – did some very good work with pieces of wire he had conjured up from somewhere that enabled the skipper to gain partial control and set course for home.'

A count the next morning revealed that Hamish had suffered '174 cannon shells up my kilt.'

Mahaddie completed his operational tour with the Pathfinders during March 1943 and, at the age of 32, was promoted to Group Captain and assigned to No.

8 (PFF) Group Headquarters. His official job was as 'Group Training Inspector' for Don Bennett. His real job was using any means he could, fair or foul, to poach the best bomber crews in the RAF from under the noses of all the other groups, an assignment for which he became notorious – the 'horse thief.'

His technique was underhand, but necessary.

As 'Group Training Inspector' Hamish regularly visited operational squadrons, giving innocent lectures to 400 or more aircrew on the changing tactics and techniques employed by the Pathfinders. Before visiting a station Hamish would already have identified crews that he felt were candidates for the PFF by studying their aiming point photographs.

'This was a pretext,' he recalled later, 'because that was only to get me in and to see the men I had secretly identified. Generally I met these people, individually and privately, in the pub that evening.

'If a pilot and crew wished to apply to be transferred to the PFF, they would have to put in a written application to the squadron commander.

'The squadron commander would look at this transfer application and say, "No fear! He's too good!" tear it up and put it in the dustbin. The pilot would put in another application and the same thing would happen.

'Next time I was around the squadron, the pilot would make quite certain that he bought me a half pint at the local boozer down the street that same day.

'He would tell me, "Look, what gives? I've put in two applications and the boss just tears them up."

'I would take his name and his crew and go back to Don Bennett, and a posting would be issued so that forty-eight hours later they would be down at RAF Warboys and starting training as Pathfinder.'

When I first met Hamish, I was flying with 617 Squadron, and I could see he had that poaching look in his eye, but the Hon Sir Ralph Cochrane, AOC 5 Group in which 617 operated, had put a blanket ban on Hamish Mahaddie getting *anywhere* near 617 crews, whatever his pretext. 'I would have had you,' he told me, which was a compliment, but then I think he would have taken virtually anybody from 617. So far as I know, none of us went, and we remained with 5 Group, known as 'Cochrane's Private Air Force'.

The 'underhand' tactics of Mahaddie were reflected in the subterfuge adopted by the PFF on operations. Tony Hiscock:

> 'Pathfinder routing would be designed to fox the Germans. You might take a direction towards another city, and then turn off at the real target at the last minute. The watching Germans expected you to go along that line, then if you turn off, you're the first one to get to the target, and by the time they have worked out which is the real target you have done your bombing and you're flying away.

'Normally, a tour of operations would be 30 trips. The trouble was, after the invasion they said, "France is now a lot safer than Germany." So they said, "If you go to Germany you get five points, and if you go to France you get three." That's why I ended up doing rather more than the usual number of ops, 68 in all.'

The proportion of Pathfinder aircraft to Main Force bombers varied enormously according to the difficulty and location of the assigned target. A ratio of 1 to 15 was common, though it could be as low as 1 to 3. By the start of 1944 the bulk of Bomber Command was bombing within three miles of the PFF indicators, a huge improvement in accuracy. The success or failure of a raid now depended overwhelmingly on the Pathfinder's marker placement and how successfully further marking was corrected.

Because of their strong personalities, each stomping on the same ground of precision bombing, a strong sense of rivalry grew up between 5 Group and 8 Group, and was driven by the personal rivalry between the leader of 5 Group, Sir Ralph Cochrane and 8 Group's Don Bennett. Cochrane was an advocate of precision *low level* marking – pioneered by Gibson on the Dams Raids, and later by Leonard Cheshire – and lobbied heavily to be allowed to prove himself. He claimed that 5 Group, with two Lancaster Pathfinder Squadrons of its own (83 and 97 Squadrons) and a Mosquito squadron (627), could attempt targets and techniques that 8 Group would not

617 Squadron was not just expert at low-level marking in their Lancasters but later, at high altitude using the new SABS, achieved an incredible and very necessary accuracy of only 94 yards at the V Weapon launch site at Abbeville at the end of December, 1943.

Don Bennett remained in command of the Pathfinder Force until the end of the war, overseeing its growth to an eventual 19 squadrons, half of them Lancasters, working relentlessly to improve its standards, and tirelessly campaigning for better equipment, in particular for more Mosquitoes and Lancasters to replace the diverse assortment of often obsolete aircraft the force started with.

Bennett was famously quoted as saying: 'I am not going to have a living Victoria Cross in the Pathfinder Force,' and he didn't. But under his leadership there were three posthumous VCs. One was a Canadian, the second an Englishman, the third a South African. They were Ian Bazalgette (25), Robert Palmer (24) and Edwin Swales (29). Their VC citations were as follows.

Ian Willoughby Bazalgette, DFC (Posthumous VC), RAFVR, A/Squadron Leader, 635 Squadron (PFF).
    4 August 1944:
    'Acting Squadron Leader Bazalgette was "Master Bomber" of a Pathfinder Squadron detailed to mark an important target at Trossy-St-Maximim for the main bomber

force. When nearing his target his Lancaster came under heavy anti-aircraft fire. Both starboard engines were put out of action and serious fires broke out in the fuselage and the starboard main plane. The bomb aimer was badly wounded. As the deputy master bomber had already been shot down, the success of the attack depended upon Squadron Leader Bazalgette, and this he knew. Despite the appalling conditions in his burning aircraft, he pressed on gallantly to the target, marking it and bombing it accurately.

'That the attack was successful was due to his magnificent effort.

'After the bombs had been dropped the Lancaster dived, practically out of control. By expert airmanship and great exertion Bazalgette regained control. But the port inner engine then failed and the whole of his starboard main plane became a mass of flames. Bazalgette fought bravely to bring his aircraft and crew to safety. The mid-upper gunner was overcome by fumes. Bazalgette then ordered those of his crew who were able to leave by parachute to do so. He remained at the controls and attempted the almost hopeless task of landing the crippled and blazing aircraft in a last effort to save the wounded bomb-aimer and help-less air gunner. With superb skills, and avoiding a small French village nearby, he brought the aircraft down safely. Unfortunately it then exploded and this gallant officer and his two comrades perished.'

Robert Anthony Maurice Palmer, DFC and bar (posthumous VC) A/Squadron Leader RAFVR 109 Squadron (PFF).
23 December 1944:

'This officer completed 110 bombing missions. Most of them involved deep penetration into heavily-defended territory; many were low-level "marking" operations against vital targets; all were executed with tenacity, high courage and great accuracy.

'He first went on operations in January 1941. He took part in the first thousand-bomber raid on Cologne in 1942. He was one of the first pilots to drop a 4,000lb bomb on the Reich. It was known he could be relied upon to press home his attack whatever the opposi-tion and to bomb with great accuracy. He was always selected, therefore, to take part in special operations against vital targets.

'The finest example of his courage and determination was on 23 December 1944 when he led a formation of Lancasters to attack the marshalling yards at Cologne in daylight (reported to be full of supplies for Von Runstedt's Ardennes Offensive). Palmer had the task of marking the target and his formation had been ordered to bomb as soon as bombs had gone from his, the leading aircraft. The leader's duties during the final bombing run were exacting and demanded coolness and resolution. To achieve accuracy he would have to fly at an exact height and airspeed on a steady course, regardless of opposition. Some minutes before the target was reached his aircraft came under heavy anti-aircraft fire; shells burst all around, two engines were set on fire and there were flames and smoke in the nose and the bomb bay. Enemy fighters now attacked in force. Squadron Leader Palmer distained the possibility of taking avoiding action. He knew that if he diverged the least bit from his course, he would be unable to utilize the special (SABS bomb aiming) equipment to best advantage. He was determined to complete the run and provide an accurate and easily-seen aiming point for the other bombers. He ignored the double risk of fire and explosion in his aircraft and kept on. With his engines developing unequal power, an immense effort was needed to keep the damaged aircraft on a straight course. Nevertheless he made a perfect approach and his bombs and marker flares hit the target. His aircraft was last seen spiralling to earth in flames. Such was the strength of the opposition that more than half his formation failed to return.'

Edwin Swales DFC, (Posthumous VC) Captain, South African Air Force, 582 Squadron.
23 February 1945:

'Captain Swales was "Master Bomber" of a force of aircraft which attacked Pforzheim, just west of Stuttgart. As master bomber he had the task of locating the target area with precision and of giving aiming instructions to the main force of bombers following in his wake. Soon after he had reached the target area he was engaged by an enemy fighter and one of his engines was put out of action. His rear guns failed. His crippled aircraft was an easy target to further attacks. Unperturbed, he carried on with his allotted task; clearly and precisely he issued aiming instructions to the main force. Meanwhile, the enemy fighter closed the range and fired again. A second engine of Swales' aircraft was put out of action. Almost defenceless, he stayed over the target area issuing his aiming instructions until he was satisfied that the attack had achieved its purpose. It is now known that the attack was one of the most concentrated and successful of the war.

'Swales did not, however, regard his mission as completed. His aircraft was damaged. Its speed had been so much reduced that it could only with difficulty be kept in the air. The blind-flying instruments were no longer working. Determined at all costs to prevent his aircraft and crew from falling into enemy hands, he set course for home.

'After an hour he flew into thin-layered cloud. He kept his course by skilful flying between the layers, but later heavy cloud and turbulent air conditions were met. The aircraft, by now over friendly territory, became more and more difficult to control; it was losing height steadily. Realising that the situation was desperate, Swales ordered his crew to bale out. Time was very short and it required all his exertions to keep the aircraft steady while each of his crew moved in turn to the escape hatch and parachuted to safety. Hardly had the last crew member jumped when the aircraft plunged to earth. Captain Swales was found dead at the controls. Intrepid in the attack, courageous in the face of danger, he did his duty to the last, giving his life that his comrades might live.'

Those VC aircrew of the Pathfinder Force who died are remembered among the greatest of heroes. There were many other deaths in PFF, and some miraculous escapes as well. One that is almost beyond belief was that of Reg Barker, a Last Witness who had joined the RAF in July 1941 after working as an insurance clerk, learned to fly in the USA and then worked there as an instructor.

Barker returned to England in 1943 and was posted to 76 Squadron flying Halifaxes out of Yorkshire. He was poached by Hamish Mahaddie for PFF with 635 Squadron flying Lancasters out of Downham Market. On 26 August 1944, by now a 23-year-old flight lieutenant, Barker's navigator was F/O 'Hannes' Vidal RCAF, bomb aimer F/O Brian Boston, w/op Sgt 'Dick' Bird, m/u gunner W/O 'Taffy' Kinsey, r/gunner Sgt 'Dizzy' Hemmings, and flight engineer Sgt Harry Bullock.

They had attacked the German port of Keil successfully and turned towards England. Reg Barker:

'Suddenly there was an explosion, a vivid flash and the Lancaster was thrown on its back. I managed to regain level flight, assured the crew that I had control, checking with each of them that they were all right. However, we could see flames coming from the starboard wing. Hoping that an increased rush of air might extinguish them, I opened up the engines to full power. As we increased speed I felt the control column go slack in my hands and I realized that the cables to the tail plane must have been severed. As I could no longer control the aircraft I immediately ordered the crew to bail out.

'At almost the same moment the nose of the Lancaster plunged violently downwards and the aircraft went into a steep, spiralling dive. Our four Merlin engines were now driving us at terrifying speed vertically towards the earth.

'The cause of our predicament – I learnt later – was that the aircraft had broken in two! The tail plane with the rear turret had split away from the fuselage. As the rest of us flew on, Dizzy Hemmings was left behind without an engine. He found himself alone in the sky, with the tail-plane fluttering gently from side to side like a leaf falling to earth, and felt sure he could descend safely that way. Fortunately he decided to climb out of his turret and to use his parachute. He landed safely.

'Without a tail-plane it was no wonder that the rest of the aircraft had nose-dived so suddenly and violently. From our flying height of 17,000ft (5,181m) we plunged in seconds to 13,000ft (3,962m). I was lifted out of my seat by the powerful G-forces caused by the behaviour of the aircraft, and I could see the altimeter needle racing around the dial as it clocked hundreds of feet a second in our headlong descent.

'Trapped in our tightly-spinning aircraft, pinned hard against the Perspex cockpit roof and unable to move so much as a finger, it would be only seconds before we hit the ground. This would be the end. There was no time for my life to flash before me, but a fleeting glimpse of the fires raging below prompted a split-second prayer.

'Before I blacked out I was aware only of the most deafening sound. The blasting and buffeting of the wind through the fuselage, the screaming of the propellers and the roaring and vibrating of four powerful engines combined in an overwhelming, thunderous, unbearable crescendo of noise.

'Then total silence. Peace.

'Instead of a fiery hell, I felt I had arrived in that heavenly abode which I believe my rightful destiny.

'Gradually the silence was broken by a persistent swishing sound. Suddenly my sight returned and nearby in the sky I could see my blazing Lancaster. The 'swishing' must have been the wind whistling through my clothing as I hurtled toward the earth. I had no sense of falling but instinctively I grabbed and pulled my ripcord.

'As my parachute opened I could see trees below me, brightly lit from above by my burning aircraft. Instantly I dropped into the trees and my Lancaster crashed a short distance away. . .

'My immediate concern was to get away from my crashed aircraft, blazing furiously close by, ammunition exploding in the intense heat of the fire. I could see the stars overhead, recognised the North Star and set off hopefully towards Denmark, a few miles to the north. I soon came to the edge of the wood in which I had landed and then crept along a ditch which ran in the direction I wanted to travel. To my dismay I heard voices coming from ahead. I might have heard them sooner had I removed my flying helmet, but I had kept it on because my head was pouring blood – as it turned out, from a superficial head wound. I hid in the hedge but it was too late, for the approaching villagers must have seen me in silhouette against the blaze.

'An excited crowd quickly surrounded me, every one grubbing my tunic or trousers, holding me as tightly as possible, no doubt so that each of them could claim to have captured the English 'terror fleiger', the name they called me. They were all very old or very young. Although one teenage boy held a revolver to my head with his hand shaking furiously, not one of them harmed me. Yet only minutes before, they must have been terrified out of their lives as my Lancaster bomber came screaming out of the sky right above.

'Perhaps because of my amazement that I was still alive, I felt an overwhelming sense of calm . . . Two uniformed men arrived and I was handed over to begin a new chapter in my life as a prisoner of war. To my great surprise and joy, in the hours that followed I met up with our rear gunner, Dizzy. Three other members of the crew had also survived, our navigator Hannes, our wireless operator Dick, and our flight engineer, Harry. Each of them described an experience identical to my own, trapped in the aircraft, blacking out, gaining consciousness in the sky while falling just in time to release their parachutes and drop into the tree tops. Hannes had unfortunately suffered a broken leg and was on his way to a German hospital.

'How did the four of us trapped under the cockpit canopy have such a miraculous escape from certain death? It must have been the G-force in the tightly spinning Lancaster that acted with the combined weight of our four unconscious bodies to break the canopy and hurl us into the sky, where we quickly regained consciousness in the cold night, just in time to pull our parachutes.

'But how did the Germans shoot us down without any warning? It was only years later that we learned that German night-fighters were able to home in on our H2S transmitters, housed in a blister under our fuselage. We learned they were equipped with upward-firing guns known as Schräge Musik – Jazz Music – to enable them to position immediately below us, completely hidden from our view and where they could inflict the greatest damage.'

The Pathfinder Force flew a total of 50,490 individual sorties against 3,440 targets. The cost in human lives was heavy. At least 3,727 PFF members were killed on operations.

Author Tony Iveson aged 23, then a flight lieutenant, just back from Africa and about to take the conversion course for the Lancaster.

The Avro Manchester, which had a 'short, unhappy life', became the father of the four-engined Lancaster.

A Lancaster prototype, all turrets fitted, is a familiar sight but when it first appeared Spitfires tried to shoot it down and Germans on the ground cheered, thinking it was one of theirs.

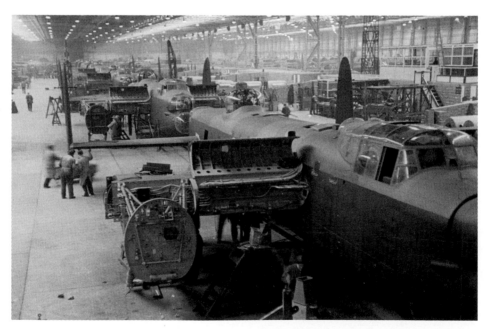

A Lancaster production line in England, which could deliver up to 26 brand new aircraft a week. There was also a Lancaster production line in Canada.

Wireless Operator, behind the navigator and in front of the Lancaster main spar, 'a very cramped position.'

Lancaster pilot, with instrument panel. Compared to 21st century aircraft they were actually very simple. Note the armour plate behind the pilot's head – absolutely non-effective against 20mm cannon rounds.

W/Cdr Guy Gibson, 24, led 19 Lancasters of 617 'Dambuster' Squadron to attack three great dams, successfully breaching two of them – Mohne and Eder – despite losing eight aircraft. Gibson is the pilot most associated with the Lancaster. He was awarded the VC, DSO*, DFC* and was killed flying a Mosquito later in the war.

Sgt Norman Cyril Jackson, 24, flight engineer, 106 Squadron. Attacked by a fighter, his Lancaster was set ablaze at 22,000ft. Jackson climbed out on the wing in a 200mph slipstream to try to put out the flames. He was pulled off the aircraft by his burning parachute but survived the fall to win the VC.

F/Lt Bill Reid, 22, 61 Squadron. Shot up twice, losing blood from a number of wounds and with dead and dying crewmen on board, flew 200 miles to bomb his target successfully. Despite fainting from loss of blood, he landed safely back in England. Awarded the VC and survived the war.

F/O Leslie Manser, 20, pilot, 50 Squadron. Shot to pieces in Harris's first '1,000 bomber raid', Manser held his crippled Manchester steady – with one engine shot away and the other failing – so that his crew could bail out. Unable to escape himself, he died when the aircraft went down. He was awarded the posthumous VC.

Sqdn Ldr John Deering Nettleton, 24, 44 (Rhodesia) Squadron led 12 Lancasters on the low-level Augsburg raid. Seven of the aircraft were shot down but the U-Boat engine factory was successfully bombed. Nettleton survived, the press hailing him as the 'Roof-Top VC.' He was killed later in the war.

W/Cdr Leonard Cheshire, 27, 'the legend', completed 100 missions in four years of fighting. Typically, in a single operation, he would dive to 1,000ft over the hottest German targets to ensure accurate marking, remaining under withering fire for 12 minutes. He was awarded the VC, DSO**, DFC*, later OM and became a Peer.

Sqdn/Ldr Ian Bazalgette, 25, Master Bomber, 635 PFF Squadron. Bombed one target with two engines shot away and his aircraft on fire. He held the aircraft steady while four of his crew bailed out. Instead of jumping himself, he crash-landed to avoid a French village and to try to save two wounded crewmen. The Lancaster exploded. He was awarded the posthumous VC.

P/O Andrew Mynarksi, 27, mid-upper gunner, 419 RCAF Squadron. When a night fighter set his Lancaster on fire, the pilot ordered the crew to bail out. Mynarski was severely burned trying to rescue the rear gunner, trapped in his turret. He only jumped, his clothes and parachute on fire, when all efforts failed. He saluted the rear gunner before exiting the aircraft but did not survive. The rear gunner did, however, and told of Mynarski's bravery, leading to his posthumous VC.

Flt Sergeant George Thompson, 24, wireless operator, 9 Squadron. Thompson suffered terrible burns rescuing two crewmen from the flames on board his burning Lancaster, beating out the fire with his bare hands. The aircraft successfully crash-landed in Holland. One of the rescued crewmen survived, but Thompson died from his injuries and was awarded the posthumous VC.

Captain Edwin Swales, 29, SAAF Master Bomber, 582 Squadron. Swales ignored repeated fighter attacks and the loss of two engines to ensure that his force accurately pressed home a raid, then held his Lancaster steady while his crew bailed out. He was found dead at the controls of his crashed aircraft and awarded the posthumous VC.

Sqdn/Ldr Robert Palmer, 24, Master Bomber, 109 PFF Squadron, with 110 ops under his belt, he ignored two engines and his bomb bay on fire to continue his bombing run, accurately to set markers for the rest of the force before falling in flames. He was awarded the posthumous VC.

CHAPTER ELEVEN

The Dambusters

The most famous of Lancaster stories is that of the Dambusters, which includes all the ingredients for a classic military adventure story. It has a mad scientist obsessed with the idea that he can build a secret weapon that can help win the war. It has a number of good-looking brave and modest young men willing to risk their lives to prove him right. It also has an extensive cast of pompous jobsworths in hats and Mackintoshes who are all quite certain that the scientist is mad and who, when they are confounded, look sheepish and leave us with a warm feeling of pleasure. It is about overcoming tremendous odds to win through, and the results are so spectacular that pictures of them flash around the world.

The scientist, Barnes Wallis, was not mad but he did have a tremendous struggle getting anyone to listen to his ideas. He was 55 years old at the time, trained first as a marine engineer, with a background in airship construction, including the geodetic design in the R100 airship in 1930. He transferred this technology to create the extremely durable Vickers Wellington bomber which first flew in 1936 and was popularly known as the 'Wimpey' after J. Wellington Wimpey in the Popeye cartoons.

When war broke out, Barnes Wallis wrote a paper advocating the use of huge bombs to attack German power supplies, and designed a bomb weighing 10 tons, far too heavy for any current bombers to carry. He went on to design a 'Victory Bomber' which would be capable of carrying one of his superbombs. In 1942 he also designed a bouncing bomb to knock out targets – dams or battleships – protected by nets that thwarted torpedo attack. Dams were normally impervious to any known bomb, but Barnes Wallis argued that explosive delivered to the right place would be really effective if aided by water pressure. His paper was entitled *Spherical Bomb — Surface Torpedo*.

In his battle to get his ideas approved it did not help that, fresh from having composed his 'de-housing' paper, the powerful Lord Cherwell was unimpressed. Wallis enlisted the help of Avro's designer, Roy Chadwick, who gave assurances that the new Lancaster could lift his bouncing bomb which, at 9,000lbs, was a heavier bomb than any aircraft had then carried. Barnes Wallis went to Bomber Command Chief Sir Arthur Harris, not a man known to be sympathetic to 'mad scientists' but who was unexpectedly impressed by a film Wallis showed him of a prototype bomb being dropped.

Churchill was enthusiastically involved in the decision to make the bouncing bomb – he had a partiality for unusual ways of fighting the war – and gave the go-ahead for full-scale trials on 28 February 1943.

The ultimate targets were the great dams of the Ruhr, and the dam-busting operation was one part of the whole Battle of the Ruhr.

Barnes Wallis stressed that whichever aircraft delivered his bouncing bomb, it had to fly at a precise speed and height, eventually agreed at 240mph and a drop height of 60ft (20m). Bomber Command decided a special squadron needed to be created and the job of choosing a leader for the new squadron was given to the new commander of 5 Group, Air Marshal the Hon Sir Ralph Cochrane, an old colleague of Arthur Harris from his fighting days in Iraq. Both men agreed the job should be given to Guy Gibson, now with a DSO and bar to add to his DFC and looking forward to a short rest after an unprecedented 174 operations as a bomber and night-fighter pilot.

Gibson was given a fairly free hand to choose his pilots for the new 617 Squadron, and immediately picked three former 106 Squadron colleagues, Flight Lieutenant J.V. Hopgood DFC and bar, the Australian Flight Lieutenant David Shannon DFC, and the Canadian Pilot Officer L.J. Burpee DFM. The old Dambuster movie gives the impression that Gibson hand-picked everyone but that is not the recollection of another of 617's founders, New Zealander and Last Witness Les Munro, who was to be the pilot of Lancaster W-Willie.

'I was 24 years old and a squadron leader when I joined, having got my wings in February 1942 and progressed through Wellingtons and Manchesters to Lancasters. I differ strongly from some authors on how 617 was founded. Some of them are wrong and so is the film, by saying that Gibson personally selected the crews. I well remember reading a letter from 5 Group headquarters, posted on the notice board for 97 Squadron, calling for volunteers to form a new squadron for a special operation. They were looking for crews nearing the end of their first tour, or beginning their second. I am emphatic on that. Gibson would not have known me from a bar of soap.

'I believe that the same applies to David Maltby and Joe McCarthy, the American. We were all volunteers. We weren't picked by Gibson, he wouldn't have known me, I had never met Gibson. The bulk of the crews were volunteers. Gibson might have picked Dave Shannon who was on 106 Squadron with him, and Mick Martin too; Mick said that Gibson telephoned him. Martin was a low-level specialist, and Gibson wanted a low-level specialist.

'I had got to 21 trips with 97 Squadron when there was this call to volunteer. I was intrigued. I talked with my crew and asked if they were happy if I volunteered as a crew? After discussing it, the majority said yes. Only one said no, the rear gunner. The only other change was my bomb aimer. The first couple of trips we did on 97, he passed out at high altitude on the bombing run, something to do with oxygen sickness; they had to take him off operations. I didn't have a permanent bomb aimer when I volunteered for 617 so I got one when I arrived at Scampton. The two new blokes to replace my bomb aimer and rear gunner were Jimmy Clay and Harvey Weekes. We stayed together for all the 38 trips I did with 617 Squadron, except Jimmy Clay left six weeks before I finished.'

It was obviously a secret operation, and as with the Pathfinders, there was a certain amount of resistance from other 5 Group squadrons reluctant to lose their best crews. Some of them also had to lose their best aircraft for a while, because it was found that Lancasters with a few operations under their belts were more reliable than those straight out of the factory. Later, when these 'loaned' aircraft were returned, as the special Lancasters capable of dropping the bouncing bombs arrived, there was disbelief at the number of hours clocked up on them, and evidence of extremely low flying… presumably bits of branches and blood stains from dead birds.

The young Canadian 'Doc' Sutherland, one of the Last Witnesses, was air gunner with Les Knight, another volunteer for 617:

'Training for the Dams attack in March to May 1943, we did a lot of incredibly low flying. I really liked that, flying low around England. You could see so much, the people on the ground, we had to be low and I guess there were a lot of complaints. We were coming to a crossroads one day at 200mph and Les pulled up so quickly that we blew this guy off his bicycle with our slipstream. We could see him when we looked back, off the road and in the ditch. We did a lot of daylight low flying, and the same thing at night.'

Les Munro:

'We had been training for six weeks at those levels, around 50ft (16.5m). On the whole we were pretty proficient at maintaining our low height. Our normal recognised height for training was supposed to be treetop height, but quite frequently the crews flew lower than tree-top height. The competency of the pilot was governed by his ability to anticipate how quickly he was approaching those trees in front of him and taking appropriate steps going over them. That was part of the training in low flying, the ability to judge obstacles in front of him, the distance approaching at 230-240 miles an hour, in the dark, in the daylight to start with obviously, then in the dark.'

The intensive training was to ensure they got to the targets and home again at low levels, away from the height at which RAF bombers normally flew. Sadly, the technique of two spotlights coned over water to achieve a height of 60ft (20m) on the actual attack was not discovered by Gibson himself after watching leggy lovelies at a London show, as portrayed in the film. It was a method transferred over from Coastal Command to judge their height at night when attacking U-boats.

All the training was aimed at being ready to go on the night of 16/17 May, when water levels in the three dams that were actually attacked – the Mohne, the Eder and the Sorpe – would be at their highest, and moon conditions were good.

Two days before the raid, the explosive-filled bouncing bombs – code-named 'Upkeep' – started arriving at Scampton. There was nearly a tragedy when one of them was dropped while loading and dozens of ground crew sprinted for their lives, but it did not explode.

In all, 19 Lancaster captains were briefed for the attack. The first group of nine, flying in three sections of three, were to attack the Mohne:

1. Wg Cmdr Guy Gibson, DSO, DFC
2. Flt Lt John Hopgood DFC
3. Flt Lt Mick Martin DFC
4. Sqdn Ldr Melvin 'Dinghy' Young DFC
5. Flt Lt David Maltby DFC
6. Flt Lt David Shannon DFC RAAF
7. Sqdn Ldr Henry Maudsley DFC
8. Flt Lt Bill Astell DFC
9. Plt Off Les Knight RAAF

The second wave, taking the northern route, consisted of five Lancasters whose main target was the Sorpe Dam:

1. Flt Lt Joe McCarthy DFC RCAF
2. Flt Lt Robert Barlow DFC RAAF
3. Flt Lt Les Munro RNZAF
4. Plt Off Vernon Byers RCAF
5. Plt Off Geoff Rice

The third wave was a mobile reserve of five Lancasters to take off two hours after the others and attack any of the dams left standing:

1. Plt Off Warner Ottley DFC
2. Plt Off Lewis Burpee DFM RCAF
3. Flt Sgt Kenny Brown RCAF
4. Flt Sgt Bill Townsend DFM
5. Flt Sgt Cyril Anderson

The last Dambuster pilot alive in the ninth year of the twenty-first century, Les Munro, pilot of W-Willie, did not actually make it to the Dams that night, but for a good reason:

'I was one of the wave of five Lancasters flying singly, not in formation, that took off and flew what they called the Northern Way, due east of Lincolnshire, and at a point just north of the island of Vieland we turned south to go over the Zuider Zee to join the others on Gibson's route, down by Hamm. I still remember the sight of the breakers on the foreshore as I approached the coast. We were flying low, probably 40 to 50ft.

'Reaching the coast I had to slightly raise height to get over the sand-dunes, and it was going down the other side of those dunes that I was hit by light flak, a single line of tracer coming up on my port side. I was hit by one flak shell which blew a hole in the side of the aircraft about 2ft (66cm) across. It cut the communications, the intercom and the electrical system.

'As a result, we were unable to communicate with each other. We could not talk to anyone outside either. The master compass was destroyed and the hydraulic lines to the rear turret were cut so we had no rear defence.

'We communicated to each other by lifting the flaps of our helmets and yelling in each other's ears. I got the flight engineer to signal the wireless operator to come up, and I asked him to go back and see if the damage could be repaired while I circled in the Zuider Zee. He came back eventually and said no. He had checked on the state of the rear gunner to see if he had been hit or not, which he hadn't been. But Percy Pigeon said to me that it was impossible to repair the damage to the communications systems. There was a hole two feet across.

'Remember we were flying singly, and it was vital that the navigator and the pilot were able to communicate. If we had carried on and got to the target area, it was essential that the bomb aimer and the pilot were able to communicate. But none of us could talk to each other.

'That German gunner must have been very alert. I was coming at him at 230mph, and he hit me. The damage had no effect on the flying ability of the Lancaster, just the communications. But without communications I could not have been directed to the target. Even if Gibson had still been around after taking out the second dam, the Eder, he could not have said, now you go to the Sorpe Dam. Assuming Gibson had still been leading and directing us on the Sorpe, we would not have been able to hear him, or communicate with him.

'Our five aircraft were not in formation. I don't know who was leading at that time. It may have been Barlow, the Australian who was shot down subsequently as he got to the Ruhr (or he may have hit a cable). The crash killed his crew but left the Germans with a strange-looking bomb, virtually undamaged.

'There was one aircraft shot down, the Canadian, Byers. He strayed off course a bit over the island of Texel. He was said to have climbed a little and flak got him. He was shot down, and he and his crew were killed.

'Then there was Geoff Rice who, I think, was adjusting his altimeter, and unconsciously leant forward on the stick to do it. I think he realised what he was doing, pulled back, and at the same moment he hit the sea, left the bomb and everything behind him.

'Geoff was incredibly lucky. He whipped the calliper arms off the aircraft, these were the arms that held the bouncing bomb and gave it spin when it operated. He was the fourth.

'Joe McCarthy had trouble with his aircraft anyway and took off half an hour after us. He was the only one from the northern flight that got to the Sorpe, and he bombed it. There was a bit of ground haze around and they had difficulty in getting a run in. The same with Ken Brown from the third wave who got there two hours later. They had difficulty in lining up their target. They were the only two who bombed the Sorpe. They didn't breach the dam.

'I got back to base at thirty minutes past midnight on 17 May. That night was the only time in the war I was directly struck by fire. You flew through fields of flak, it was just the luck of the gods as to whether you were hit or not. Sometimes we would come back with little shrapnel holes, but we had been far enough away from the explosions for the flak not to do any serious damage.

'On the Dams Raid I had no alternative but return to base. I felt disappointed we couldn't go on. But I think Lady Luck was on my side even at that stage. . . People have said that maybe if I had gone on I might have been one of those eight that didn't come back, and I look at it from that point of view.'

Sgt 'Doc' Sutherland was mid-upper gunner, and another of the Last Witnesses, Sgt Ray Grayston was flight engineer to Pilot Officer Les Knight, the only undecorated pilot in Gibson's first wave of nine aircraft. Sutherland:

'We were lined up at Scampton for the takeoff of the first wave, each of us a formation of three; we were in the third formation. David Maudslay was our leader, and Bill Astell was the other pilot. Most books say Shannon was our leader, but somehow it was changed and Shannon was in David Maltby's flight. We were given the green light from the controller at the end of the runway, and everybody poured it on. We roared off that grass strip, it was very impressive to watch, it must have made a terrific racket. We had a little trouble getting over the fence at the far end, but everybody made it.

'We observed complete radio silence, all our communication with each other was done with signal lights and Morse code. Within our own formation we had sight of each other, but the two earlier formations had gone and were out of sight of us.

'We flew in formation until we got to the Dutch coast and then things started happening. We broke up and did not see Maudslay again for a long while. The interesting story to me was our engineer Ray Grayston's account of the flight, after we tested the 60-foot spotlights over the North Sea.

'Grayston looked at Maudslay testing his, and told me later that Maudslay was 20ft (6.6m) below us when his lights coned on the water!

'Either we were at 80ft (26.5m), or he was at 40ft (13.2m). Years later I asked Ray Grayston if he remembered saying that, observing that Maudslay coned 20ft below us, and he didn't remember at all! But this did happen.'

Grayston:

'I am surprised Doc Sutherland said that about Maudslay's aircraft not being at the right height, 60ft (20m), when the two lights lined up on the water. Looking sideways on to another aircraft with its lights on, you would have no idea how high he was unless you were closer to the lights.'

Sutherland:

'When Maudslay crossed the coast, we don't know if he hit something, or what happened, but we didn't see him again until we got to the Eder Dam. I think at the Mohne Dam Gibson called up Maudslay, and Maudslay didn't answer, but he did answer later at the Eder

'In England low flying was good, like going on holiday, but on the actual raid itself the problem was the power lines, seeing them in the dark. They got a lot of guys. You could see them coming up, and the call, power lines! Pour on the petrol and it seemed to take forever to climb up over them with a full bomb load. Some pilots went under them.

'We were by ourselves when we got to the Mohne. Gibson had put his bomb down already and it should have blown the dam, one bomb. But it was so hard, somebody shooting at you, it was very difficult. Hopgood had just been blown up and his aircraft was still burning underneath the dam. His bomb had gone over the dam, but he was hit by flak on the way in to bomb. When he crossed over the dam he was on fire.

'Gibson said, "Get out if you can."

'Hopgood said, "For Christ's sake get out," This quote is from Fraser, his bomb aimer, after the war. Fraser went out of Hopgood's Lancaster through the front turret. The rear gunner, an Australian called Burcher, got out through the back. They baled out at the height of the dam and then pulled their ripcord. Fraser said he opened the parachute before he got out and it pulled him out of the aircraft. They both lived. Burcher was pretty badly hurt, but Fraser, the bomb aimer, he was OK. They both became PoWs.'

Grayston:

'What happened was that we were all within the target area, and we were called up as numbered crews. Gibson was number one and I think we were number 8 in the order of attack on the Mohne. We stayed on the Mohne Dam until number 5, when it cracked, then the three remaining available crew moved on to the Eder. Dave Shannon was one of them, just ahead of us, Maudsley and our crew. Gibson was with us, of course.'

Sutherland:

'We watched Mick Martin go in on the Mohne and he got hit just before he was due to drop his bomb. It blew a hell of a hole in his port wing, though other reports say his starboard wing. But Tam Simpson, Martin's rear gunner, survived the attack and the war and wrote an account of it in a book and he said Martin's Lancaster was hit in the port wing and it blew out the empty petrol tank.

'Martin dropped his bomb. I think his aircraft was tilted and the bomb didn't quite land in the right place. He survived anyway. He was the third guy in. The rest of us were flying in a square formation to the south until it was our turn to bomb.

'Dinghy Young went next. It seemed to be a successful run, there was an explosion but the dam did not break. Gibson and Martin had gone in with Young, despite Martin's damaged aircraft, drawing fire. We were listening on the radio.

'We could see the flames from Hopgood's plane and the flak from the two towers on the dam. I don't think they were very good gunners. We were coming down to 60 feet, maintaining a straight course to line up and with our lights on, so they should have nailed us. I guess the guys who were shooting back at them must have put them off.

'The way it is credited now, it was Maltby's bomb in J-Johnny, that got the dam. They have since been able to work out which bombs hit the wall of the dam, and which ones didn't. The Germans were recording seismic shocks and they could tell which bombs made solid contact with the wall.

'Dave Shannon was lining up to bomb, and then Gibson called him off because Maltby had broken it. Everybody was happy the dam was gone, but it was a disaster losing all the men we lost, especially Hopgood and my personal friend Al Cottam.

'It was a blow.

'Gibson called up Maudslay, our own pilot Les Knight and Dave Shannon, then called Dinghy Young and said, "You will be second in command if something happens to me."

'Dinghy Young – I know he was there, though I never heard him after he acknowledged this signal.

'The Eder Dam was not far away, 15 minutes flying time, but it was difficult to find. It was in a hole in the mountain. We found our own way to the Eder and met up there. Gibson called Maudslay, leader of our flight, and Maudslay went in and had difficulty getting down to the right height of 60ft (18.3m).

'Things weren't quite right. Gibson said, "That's very nice flying, Henry, but you will have to do better."

'Maudslay said, "Sorry, Sir."

'He had another go, and his bomb skipped over the dam. And I think, personally, that's because his lights were not set right, he was too low. The bomb skipped over the dam and blew up the power station.

'Gibson kept calling, "Henry are you all right? Henry are you all right?"

'Maudslay came back in a very weak voice and said, "Yes, Sir, returning to base." He died about 60 miles away on his way home; we think he was hit by flak.

'Gibson said, "Dave, you go in and have a go."

'Dave Shannon went in and made a couple of dummy runs. Gibson was agitating, saying daylight is coming, we've got to get out of here, but Shannon got his go. It wasn't quite right, but he never said so. He sent a message back that he had made a crack at the dam, but it wasn't quite right. Then it was our turn. We made a dummy run, we didn't have the proper height, and in any case everything wasn't just right.'

Grayston:

'The actual attack on the Eder was not all that difficult. We did not get fired at – they fired at Gibson but nobody shot at us at any time, there was no flak – it was just an ordinary run to the target. We went around twice.

'The difficult thing was getting the altitude down to 60ft. Other crews had struggled. We were at the end of the line and learnt a lot watching them trying to control their speed.'

Sutherland:

'The next time Les Knight brought us in his airspeed was right on, the height was right on, and Johnny Johnson let the bomb go and it was perfect. It rolled up against the wall and it blew right through.'

Grayston:

'What happened with us is that as flight engineer, I chopped all four engines back to idle and let her glide down to 60ft and then opened them up again. It worked a treat. Two seconds miscalculation could have been disastrous, but if you know your machine as I did, you know how reliable they are. Glide down to 60ft and then open the taps up to maximum immediately. We only had a few seconds just to level up, and luckily Les Knight got it spot-on to the target straight away on the second run.

'We hit it and took the bottom out of it.'

The third wave fared very badly, and their stories went almost untold in the public euphoria over the success of the first wave. They took off at one minute intervals

just after midnight. First off was Pilot Officer Warner Ottley DFC, and though he flew through some heavy flak, he and his crew got past the Rhine.

He acknowledged a signal sent to him at 02.30 to attack the Lister Dam, the most southern of the targets, 50 miles south of the Mohne. Two minutes later a signal was sent telling Ottley to change his target and head for the Sorpe, halfway between the Mohne and the Lister, but was not acknowledged.

Flight Sergeant Ken Brown in one of the following Lancasters saw an aircraft coned and hit by flak north of the city of Hamm, the fuel tanks and the bouncing bomb exploding. Astonishingly, Ottley's rear turret gunner, Sergeant Freddy Tees survived when his rear turret, with Tees still inside, was thrown clear. Freddy suffered severe burns, but ended the war as a PoW.

Sadly, he later committed suicide, perhaps because of guilt at being the only one of his crew to live.

The Canadian pilot, Flying Officer Lewis Burpee DFM, brought in to 617 personally by Gibson, drifted slightly off track over Holland. He was seen by a following aircraft to go into light flak, turn right, get coned and crash in a huge ball of flame causing a lot of damage and with no survivors.

Flight Sergeant Kenny Brown, another Canadian, witnessed the loss of both his colleagues and he, too, was then ordered to attack the Sorpe. On the way he flew over the Mohne Dam and must have been reassured that, despite the losses, the operation was working.

There was a great deal of mist at the Sorpe, as Joe McCarthy had found, and it was only after several runs and dropping flares that the 'Upkeep' bomb was dropped at 03.14, hitting the water a few yards from the parapet. Brown logged that there was more delay than they expected before the explosion, but that no breach was caused. They ran into a lot of flak on the way back near Hamm and on the coast, but got back safely at 05.33.

This was three minutes ahead of Flight Sergeant Cyril Anderson, who was still carrying his bouncing bomb! Last to take off, Anderson had fallen further and further behind schedule, and with the moon behind him and gathering mist, appears to have got lost. In addition, his rear turret was out of action so he had lost his best defensive weapon. He acknowledged an order at 02.28 to attack the Sorpe but was now seriously lost, and deep inside Germany with 90 minutes to daybreak, he flew home along his reciprocal route.

Most of the other survivors endorsed this decision as the only one he could have taken in the circumstances but Gibson fired him that morning. Anderson may not even have had breakfast. He and his crew were sent straight back to a Main Force squadron and were later killed on ops.

The last of the crews to land was that of Flight Sergeant Bill Townsend, after an epic low-level flight there and back. His aircraft was coned and attracted a storm of flak 15 minutes after crossing the Dutch coast, which he escaped by throwing the aircraft all over the sky at very low level. They were set to attack the Mohne but then orders came through to attack the Ennepe, 30 miles west-southwest of the Mohne. They got lost near the Mohne Dam because by now the lake that had been contained by the dam had half-drained, confusing their navigation, but Townsend persisted and identified a lake he felt sure was the Ennepe – but which was probably a dirt dam called the Bever, five miles away. Townsend made three dummy runs to ensure he could hit his target, and released his 'Upkeep' on the fourth run at 03.37, safely steering his aircraft over the dam and clearing the hills around it. The mine made two bounces and then disappeared, exploding 30 seconds later, but short of the actual dam itself, so no breach. With 40 minutes left before daylight, he set off home at top speed, up to 270mph, almost 'on the deck' and twisting and turning to avoid houses, trees and power cables. Going across the North Sea one engine was shut down after over-heating, he made a shaky landing at Scampton after a few bounces.

Townsend was awarded the CGM, the Conspicuous Gallantry Medal, as was Kenny Brown, a medal ranking second only to the Victoria Cross. The surviving officer pilots who attacked the Dams – Knight, McCarthy, Maltby, Martin and Shannon – all won DSO's. Fourteen DFC's, including four bars, and 12 DFMs, including one bar to Franklyn, were awarded.

Les Munro got nothing for that night's work, but went on to a distinguished career with 617 as a flight commander, and later won a DSO and a DFC.

Guy Gibson, 24 years old, who then had two DSO's and two DFC's, was famously awarded the Victoria Cross. The citation read:

'16-17 May, 1943. This officer served as a night bomber pilot at the beginning of the war and quickly established a reputation as an outstanding operational pilot. In addition to taking the fullest possible share in all normal operations, he made single-handed attacks during his rest nights on such highly-defended objectives as the German battleship *Tirpitz*, being completed in Wilhelmshaven. When his tour of operations was concluded he asked for a further operational posting and went to a night fighter unit instead of being posted to instructional duties. In the course of his second operational tour he destroyed at least three enemy bombers and contributed much to the raising and development of new night-fighter squadrons. After a short period in a training unit, he again volunteered for operational duties and returned to night bombers. Both as an operational pilot and as leader of his squadron he achieved outstandingly successful results and his personal courage knew no bounds. Berlin, Cologne, Danzig, Gdynia, Genoa, Le Creusot, Milan, Nuremberg and Stuttgart were among the targets he attacked by day and by night.

'On the conclusion of his third operational tour, Gibson pressed strongly to be allowed to remain on operations and he was selected to command a new squadron, 617, formed for a special task.

'Under his inspiring leadership, this squadron executed one of the most devastating attacks of the war, the breaching of the Mohne and Eder dams. The task was fraught with danger and difficulty. Gibson personally made the initial attack on the Mohne dam. Descending to within a few feet of the water and taking the full brunt of the anti-aircraft defences, he delivered his attack with great accuracy. Afterwards he circled very low for 30 minutes, drawing the enemy fire on himself, in order to leave as free a run as possible to the following aircraft which were attacking the dam in turn. He then led the remainder of his force to the Eder dam where, with complete disregard for his own safety, he repeated his tactics and once more drew on himself enemy fire so that the attack could be successfully developed.

'Wing Commander Gibson has completed over 170 sorties, involving more than 600 hours operational flying. Throughout his operational career, prolonged exceptionally at his own request, he has shown leadership, determination and valour of the highest order.'

Doc Sutherland:

'It was quite a party they had after the raid. I was in the Sergeant's Mess so we had to go to bed, but those other guys, the officers, had a real wing-ding.

'Les Knight had been a sergeant most of the first tour with 50 Squadron, and then he got commissioned and promoted rather quickly. He didn't drink like most of the rest of us. He was always thinking, a really smart person. He had things figured out and he studied a lot. He never flew a straight course, so we were never caught by a night fighter. He was always weaving.

'When he was killed he was a flight lieutenant with a DSO. Grayston and I were still in this crew, but we lived. Gibson had left the squadron by then, after his VC.'

An unusual insight into Gibson appeared in the 2009 obituary of Joan Bright Astley, personal assistant to General Sir Hastings 'Pug' Ismay, Deputy Secretary to the War Cabinet and a confidant of Winston Churchill's.

On a voyage by liner to the Quebec Conference in 1943, Miss Bright, as she then was, met Gibson as he went on his promotional tour after the Dams Raid, in which, in her words, he had continued… 'to direct his bombers after half his own squadron had been shot down.'

What had he felt? She asked him.

'Nothing much,' Gibson replied, 'but I let loose vile oaths – "Here it is, you *****s" "Take that you ******s!" I shouted.'

CHAPTER TWELVE

The Ruhr, Hamburg and Peenemunde

Lie in the dark and listen.
City magnates and steel contractors
Factory workers and politicians
Soft hysterical little actors,
Ballet dancers, reserved musicians
Safe in your warm civilian beds,
Count your profits and count your sheep
Life is passing above your heads,
Just turn over and try to sleep.
Lie in the dark and let them go
There's one debt you'll forever owe,
Lie in the dark and listen.

Noel Coward

The Ruhr was known as 'Happy Valley' to RAF bomber crews, and the battle between March and July 1943 was one of four major bombing offensives launched by the Bomber Command that year. Its targets were the cities and towns of the Germany's industrial heartland, a difficult objective due to the haze generated by its industrial plants and a high concentration of German defences. Increasing numbers of German night-fighters, equipped with radar and various electronic targeting devices, took a heavy toll on the attacking bombers. The bombers, with Lancasters outnumbering Halifaxes and others by the summer of 1943, were still able to inflict significant damage to disrupt a great deal of the Happy Valley industry (though not as great as was thought at the time).

Nearly everyone with influence in the armed forces had an opinion on what *should* be Bomber Command targets, if only Arthur Harris would see sense:

- Experts in economic war proposed one class of industrial target after another, the destruction of which would, they said, cripple the German war effort.

- Experts in maritime war called for attacks on the enemy ports, on ships in harbour, on U-boat bases and shipbuilding yards.
- Experts in land warfare called for attacks on tank factories, on fuel dumps, ordnance depots and so on.
- Experts in air warfare had their own target systems as part of their campaign for air superiority.

When the expected spectacular results failed to materialise, it was put down to faults in the bomber forces. There were doubts, criticisms, and even opposition to the whole bombing campaign. Arthur Harris conducted a stubborn, hard-fought battle in which new and ever-changing tactics had to be hammered out through painful experience. He wanted to concentrate his forces to have the most effect, and in general he succeeded in his aim. It took until the middle of 1943 for RAF Bomber Command to become strong enough to launch a heavy attack on Germany, to *hurt* them as much as Harris felt Britain had been hurt in the earlier years of the war.

The effects of the bomber offensive were only gradual, slowly cumulative. There were few spectacular events like the Dambuster raid, but gradually the Germans changed their armed forces from the offensive – bombers and tanks – to the defensive – fighters and anti-aircraft guns – an expensive move that Albert Speer, Hitler's Minister for Armaments and War Production, identified as 'Germany's Lost War.'

Anti-aircraft defences in Germany numbered 600,000 in 1943, and rose to nearly a million a year later. Anti-aircraft guns took an ever-increasing part of Germany's total weapon production, while the German night-fighter force – pitched against the RAF rather than the USAAF – grew from virtually nothing to 150 aircraft in November 1940, 250 by July 1942, 550 by July 1943, 800 by the spring of 1944, and 1,250 by the end of 1944.

The Battle of the Ruhr, the real beginning of Bomber Command carrying the war to the Germans, opened on the night of 5 March, 1943 with an attack on Essen by 442 aircraft, mainly Lancasters and Halifaxes, but Stirlings and Wellingtons were also used. They were aided by the Pathfinder Force, 'Oboe' blind-bombing system and 'H2S' navigation and bombing radar. In all, 14 aircraft were lost. A similar-sized raid on Essen followed on the night of 12 March with 23 aircraft lost. Duisburg was attacked with a large force on 26 March, but cloud cover and problems with the Oboe Mosquitoes gave a 'widely scattered raid.'

Concentrated attacks against all of the major industrial cities of the Ruhr continued up to the middle of July. On the night of 12 May, Alliot Veron Roe's son, Lighton, failed to return from a raid on Duisburg. He was on his third operational tour, an acting Squadron Leader with 156 Squadron, flying a

Lancaster as a Pathfinder Marker. Lighton had previously been awarded a DFC when, having lost an engine on take-off, he pressed on to bomb the target and return on only three engines. His death left Avro's founder with two remaining sons, Geoffrey and 17-year-old Royce, the latter intent on joining the RAF as soon as he was 18.

By the night of 23 May and a heavy raid on Dortmund, the total weight of bombs dropped by Bomber Command on Germany had passed 100,000 tons.

Bomber Command Chief Arthur Harris publicly taunted Goering:

'In 1939, Goering promised that not a single enemy bomb would reach the Ruhr. Congratulations on having delivered the first 100,000 tons of bombs on Germany to refute him.'

Last Witness Stan Bradford DFM, was then 19:

'We were on our way to Nuremburg, it was 1943, I was a mid-upper gunner with 57 Squadron, 5 Group, and there was lots of flak around. I spied an aircraft, obviously a Lancaster, that burst into flames and I could see by the light of the flames that he had been shot down by a Focke Wulf.

'I thought, oh dear, here we go.

'As the Focke Wulf got a bit closer I alerted the skipper to what tactics we were going to use, corkscrew to the left. I warned him what was happening. "Prepare to dive to port," I told him, but the signal was "Go!" and I still hadn't said it so he carried on as normal.

'This German fighter looked like he was stalking us, but he got a bit close and I had him immediately, no bother at all. I know he had a cannon but I had two 0.303 machine guns in the mid-upper turret. He went straight down in flames.

'A little later in the flight we were attacked again, and Chick, our rear-gunner, a Canadian, he picked up a German fighter, and now he gave our pilot instructions. Then he shot at the German who was obviously in trouble. . . I dealt with him as well, just to make sure.

'The risk was always that he was going to fire before I did. I used to let them get within 250 yards (227m) and then a quick burst, straight at him. In the first two attacks I know I got the engine and he went down in flames. They were both flamers. The second was a Me109. There was an hour to 90 minutes between the two kills. I got the credit for both.'

There were large raids on Essen on 3 April, on Duisburg on 8 April and later on 26 April. Essen caught it again on 30 April. In the month of May, 826 of Harris's bombers raided Dortmund, 729 hit Düsseldorf, 518 bombed Essen and 719 attacked Wuppertal, the last destroying a thousand acres of the old town by fire.

Last Witness Sergeant Don Briggs, Flight Engineer, 156 Pathfinder Squadron:

'I can remember the nearest thing you will ever get to a direct hit with heavy flak. . . This flak exploded right above the canopy, pieces of shrapnel punctured the wing. Thankfully there was no fuel tank leakage, but a chunk of shrapnel flew through the cabin, missed my right ear by inches, and landed on the cockpit floor. When we got back the aeroplane was like a pepper-pot. The poor old guys on the ground were aghast. No one was injured. I was the nearest, but the navigator was more or less as close. I had just reached my twentieth birthday.'

Last Witness LAC George Hart, RAF ground crew on Lancasters with 83 Pathfinder Squadron at Scampton:

'Almost all our work, winter and summer, was out in the open. Being up on an aerodrome, especially in Lincolnshire, is pretty draughty, and dealing with tiny nuts and bolts when your fingers were frozen was a bit difficult.

'When there was a night operation, certain numbers of our flight were on night duties. We had to start the aircraft up, see them off and be there when they returned. We had a Nissen hut – well over a mile or more from the main camp – and when the aircraft were off, we would go to the NAAFI and have something to eat. Then we would be brought back and have a bit of a kip in the Nissen hut on dispersal until the bombers came home. We would meet them off the edge of the runway with two little torches and navigate them back to their dispersal stands.

'Some of the time returning aircraft were shot up quite badly.

'We were great friends with the aircrew – I am still friendly with some of our pilots now. You got to know them and when they didn't come back, you felt a real loss of a friend. The number of times you start the aircraft and wave them off, and they don't come back...

'When you were on a squadron you were part of a family. When you lost anybody, you felt it deeply.'

In all, there were 43 Ruhr attacks to the end of July 1943, hitting 26 German cities. They were all central to Germany's war production. Essen housed the Krupp works and on the night of 22 July, Arthur Harris sent 600 bombers to Essen over a period of less than an hour, which, according to the Nazi propaganda chief Josef Goebbels caused 'a complete stoppage of production in the Krupps works.'

The Germans increased air defences in the Ruhr area and Bomber Command losses increased to 4.7 per cent of the aircraft dispatched.

The Battle of the Ruhr ended when mounting RAF losses caused the offensive to be called off. On 11 June 1943, Bomber Command had 726 bombers crewed and operational. By the last raid of the offensive, on 9 July, this had fallen to 623. The battle killed around 15,000 Germans with the loss of 5,000 British and Commonwealth aircrew. Other German targets were largely spared during this battle, before Harris – with Churchill's urging – switched the attack to the great Hansiatic port of Hamburg.

The Battle of Hamburg ['Operation Gomorrah']

Churchill and Harris jointly conceived the idea of a series of massive raids on the port of Hamburg, Germany's second largest city and its largest port. As it was threequarters of the way to Berlin, lessons could be learnt about the forthcoming attack on the German capital. It also had one great navigational advantage; as a very distinct shape on the Baltic coast, it was easily discernable on H2S radar.

The major raids, in July and August 1943, devastated Hamburg, virtually destroying it. Albert Speer, Nazi Minister for Armaments and War Production, said later that what happened to Hamburg was exactly what Hitler and Goering had wanted to see happen to London. When the Blitz had not done it, they had gone on to pin their hopes on the secret 'Vengeance' weapons.

Between the 'Battle' nights of 24 July and 2 August, RAF Bomber Command subjected Hamburg to four intense raids, aided and abetted by what, by comparison, were pin-prick daylight raids from the US 8th Air Force. It was the first RAF raid when 'Window' was used, the dropping of thousands of tinfoil strips to confuse German radar, and also the first use of the H2S radar scanning system that provided the Pathfinders with a crude TV-like image of the ground below. It was to be quite some time, nearly a year, before the RAF discovered that the Germans were able to detect individual H2S scanners, even at long range, with deadly effect for hundreds of RAF bombers, including at least one of the Last Witnesses later in the war.

On the night of 24 July 1943, 791 RAF bombers took off for the attack on Hamburg, including 354 Lancasters, 239 Halifaxes, 120 Stirlings and 68 Wellingtons. Lancasters were now providing 46 per cent of Bomber Command's strength, but in terms of the tonnage of bombs delivered, Lancasters took more than 70 per cent. RAF losses that night were light, amounting to 12 aircraft, a loss rate of 1.5 per cent, only four of which were Lancasters.

This raid was followed up the next day when 68 American B-17's struck Hamburg's U-boat pens and shipyards, while Harris sent 705 bombers that evening – 294 of them Lancasters – to attack Essen. He lost 26, of which 5 were Lancasters.

On 26 July, another American attack destroyed Hamburg's power plant, and that night Bomber Command mounted a raid that was later dubbed the 'Hiroshima of

Hamburg'. A total of 736 aircraft, including 356 Lancasters, were approaching the city from the northeast, rather than following the Elbe, carrying a higher proportion than before of fire-bombs. With streets still blocked by collapsed buildings and water mains destroyed, fire services were unable to reach the thousands of fires that sprang up. These joined together to become a single fire-storm in which temperatures of 1,000 degrees were reached, along with winds of 150mph.

The Luftwaffe countered the chaos that had been caused by 'Window', sending up single-seater Me 109s and FW-190s, 'Wild Boar' missions led by a Major Hajo Hermann, in contrast to the new name for two-engined, radar-guided night-fighters as 'Tame Boars.' The 'Wild Boars' gained great height and singled-out RAF bombers as they flew over the conflagration. RAF losses were 17, including 11 Lancasters, ironically more at risk for flying higher than other bombers because they were closest to the even-higher flying 'Wild Boar.'

By the third attack on Hamburg on the night of 29 July, more than a million people had fled the city. The RAF sent 777 bombers, 355 of them Lancasters, and defence tactics changed; searchlights appeared to be trying to create a sheet of light against which the high-flying 'Wild Boars' could work on the bombers silhouetted below them.

The fourth and last major attack on Hamburg – there would be a further 69 before the end of the war – happened on 2 August, in weather conditions so bad that Lancasters were sent to go it alone. Halifaxes, Stirlings and Wellingtons could not climb above the violent storm conditions in the North Sea, and even the 318 Lancasters sent had an enormous number of aborted attacks, 71 in all, due to severe icing. Thirteen Lancasters failed to return, two of which were struck by lightning and seen to break up. Number 97 Squadron RAF, in which 12 of 18 Pathfinder Lancasters aborted, was the subject of particular wrath, and its CO replaced. Yet the bombers that did get through dropped 1,429 tons of explosive on their targets.

Totting up the bill for the Battle of Hamburg, the RAF carried out 2,630 operations and lost 87 aircraft, 552 British and Allied airmen were killed, 65 captured and 7 interned in Sweden. Nearly half the aircraft losses, 39, were Lancasters with 273 crew members.

The German losses came to an estimated 41,800 killed and 37,000 seriously injured – many of whom were to die from their wounds. The Germans lost 40,000 houses, 275,000 flats, with 580 armament and other industrial factories destroyed or made unsafe. The same fate befell 2,632 shops, 277 schools, 58 churches, 24 hospitals, 96 municipal buildings and 12 bridges. More than 6,000 acres of the city was reduced to smoking rubble.

Truly a whirlwind was being reaped.

The RAF attacks severely shook the Nazi leadership, leading Josef Goebbels to worry that five or six similar raids on other cities could force Germany out of the war. Hitler continued to make a point of never visiting any bombed areas of Germany, but was reportedly so enraged that he signed off papers to begin full-scale production of the V-2 rocket weapons being designed at Peenemunde. It is hard to believe he would not have done that anyway, whether Hamburg happened or not.

Peenemunde, night of 17 August, 1943

There had been clues about top-secret weapons being made by brilliant German scientists since the so-called Oslo Report in 1939, but attention did not really focus on them until 28 June 1943.

That night RAF photographic reconnaissance revealed that rockets with an estimated range of up to 130 miles were being developed at the research facility at Peenemunde on the Baltic coast. The photos seemed to verify intelligence reports from PoWs and the Polish Home Army. The following day, Churchill's son-in-law, the MP Duncan Sandys, Chairman of a War Cabinet Committee for defence against German flying bombs and rockets, addressed a meeting in the Cabinet War Room. Sandys said the Germans were building rockets. Lord Cherwell said, in effect, stuff and nonsense! 'Putting a four-thousand horsepower turbine in a twenty-inch space is lunacy: it cannot be done.'

What the photos showed, he said, were balloons! Lord Cherwell went on to make a strong case about an 'elaborate cover plan' by the Germans, and ridiculed the credibility and existence of rockets. 'At the end of the war we will find that the rocket was a mare's nest!'

One of Cherwell's protégés was a young scientist called R.V. Jones who had already shown how RAF Fighter Command could win the 'Battle of the Beams', the German radio signals guiding Luftwaffe bombers to targets in Britain in 1940. Jones demonstrated that the 'beams' existed, and how they could be bent to lead to the Germans missing London.

Jones was at the Sandys meeting, as was Winston Churchill, who must have had a twinkle in his eye when he turned to the young scientist who had been ridiculed by Lord Cherwell and said: 'Now, Dr. Jones, may we hear the truth?'

Jones set about demolishing each of his patron's points, with a mischievous running commentary from Churchill – keeping a keen eye on Cherwell's reaction – along the lines of 'isn't he doing well?'

R.V. Jones made so certain a case that the Sandys Committee recommended the heaviest attack on Peenemunde at the earliest possible time when conditions were suitable. Cherwell recovered enough to be part of the planning for the Peenemunde raid.

The attack, code-named 'Operation Hydra', on the night of 17 August 1943, opened the strategic bombing phase against long-range German weapons programmes.

Its primary aim was simple, to kill boffins.

The secondary aim was to destroy their laboratories.

The third intention was to wipe out as much research paperwork as possible.

Bomber Command sent more than 600 bombers, including 324 Lancasters, 218 Halifaxes and 54 Stirlings, along with 28 Mosquitoes and 10 Beaufighters. All the air groups, including the Canadian 6 Group provided squadrons. Aircrews were told that if they did not destroy Peenemunde that night, they would go back every night until they had destroyed it.

It was a difficult target, 600 miles from the nearest British airfield, too far for radio navigation beams, and it had to be a moonlight raid just to ensure they hit the right place. It was to be a relatively low-level raid, bombing from 8,000ft (2,438m) rather than 20,000ft (6,096m), making the attackers easier to shoot down, but accuracy and precision on this attack were everything.

Guy Gibson's 'Master Bomber' tactic, pioneered on the Dambuster raid, circling to conduct the bomber stream over the target and adjusting Pathfinder crews to correct their aim, was used for the first time with Main Force. Conducting operations was Group Captain John Searby, who had come up through the ranks, starting as a 16-year-old apprentice in 1929, and who won a DSO that night.

A diversionary raid by Mosquitoes to draw off German night-fighters, called 'Whitebait', was sent to Berlin.

The first attack, on the Peenemunde sleeping and living quarters, went in at ten minutes past midnight with 16 Blind Illuminator aircraft dropping white parachute flares and long-burning Target Indicators. But there was uncertain visibility with patchy cloud, and the 'red datum' lights were two miles from target. Searby saw the mistake, identified one of the yellow markers as 'well-placed', and was able to steer more markers to join it. Two thirds of the 227 bombers in the first wave made an accurate bombing run, leaving one third of the bombs dropped inaccurately, a problem compounded as the night went on.

The second attack, on the factory workshops, started at 12.27 on a line northwest of the first markers dropped, but the correct marker was ignored by bombing crews until Searby saw the overshoot and notified those still waiting to bomb to change their aim. This included a bombing force of 113 Lancasters from 5 and 6 Groups.

The third wave started at 12.48, targeting the experimental station, and a Pathfinder Backer-up accurately placed a green flare load in the heart of the Development Works, where a few bomb-loads caused serious laboratory and office damage. Blind bombing after smoke concealed the main target indicator was called for, but sadly the Lancasters and Halifaxes droned 20 and even 30 seconds past the timing point, aiming for the wrong markers and killing slave workers in the concentration camp. Included among the dead were some of the informants who had alerted the RAF to the importance of destroying Peenemunde in the first place.

About 1,800 tons of bombs were dropped, all but 15 per cent high explosive. Two of the key boffins died, Doctor Walter Thiel and Chief Engineer Walther, buried in one of the air-raid trenches. But the most important boffin, Werner Von Braun, was not harmed. He would go on after the war to lead America's space race to the moon in the 1960s. One result of the raid was the whole works were moved from Peenemunde to a large cave in Bavaria. Bomber Command lost 6.7 per cent of the Operation Hydra force. After the Luftwaffe realised the 'Whitebait' deception, 30 FW-190 'Wild Boar' night fighters raced to Peenemunde. Most of the casualties were suffered by the aircraft of the last wave when the German night-fighters arrived in force.

The Groups involved in this raid were 5 Group, which lost 17 of its 109 aircraft (14.5 per cent) and the Canadian 6 Group, which lost 12 out of 57 aircraft (19.7 per cent). The counterattack included the first operational flights of 'Schräge Musik' fighters, two Me110s piloted by Leutnant Peter Erhardt, the Staffelkapitän, and Unteroffizier Walter Höker. These two pilots found the bomber stream flying home from the target and are believed to have shot down six of the bombers lost on the raid. This fearsome weapon was said by German sources to have destroyed four out of five of the RAF bomber losses in the period between Peenemunde and the end of the war.

One other consequence of the success of the 'Whitebait' deception in pretending to attack Berlin, was that Luftwaffe Chief of Staff General Hans Jeschonnek shot himself on 19 August. Every little helped.

The British Official History states that the attack 'may well have caused a delay of two months' in the development of V-2 rockets, consistent with the German assessment by Joseph Goebbels of 'six to eight weeks.' But it is also estimated that instead of producing the planned 1,800 V-2 rockets per month that Hitler had demanded, the Peenemunde Raid reduced that fearsome weapon to just 400 a month.

A Victoria Cross Flight

Sergeant Jim Norris, one of the Last Witnesses, was born and brought up in Wales and, at 22 was flight engineer to 61 Squadron pilot Bill Reid in 1943:

> 'In all, I did eight tough trips with Bill Reid in the Summer and Autumn of 1943. Bill was a good pilot and we co-operated with each other. He would ask me something, I would ask him something, there was no rank consciousness.

'All the trips, except the last one, were uneventful. No attacks by fighters, nothing serious with flak. It was on my sixteenth trip that things changed.

'The weather was good on 3 November 1943, when we were briefed to attack Düsseldorf. We took off from Syerston near Lincoln at about 7 o'clock in the evening. It was a big raid that night. We set course over the North Sea, and soon hit the Dutch coast. I used to sit on the floor to write the log, it was better than kneeling down, and all of a sudden there was a loud bang. As I went to get up, so the navigator fell and hit me in the back. We were being blasted from behind by a fighter, an Me 109. Then from the front came the Focke Wulf 190, smashing the windscreen. The rear gunner, Emerson, told us about the two different aircraft, because he thought he had hit one of them, the Focke Wulf, before the guns froze. We were high that night, over 20,000ft (6,096m).

'We went into a dive. I had been hit in the left arm, some of the metal is still there all these years later, and I had some shrapnel in my back. I don't remember being in pain, but my left arm locked into a crook. I went around the aircraft to see what our state was. The navigator, Jeffreys, an Australian, was killed immediately, the wireless operator was seriously injured – he died the next morning – while Bill Reid was cut in the head and bleeding badly.

'We had no navigator, but Bill decided to fly on to the target, even though it was 200 miles away. The attacks had knocked out the intercom and the oxygen. I collected the spare bottles and was giving them to Bill, as he was the main man to keep going. The rear gunner and the mid-upper gunner were uninjured. I didn't do my normal job, monitoring the instruments, never even looked at them again that night. I stuck by Bill all the time, he was sitting in his pilot's seat and I was standing beside him.

'Bill was all right going to Düsseldorf despite his injuries, and although we were using sign language between each other, we believe we had a direct hit on the target. But as we left the target, I knew Bill had to make a steep turn and the aircraft went into a dive.

'Something's gone wrong here, I said, so I pulled it back, and I kept digging Bill Reid in the ribs. He had fainted. It could have been blood loss or lack of oxygen, even though we had lost height after having been hit by those fighters.

'I remember there had only been one alteration of course on the way to the target – four or five degrees – so I took the reciprocal and kept the Pole Star on my right. We could not have got his unconscious body out of the pilot's seat anyway, so I remained standing beside him, holding the wheel. Bill's only injury that I could see was the gash across his forehead.

'It was freezing cold, the windscreen had been shattered by the Folke Wulf, and both of us were suffering. The fighters which had attacked us left us alone because they may have thought we were a goner anyway, or the rear gunner was right and he had hit one of the fighters. We ran into heavy anti-aircraft fire over the Dutch coast, but we were not hit.

'Then the engines cut out.

'I tried telling the bomb aimer to change the tanks, but he didn't have a clue what I was saying. I couldn't leave the steering column, so I made the bomb aimer hold it while I dived over and changed the petrol cocks.

The engines did not need to be re-started electrically, they start automatically when the fuel begins to flow again. The aircraft went into a dive again. I have no idea how high we were, though I could see the sea. I pulled it out of the dive while Bill was just lying there. Every now and again I would dig him in the ribs with my elbow, but I was concentrating too much.

'The thought in my mind was that I was still in the air flying this thing, not even in the pilot's seat; how was I going to land it? I had no real idea. Then we got a sight of Shiphon, an American base near East Dereham in Norfolk, and Bill woke up!

'He took over, despite his loss of blood. By now we had discovered that the hydraulics had gone. I put the under-carriage lever down, and nothing happened. I went back to the hydraulic pump and pumped and pumped and pumped. Then I went back to Bill and all I could do was shrug.

'We went in to land, prepared for a belly landing, partly on the tarmac and partly on the grass. As it happened one wheel was halfway down, and the impact drove the wheel up through the wing. But we were able to walk out of the aircraft, there was no fire. Bill and I walked out, though wounded, and they carried out the dead navigator and mortally wounded wireless operator. The other crew were unwounded. I was taken to hospital, covered in blood. I was all right, but my left arm was locked. I had wrapped it around the steering column for so long, that it locked into position and I couldn't move it.'

Citation – Conspicuous Gallantry Medal - Sergeant James William Norris RAFVR (1411327), 61 Squadron:

'This airman was the flight engineer of an aircraft detailed to attack Düsseldorf. Soon after crossing the enemy coast, the aircraft was attacked and sustained damage. A few minutes later another fighter attacked. The bomber was struck by a hail of bullets. The windscreen was broken, the wireless apparatus and other important equipment were destroyed and the oxygen system was rendered useless. The pilot, wireless operator and flight engineer were wounded, and the navigator was killed. The aircraft became difficult to control, but, despite this, the pilot continued to the target, being greatly assisted by Sergeant Norris, whose strenuous efforts were invaluable. Shortly after the target had been successfully attacked, the pilot collapsed, owing to wounds. Sergeant Norris took over the controls, and at times aided by another member of the crew, succeeded in flying the damaged aircraft to this country. When an airfield was sighted, Sergeant Norris and his comrade succeeded in rallying the semi-conscious pilot sufficiently to take over and land the aircraft safely. Not until then did Sergeant Norris disclose that he had been wounded in his arm. In circumstances fraught with great danger, this airman displayed courage, fortitude and determination of the highest order.'

His pilot, Bill Reid, had his Victoria Cross posted in the *London Gazette*, 14 December 1943

'Raid on Düsseldorf, Germany, 3 November 1943, Acting / Flight Lieutenant William Reid, 61 Squadron, Royal Air Force Volunteer Reserve.

'On the night of 3rd November 1943, Flight Lieutenant Reid was pilot and captain of a Lancaster aircraft detailed to attack Düsseldorf. Shortly after crossing the Dutch coast, the pilot's windscreen was shattered by fire from a Messerschmitt 110. Owing to a failure in the heating circuit, the rear gunner's hands were too cold for him to open fire immediately or to operate his microphone and so give warning of danger: but after a brief delay he managed to return the Messerschmitt's fire and it was driven off.

'During the fight with the Messerschmitt, Flight Lieutenant Reid was wounded in the head, shoulders and hands. The elevator trimming tabs of the aircraft were damaged and it became difficult to control. The rear turret, too, was badly damaged and the communications system and compasses were put out of action. Flight Lieutenant Reid ascertained that his crew were unscathed and, saying nothing about his own injuries, he continued his mission.

'Soon afterwards, the Lancaster was attacked by a Focke Wulf 190. This time, the enemy's fire raked the bomber from stem to stern. The rear gunner replied with his only serviceable gun but the state of his turret made accurate aiming impossible. The navigator was killed and the wireless operator fatally injured. The mid-upper turret was hit and the oxygen system put out of action. Flight Lieutenant Reid was again wounded and the flight engineer, though hit in the forearm, supplied him with oxygen from a portable supply.

'Flight Lieutenant Reid refused to be turned from his objective and Düsseldorf was reached some 50 minutes later. He had memorised his course to the target and had continued in such a normal manner that the bomb-aimer, who was cut off by the failure of the communications system, knew nothing of his captain's injuries or of the casualties to his comrades. Photographs show that, when the bombs were released, the aircraft was right over the centre of the target.

'Steering by the pole star and the moon, Flight Lieutenant Reid then set course for home. He was growing weak from loss of blood. The emergency oxygen supply had given out. With the windscreen shattered, the cold was intense. He lapsed into semi-consciousness. The flight engineer, with some help from the bomb-aimer, kept the Lancaster in the air despite heavy anti-aircraft fire over the Dutch coast.

'The North Sea crossing was accomplished. An airfield was sighted. The captain revived, resumed control and made ready to land. Ground mist partially obscured the runway lights. The captain was also much bothered by blood from his head wound getting into his eyes. But he made a safe landing although one leg of the damaged undercarriage collapsed when the load came on.

'Wounded in two attacks, without oxygen, suffering severely from cold, his navigator dead, his wireless operator fatally wounded, his aircraft crippled and defenceless, Flight Lieutenant Reid showed superb courage and leadership in penetrating a further 200 miles into enemy territory to attack one of the most strongly-defended targets in Germany, every additional mile increasing the hazards of the long and perilous journey home. His tenacity and devotion to duty were beyond praise.'

When asked later in hospital why he had not turned back, Bill Reid said it was safer to go on, because turning would have put him in danger of collision with all the other RAF Lancasters heading for Düsseldorf. He was invested with his Victoria Cross by King George VI at Buckingham Palace on 11 June 1944.

CHAPTER THIRTEEN

The Boffins' War

'The combination of the Pathfinders' operations, the activities of No. 100 Group, the British advantage in radar, jamming and Window techniques, combined with intelligent attacking tactics, as well as the discipline and bravery of the RAF crews, have been remarkable. We had our severe problems in trying to defend Germany in the air.'

General Adolph Galland,
Luftwaffe leading fighter ace

War was being researched and planned within weeks of Hitler's election as German Chancellor. Through the 1930s, German boffins developed a 'guiding beam' which became known as the Lorenz, after the firm that made it. It worked through two signals broadcast at the same frequency, through antennas along a radio beam a few degrees wide. The signal on the left broadcast the Morse code A – dit-dah – the signal on the right broadcast Mode code N – dah-dit. So long as the aircraft flew along the beam, the pilot would hear a continuous signal. If he strayed to the left he would hear dit-dah, to the right dah-dit, so he knew which way to steer to stay in the centre of the beam.

Its peaceful use was as a night or bad-weather landing system, but Lorenz was developed for long-range night bombing, and after Dunkirk was used to target British cities. The young R.V. Jones came to real fame by proving such beams existed and working out how to bend them so German bombers headed for the country to frighten farmers and their livestock rather than more vulnerable cities. It was an early manifestation of the Boffins' War, estimated by 1945 to have 'saved' a thousand Allied aircraft and seven thousand aircrew.

After the Battle of Britain, RAF Bomber Command began night attacks against German cities. As we have seen, the only way of judging how effective such raids were came from the individual reports of the aircrews, and the Butt Report showed how little effect they were having on the German war effort. Only one aircraft in ten was getting to Ruhr targets, and on moonless nights, it was only one in 15.

'Dead reckoning', calculating position by estimating wind-speed and ground speed and compass bearing, or using sextants through the astro-dome, just did not work. It did on paper, but out in the cold nights over enemy territory it was pretty useless. As the Lancaster was coming on stream, and with vigorous leadership from Sir Arthur Harris, two invaluable new technical aids were produced by the boffins to help pilots reach their targets. They were called GEE and OBOE.

GEE

GEE measured the difference of signal arrival times from two or more locations, a so-called hyperbolic system. GEE used a number of transmitters which sent out precisely timed signals. An on-board set received the radio signals transmitted from ground stations in different locations in England. Two signals gave the navigator a 'fix', three would be even more accurate. The navigator could work out his aircraft's position on the route to the target at any time. When flying near ground stations over home territory, GEE's accuracy was good. When the aircraft entered Germany, the accuracy was reduced. With a range of about 300 miles, providing the Germans were not jamming signals, GEE was accurate to about 165 yards (150m) at short ranges, and up to a mile at longer ranges over Germany.

GEE could give a bomber crew a reasonable amount of confidence that they were entering Germany on an accurate fix. After a time, the Germans worked out how to jam the system, and the boffins were forced to develop new GEE systems, new frequencies and jamming techniques of their own.

OBOE

OBOE came into service in December 1942 as an accurate bombing device against shorter range targets. Two OBOE ground stations in England sent out radio signals, picked up by an OBOE-equipped bomber and then sent back. One station guided the bomber along a pre-determined track, the pilot being told when he steered left or right of track. The second OBOE station measured the speed of the bomber over the ground and, with an early form of calculator, deduced the right time for the bomb to be dropped. One drawback was that only a single aircraft could be controlled at a time, so it was primarily used by Pathfinders to mark the target for the Main Force following them. Another drawback was its range of just 300 miles. Following the Normandy Invasion in June 1944, the RAF sent mobile ground stations to mainland Europe to extend OBOE deep into Germany.

H2S

This was a primitive form of airborne radar. The Lancaster carried a parabolic rotating dish in a bulge below the fuselage between the mid-upper turret and the rear gunner. It scanned the ground beneath and showed the image on a screen. To modern eyes the image was very poor, but it did show the sea or a lake as a dark area, a brighter area for countryside and built-up areas were very bright. It worked best on coastal targets like Hamburg. A team called Telecommunications Research Department (TRE) was set up under Bernard Lovell, later the great astronomer, to develop H2S.

There is an odd story about how it came to be known as H2S, and it involves two characters who were later to clash over the Peenemunde raid. One was the powerful Lord Cherwell, the other his protégé, R.V. Jones. According to Jones, H2S had started and then faltered because it was thought that Cherwell – a great and opinionated disapprover – was not keen on the idea. When Cherwell later asked the boffins how H2S was progressing, he was upset to hear it had not developed very far because of his perceived lack of enthusiasm, and was said to have used the phrase about the delay – a number of times – that 'it stinks!' H2S is an acronym for hydrogen sulphide, which does, indeed, stink of rotten eggs, and Jones says that when Cherwell asked what H2S stood for, no one had the courage to tell him it was based on his furious comment at its delay. He was told instead it stood for 'Home Sweet Home'.

The first H2S flight was on 23 April 1942, the equipment carried in a big bulge under a Halifax bomber.

One 'flap' at that time concerned an Intelligence report that the Germans had moved a company of their best paratroopers to a secret base near Cherburg, looking to raid TRE and nobble its secrets. British Commandos had successfully raided Bruneval on the French coast in February 1942, storming a villa where the German 'Giant Wurzburg' radar was situated. The leader of the raiding party, Major John Frost, was under orders to shoot the British technical expert they had brought with them – who had no idea of his potential fate – if the Germans looked like capturing him. The raiding party grabbed one of the German technicians and loaded him and his British counterpart and other bits and pieces into small boats, making a clean getaway to England.

There was no reason why the Germans could not do the same thing back, so the whole TRE group was moved inland from Swanage to Malvern College.

There, two weeks later, Alan Blumlein, the best and the brightest of scientists performing tests on the H2S, was working in the Halifax when it crashed, killing him and everyone else on board. The whole matter was hushed up; it was a huge blow to the project.

Churchill, however, was on the case of H2S and in early July 1942 reviewed the situation. He gave it the highest priority, and demanded 200 H2S sets to be built in 10 weeks! This did not happen, despite extraordinary efforts – who would want to cross Winston Churchill in a fury? – but by the first day of January 1943, 12 Stirling and 12 Halifax bombers had been fitted with it. On 30 January 1943, 13 Pathfinder bombers used H2S to drop fire-bombs or flares on Hamburg. Seven of the Pathfinders aborted but six got to the city, marked it, and Hamburg was then hit by 100 Lancasters.

There were disadvantages. It took time to discover that, since both H2S and OBOE transmitted a signal, the Germans could identify them as an enemy. Also, as was feared, it was not long before a Stirling carrying one of the top-secret sets crashed on a raid on Cologne on 2 February 1943 and the Germans could examine the H2S equipment. The set was damaged but not beyond repair, and German boffins were able to reassemble it well enough to develop the Naxos radar detector, enabling them to home in on the transmissions of H2S

Nevertheless, H2S came into its own that summer, fitted to Lancasters at the start of Operation Gomorrah, the 'Battle of Hamburg.' It was vital in the 'Battle of Berlin' from November 1943 until March 1944, because the German capital had been out of range of GEE and OBOE and often obscured by cloud in the winter. It was hoped that H2S would identify Berlin's many lakes and rivers and be a crucial aid to navigation. The early H2S was not up to the job, and it was not until the night of 2 December 1943, and the introduction of H2S Mark III, that Berlin was bombed accurately, whatever the weather.

GH

In the constant struggle to find an edge over the Germans, the boffins produced the extremely advanced GH in 1944. RAF bombers fitted with GH sent radio pulses to two ground stations in Britain, which re-transmitted them back to the aircraft. The navigator could measure the time interval between the outgoing and returning pulses on an oscilloscope display, and guide the pilot towards the target and even tell him the precise point to drop his bombs. Only a limited number of aircraft could use GH at any one time, and it had the same 300-mile range as OBOE, but it was another tool for getting Bomber Command to its intended targets.

IFF

A system still in use in much more sophisticated ways in modern Iraq and Afghanistan, IFF stands for Identification, Friend or Foe. Special signals from a 'friend' showed on radar screens. It was introduced as far back as 1 January 1940. In September 1941, R. V. Jones had warned Bomber Command that the Germans could trigger British IFF sets if these were left on, to home in on the bombers. He was largely ignored but by June 1942 IFF sets were fitted with a jamming switch which enabled them to transmit continuously, followed by the short-lived 'Shiver' set incorporating a true jammer. RAF aircrew also took to the erroneous idea that pulses from their IFF sets could jam German searchlights. Bomber Command was said to have encouraged this idea on the grounds of morale.

All the boffins' weapons had code names, British and German:

Window – foil strips, silver on one side, dropped from RAF aircraft to form reflective clouds that swamped German radar with false signals. Both sides knew about Window for at least two years, each worried that the other would use it, but it was the Japanese who were the first to deploy it operationally, in night raids on Guadalcanal in May 1943. They called it *giman-shi* (deceiving paper), but apparently neither the Germans nor the British were informed about this by their respective allies. Window was first used operationally by the RAF in the 23 July raid on Hamburg. RAF losses dropped that night to 1.5 per cent from 6 per cent as the Wurzburg radar was blinded.

Mandrel, Carpet, Shiver – the names of three airborne radio transmitters used to jam and swamp the standard German ground radar. Mandrel's radar noise jammer countered the German Freya radars by radiating signals to swamp the normal return echo, obliterating formation size and range information.

Boozer – on-board equipment that warned RAF bomber crews when they were being tracked by German radar.

Monica and Fishpond – fitted to bombers to give warning of approaching German fighters. Monica, the RAF's tail warning radar, entered service in early 1943. It was mounted on the tail and pointed backwards, providing audible bleeps if an aircraft approached from the rear. But a German night fighter could 'hide' among the bleeps generated by other bombers in the stream and by March 1943 the Germans had examples of Monica from shot-down aircraft. It became dangerous to use once the Luftwaffe equipped their night-fighters to track Monica emissions. Although partly superseded by Fishpond, Monica remained in use until mid 1944. Monica turned out to be almost a standing invitation for a German fighter to shoot this particular RAF bomber down, but for at least six months British boffins knew nothing of its real effect. One estimate has it that Monica downed more RAF bombers than any other invention, although Schräge Musik probably claims that title.

Tinsel and Gaston – provided airborne jamming of German defence R/T. It disrupted voice communications between ground control stations and night-fighter crews. Tinsel used a microphone mounted in an engine nacelle, linked to a radio transmitter. A German-speaking crewman used the aircraft's normal radio receiver to search for fighter control R/T, then tuned Tinsel's transmitter to broadcast the engine noise on the same frequency. Gaston was an early version of Tinsel.

Cigar and Corona – In raids later in the war, a number of RAF bombers carried brave German-speakers who were assigned to transmit false and contradictory directions to German fighters. Bitter arguments often developed as each operator, true and false, tried to convince Luftwaffe night-fighters they were the real thing.

Serrate – airborne radar fitted to RAF night-fighters on intruder operations, to enable Allied fighters such as the Mosquito to track and attack German night-fighters.

On the German side there were:

Freya – ground-based, long-range radar.

Wurzburg and Giant Wurzburg – ground-based, shorter range radar giving information on approaching bombers to searchlights, flak and fighters.

Naxos and Flensburg – fitted to German fighters to permit them to home onto radio transmissions from the bombers, from, say, H2S. The Germans developed Naxos to pick up H2S. There were two different types of Naxos. The first, the Naxos Z, was used by night-fighters and mounted under a blister on top of the fighter's canopy. The second type was the Naxos ZR fitted to the tails of German night-fighters to warn them if they were being tracked by radar-equipped RAF Mosquitoes. Flensburg was a longer-range system.

Lichtenstein – airborne radar fitted to fighters to allow the Luftwaffe to detect RAF night bombers. Until Window was introduced, Lichtenstein worked efficiently, but the floating strips of metal foil and paper gummed the system up. The Serrate sets increasingly used by RAF Mosquito intruders were also picking up German night-fighters. In the early months of 1944 a new German radar called SN2 was introduced. Window did not work against the SN2, and the radar had a 4-mile range against Lichtenstein's two miles. SN2 was also immune to the Mosquito Serrate sets. Coupled with the increasing use of Schräge Musik cannon, the first half of 1944 was a harrowing time for Main Force crews.

SN2 was especially galling to British boffins like R.V. Jones:

'SN2 showed up only rarely in the ultra-secret Enigma traffic of February 1944: this may be explained by the fact that at the beginning of that month only 90 out of 480 German night fighters were completely fitted with it. But it was given first to the best night fighting crews, so its effect was greater than the simple numerical proportion.'

In March 1944, Jones had identified SN2 as one of his most urgent problems. He had worked out the wavelength at 3-4 metres, but all his listening searches failed to pick it up. He had proof in May that his deductions were correct when

American camera guns caught Ju88s and the Me110s fitted with the ponderous aerials used by the SN2. But it was not until one of the greatest coups of the Intelligence war happened – by accident – that the tables were turned on the German night-fighter forces.

On the morning of 13 July 1944, three young Luftwaffe aircrew flew their night-fighter, a brand new Ju88G-1 of 7.Staffel//NJG2, the latest type but not yet fitted with Schräge Musik, into RAF Woodbridge airfield. The crew had just completed 100 hours of training and been on night-fighter duty but, tired and inexperienced, they had made a mistake about a navigation beacon. They seem to have flown the reciprocal rather than the true bearing, flying West and not East. They circled Woodbridge, one of the three RAF emergency airfields and often cluttered with wrecked bomber carcasses, received a green signal to land and did so. An RAF Flight Sergeant who ambled out to pick them up in the crew bus had the surprise of his life, but nothing like the shock suffered by the unfortunate young Germans, who did not have enough fuel to get away. The Flight Sergeant, armed only with a flare pistol, took them into custody.

According to Francis K Mason's book *The Avro Lancaster*, which painstakingly recorded the fate of every Lancaster ever built, one of the boffins developing radar and radio countermeasures, Wing Commander Derek Jackson, immediately undertook test flights with the Ju88G. He began by trying the passive homer called Flensburg against the Monica radar of a single Lancaster and found it gave clear bearings out to a range of at least 130 miles!

Jackson then tried it against five Lancasters flying in a loose gaggle and found that he could home in immediately on to any one of the five. Bomber Command kept arguing with this evidence so, six weeks after the capture, Jackson managed the final evaluation against a 'bomber stream' of 71 Lancasters orbiting between Cambridge and Gloucester. Far from being smothered or confused by the large number of aircraft – the aim of the bomber stream tactics – the Flensburg continued to give a clear indication of the exact positions of the nearest bombers. Clearly, this one aid alone could guide a night-fighter crew straight to any bomber using its tail warning radar. At once 'Bomber' Harris ordered the Monica sets not to be switched on and their frequency changed immediately.

At a stroke the RAF bombers stopped issuing a very public invitation for the Germans to come and shoot them down. Navigation and airborne weapons like H2S, Airborne Cigar, Mandrel and Tinsel were banned from use until over enemy airspace. IFF could only be used in an emergency.

The captured night-fighter also had SN2 radar fitted, and when the boffins came to study it they realised it worked on a frequency of 85 MHz (a wavelength around 3.2 metres). This meant that standard 25 cm Window foil strips would not work against it. However, a concertina strip around 160 cm long had been developed to fool sea-search radars during the D-Day invasion and could be adapted for use against SN2. Within 10 days of the Ju88's capture, the new 'Type M' Window was being used to blind the SN2 radars of the night-fighters.

Design changes were immediately ordered on Serrate IV to home on to the German radar, and another anti-fighter weapon, Pipecrack to jam it. Intruder Mosquitoes were also given a device called Perfectos to interrogate the latest Luftwaffe IFF sets. Perfectos supplied the hunting RAF airmen with the range and bearing of their targets.

All the formidable developments that the Germans made could be largely countered by switching off H2S and Monica, keeping a sharp lookout and having the guts to corkscrew better than the average Luftwaffe fighter.

Yet it was not a one-sided battle. From mid 1943, no Luftwaffe night-fighter pilot ever felt safe in his own night sky and far more were killed in crashes, often caused by fear of the omnipotent Mosquito, than in combat.

RAF Bomber Command loss rates fluctuated, depending on the interplay of initiatives from both sides: in mid-1943 RAF losses averaged around 5 per cent. In human terms this meant that on a typical operation involving 750 bombers, the RAF would lose about 37 aircraft – and 260 airmen. In the one year period to September 1944, RAF aircrew deaths reached their peak, at 18,948. These were real sacrifices in an intense battle in which the outcome could not yet be determined. But Bomber Command was growing more sophisticated.

100 Group – Spoofs & ghost bombers and Decoys
A new group was formed in November 1943, to direct all the boffin's weapons at the Luftwaffe. 100 Group had no Lancasters among its first 100 aircraft, but the bomber stream they were assisting now had a majority of Lancasters, a situation that lasted until the end of the war. A number of American aircraft, B-17 'Flying Fortresses' and B-24 'Liberators', carried jamming equipment inside the bomber stream. Stirlings and Halifaxes flew spoof missions to create decoy raids by 'ghost' squadrons using Window. The Group also sent out Mosquitoes and Beaufighters with airborne radar to hunt down and kill German night-fighters.

100 Group grew in size to control eight airfields with 260 aircraft, 140 of which were various marks of Mosquito night-fighter intruders, and the remainder 80 Halifaxes, 20 Fortresses and 20 Liberators, all carrying electronic jamming equipment.

The B-17s and Liberators were able to fly a mile above the bomber stream, providing a protective electronic 'cloak' to help conceal the attack. They carried radio transmitters that jammed German early warning radar and fighter control communications. It was in aircraft like these that German-speakers sent out false instructions to Luftwaffe pilots.

Tallboy and Grand Slam

Most British bombs in the early part of the war had thin skins for maximum explosive force. Barnes Wallis upset all the calculations that Hitler and his cronies had about their personal safely when he set out to find a way to penetrate targets deep under the earth beneath hardened concrete. His 'superbomb', soon to be called Tallboy, had to penetrate without exploding first. To do this, his 12,000lb Tallboys were cast in one piece of high tensile steel, strong but also aerodynamic to make them fast. The tail of the Tallboy bomb, 10ft (3m) long, was nearly half the length of the finished 21-foot weapon. Its fins were given a slight twist to spin the Tallboy, making the bomb more accurate.

When dropped from 20,000ft (6,096m) a Tallboy made a crater 80ft (24.4m) deep and 100ft (30.5m) across. It could go through 16ft (4-9m) of concrete, was capable of displacing a million cubic feet of earth in a crater which would take 5,000 tons of earth to fill. It was ballistically perfect and fell at about 2,500mph, three times the speed of sound.

Barnes Wallis wanted the Tallboy dropped from 40,000ft (12,195m) but the Lancaster could not climb that high, even after removing some of our armour and guns. We dropped our Tallboys from between 15,000 and 20,000ft. On underground targets Tallboy was fitted with three separate inertia fuse-pistols to allow deep penetration. The time delay could be set to 30 seconds or 30 minutes after impact. Three separate long-delay fuses were fitted into the bomb; we used the 30-minute fuse on the Kembs Dam, for example, so that even if two of the fuses failed, the third would do the job.

The primary intention against hardened concrete was not to hit it, but to penetrate the ground next to it, so the explosion caused an earthquake; Tallboy was known as the 'Earthquake Bomb.' This caused far more damage to the whole structure of the building than a direct hit.

Tallboys were very expensive and not considered expendable. If we did not use it on a raid we were expected to bring it back rather than toss it into the sea.

In all, 854 Tallboys were made and dropped.

Barnes Wallis went on to make a 'Big Brother' to the Tallboy, the 10-ton 'Grand Slam' which 617 Squadron started using in March 1945.

Only 41 of the 22,000lb 'super-earthquake' Grand Slams were built, but they were all dropped, to great effect.

D-Day

Sixteen Lancasters from 617 Squadron led by Leonard Cheshire, and a force of five B-17's from 100 Group set out of the night before D-Day, 5/6 June 1944, flying meticulous patterns and dropping bundles of Window. They were simulating the effect of an invasion fleet aimed at the Calais area, closest to the coast of England. It was technically an extremely difficult 'spoof'. The eight 617 Lancasters, including F-Fox which I was to take over later that summer, took off at 11.00 pm on 5 June and flew for four hours, to be relieved at 3.00 am the following morning by the second wave of eight Lancasters. Each carried a normal crew of seven, plus a skeleton reserve crew and three men, thirteen in all, to throw out Window every four seconds.

The effect on German radar was of a huge fleet of ships moving towards Calais at 7 knots. The 'spoof' stopped just before dawn to reveal an empty sea; all the invasion fleet were 100 miles away in Normandy, where there was an electronic wall blocking all German radio communications.

Spoofing

A technique was developed by 100 Group which they called 'conditioning'. Hundreds of RAF bombers were seen on German radar in the middle of August 1944 heading for the port of Keil, attracting a lot of attention from Luftwaffe night-fighters. They chased down a 'ghost' squadron, a small number of 100 Group aircraft dropping Window and the Luftwaffe shot down nothing. A day later a similar raid was seen developing on radar screens but this time it was real, passing through the same area as yesterday's spoof, but it was ignored.

There is a feeling, looking back, among many of those not involved in the war, that by the second half of 1944 it was all over bar the shouting. The terrible battles against the V-1s and V-2s are virtually forgotten. What is remembered is that RAF Bomber Command were giving Germany a pounding and went on doing so until close to the end of the war, and that Germans were now suffering far more than Britain had during the Blitz. A proportion of the chattering classes felt that we were now 'being beastly to the Germans.'

As one of the few young men from my generation of pilots who survived the conflict, that is not how I feel at all. By 1944 the Germans had created and were skilled at using terrible weapons against Bomber Command, one being the virtually unknown Schräge Musik – Jazz Music – through which we aircrew became as geese to hunters.

CHAPTER FOURTEEN

Bomber Command's Darkest Hour — Battle of Berlin

'The real importance of the air war consisted in the fact that it opened a second front long before the invasion in Europe. . . Defence against RAF and USAAF air attacks required the production of thousands of anti-aircraft guns, the stockpiling of tremendous quantities of ammunition all over the country, and holding in readiness hundreds of thousands of soldiers, who in addition had to stay in position by their guns, often totally inactive, for months at a time... No one has yet seen that this was the greatest lost battle on the German side.'

Albert Speer, Hitler's Minister of Armaments

There had been huge changes in Bomber Command in the 30 months to the end of 1943, most of them under Sir Arthur Harris. Official figures show that in July 1941 Bomber Command had 732 operational bombers, of which 253 were Wellingtons, 40 Halifaxes, and 24 Stirlings. RAF aircrews were still setting out to fight and often die in the other 415 RAF bombers like Whitleys and Blenheims. Of this assortment, only the Halifax remained in the main force by the end of 1943. Harris commanded a totally different force, much more powerful both in numbers and in the higher quality of its new bombers. He now had 1,249 operational long range bombers, of which 1,008 were of new types – 573 Lancasters, 363 Halifaxes, and 72 Mosquitoes. Only 241 were the older types – 208 Stirlings and 33 Wellingtons used for secondary missions.

The Battle of Berlin started in the winter months because of the length of time RAF bombers were forced to spend over enemy territory to get to their targets; darkness was concealment. In the summer months the bombers would be exposed in the short nights to attack from both day and night-fighters. However dreadful the weather conditions and the cold, winter was safer.

The campaign raged from 18 November 1943 to 31 March 1944, and was Arthur Harris's great throw of the dice to bomb Germany out of the war. 'It will cost us between 400 and 500 aircraft. It will cost Germany the war.'

He could now deploy over 800 long-range bombers on any given night, more

Lancasters than any other type, equipped with new and sophisticated navigational devices. Over a 19-week period Bomber Command made 16 massed attacks on Berlin. Great sacrifices were made and a great many people killed.

The 'Battle of Berlin' was predominantly a Lancaster battle because of their range and bomb capacity, aided by speedy Mosquitoes and with a smaller role played by the Halifax, although the only Victoria Cross of the battle was awarded – posthumously – to a Halifax pilot of 578 Squadron, Pilot Officer Cyril Barton. The battle also forced the Stirling out of the front line because it was so vulnerable, suffering losses of 13 per cent in the initial stages. Not many Stirling crews were surviving 30 operations.

As a backdrop, and a spur to British bomber crews setting out on their nightly operations, Luftwaffe chief Hermann Goering was determined to dish out to Britain what Germany was suffering, and staged what came to be known as the 'Baby Blitz.' Throughout November, German bomber forces, still using twin-engined aircraft, re-launched their campaign against the south of England. During the winter months the Luftwaffe gathered some 515 aircraft of widely differing types on French airfields, and 447 of these bombers, including Ju88s, Ju188s, Do217s, Me410s and the new He177 were used on the first mass attack on London on 21 January 1944.

The German bomber crews were now unpractised at night flying, and the very different aircraft types required pathfinder aircraft to be used to mark targets within the London area. The raid was a disaster for the Luftwaffe. Out of the 282 bombs they dropped, only 32 hit the capital.

In the next four months the Luftwaffe continued its bombing campaign, a pale shadow of the great 1940/41 Blitz. Of the 515 gathered together on French airfields to begin the campaign, 329 aircraft were lost by March 1944, with little effect on the forthcoming preparations for the Normandy Invasion. Goering's fightback meant that Germany had fewer aircraft – just 144 – to carry out operations against the Allies as the invasion approached.

Why didn't the Germans build a fleet of heavy four-engine bombers? Last Witness Captain Eric Brown DSC, RN (fluent in German and French):

'This was a question I asked Hermann Goering personally, because it has always intrigued me. Why didn't the Germans have a specialist heavy bomber fleet? They were building one up pre-war, of course, when Walther Wever, the General who was building it was killed in a silly light aircraft accident in 1936, and with him died the interest in heavy bombers. The Russians, early on, pushed everything back out of range of the invading Germans, and built aeroplanes and tanks by the thousands. Goering told me that Hitler decreed that Germany would never get involved in a lengthy war. Blitzkrieg was to be the order of the day. We were to do it all in a couple of months, he said, three months. But that was it, finish, hammer them to death, that was Hitler's view. This happened brilliantly in Europe, and it damn near succeeded in Russia.'

In the minds of the German leaders this 'Baby Blitz' was a mere stop-gap operation because they were pinning their faith in victory in un-manned weapons developed at Peenemunde, which they were to unleash as terrible 'Vengeance' weapons in the middle of 1944. However much Germany was hurt by the RAF at night and the USAAF by day, Hitler and most of the German people were assured that they still had an adequate response.

The first of Harris's Berlin attacks was on 18 November 1943, with 440 Lancasters and 4 Mosquitoes hitting the city under cloud. There were diversionary raids on Mannheim and Ludwigshaven by 395 other aircraft and Mosquitoes attacked several other towns; among 884 sorties, 32 aircraft (3.6 per cent) were lost. Michael Beetham:

> 'I came back to England from training in America at the age of 20 and joined 50 Squadron in 5 Group flying Lancasters in October 1943. The Battle of the Ruhr was coming to an end, the Battle of Berlin was just starting. I did a second dicky trip to Düsseldorf with an experienced crew and thought we were all set to go. But the next night when a crew list went up, we weren't on it!
>
> 'Why?
>
> 'The CO said the target is Berlin, and that's a bit of a tough one to start on so I think we'll leave it. OK, we thought, we're disappointed… but Berlin… perhaps it's not a bad idea not to do that on our first operation.
>
> 'Next night, crew list, we were going, we wanted to get started, but when the target went up at briefing, there it was, Berlin! The CO said to me, "It's going to be all Berlin now so you had better get in on it." I did my first three operational trips to Berlin.'

Four nights later RAF bombers returned to Berlin with 469 Lancasters, 234 Halifaxes, 50 Stirlings and 11 Mosquitoes. Of the total of 764 aircraft, 26 were lost, 3.4 per cent of the force. This was judged the most effective raid on Berlin of the war so far, though most of the damage was done to residential areas west of the centre – Tiergarten, Charlottenburg, Schoneburg and Spandau. But because of the dry weather conditions several 'firestorms' were ignited, 175,000 people were made homeless and the Kaiser-Wilhelm-Gedächtniskirche was destroyed (the ruins of the old church are now a monument to the horrors of war).

Several other buildings of note were either damaged or destroyed, including the British, French, Italian and Japanese embassies, Charlottenburg Palace and Berlin Zoo, plus the Ministry of Munitions, the Waffen SS Administrative College, barracks of the Imperial Guard at Spandau and several arms factories.

RAF Bombers turned up in force the following night, attacking with 365 Lancasters, 10 Halifaxes, and 8 Mosquitoes, but Berlin was left alone on 24 November for Harris's analysts to assess results. Three Mosquitoes flew there on 25 November to disturb the sleep of Berliners.

On the night of 26 November 1943 Berlin was attacked by 443 Lancasters and 7 Mosquitoes. Most of the damage was in the semi-industrial suburb of Reinickendorf, and Stuttgart was a diversion, attacked by 84 aircraft. Total sorties for the night was 666 with 34 RAF aircraft (5.1%) lost.

Last Witness Michael Beetham:

> 'There was a raid on Berlin which I had thought was quiet and uneventful, and I got back and de-briefed. There had been a bit of clanging, I reported, but all OK. Next morning the flight commander said, "I understand you had an uneventful trip?"
>
> 'I said yes, I had.
>
> 'He said, "Come with me."
>
> 'We went out to the aircraft, and from above someone had dropped an incendiary right through the wing. Luckily it was through an outer fuel tank and the fuel had been emptied. It might have been tricky otherwise. The incendiary bomb had gone right though and I didn't know it. On a bombing raid there are bombs, ack-ack, there's slipstream, it obviously happened and I must have felt something, but it did not feel out of the ordinary until I saw the damage the next day. It meant a wing-change to repair it.'

Berlin returned as the main target on the night of 2 December, attacked by 425 Lancasters, 18 Mosquitoes, and 15 Halifaxes. The Germans correctly identified the target, cross winds scattered the bombers and German fighters shot down a total of 40 bombers — 37 Lancasters, 2 Halifaxes and 1 Mosquito (8.7 per cent of the force). The cross-winds also rendered the bombing inaccurate, scattered around the south of the city, but two more of the Siemens factories, a ball-bearing factory and several railway installations were damaged.

On the night of 3 December, Leipzig was the main target, attacked by 307 Lancasters, 220 Halifaxes (527 aircraft). Michael Beetham:

> 'After the first few raids on Berlin we were full of confidence, and had not been attacked by fighters. The next time the target went up, it was Leipzig, and we thought, we've done Berlin, this is going to be easy. That's when we got attacked, having just dropped our bombs, an attack by a fighter. He put a hole though the port outer fuel tank, but we corkscrewed away and lost him. Then the fuel was a bit short. If you got a hole, you used the fuel from that tank first, which we did, and then we were watching and monitoring all the way back, and scraped into Wittering.
>
> 'We were attacked a few times but managed to survive. If you kept a good look-out and a banking search going, always active, I think fighters would tend to go more for the sitting duck who flew, as some people did, straight and level the whole time. I never stayed straight and level for more than a few seconds.'

On the night of 16 December, Berlin was attacked by 483 Lancasters and 15 Mosquitoes, but night-fighters made a successful interception, and 25 Lancasters, 5.2 per cent of the Lancaster force, were lost over enemy occupied territory. A further 29 RAF aircraft were lost landing in England due to very low cloud. The damage to the Berlin railway system that night was extensive, and 1,000 wagon-loads of war material destined for the Eastern Front were held up for six days. The cumulative effect of the bombing campaign had made more than a quarter of Berlin's total living accommodation unusable, vindicating Lord Cherwell's theories.

Berlin caught it again on the night of 23 December, attacked by 364 Lancasters, 8 Mosquitoes and 7 Halifaxes. Poor weather handicapped the night-fighters who shot down only 16 Lancasters, 4.2 per cent of the force. Damage to the city was relatively small.

Three days after Christmas 1943, Berlin was again the main target, hit by 457 Lancasters, 252 Halifaxes and 3 Mosquitoes (712 aircraft). RAF losses were light (20 aircraft, 2.8 per cent), but heavy cloud frustrated both the RAF and the Luft-waffe.

Harris welcomed Berliners into the New Year of 1944 by sending them 421 Lancasters on 1 January. German night-fighters responded by shooting down 28 RAF aircraft, a steep loss rate of 6.7 per cent. Anything above 4 per cent was a win for the Luftwaffe.

The next night it was Berlin again. 362 Lancasters, 12 Mosquitoes, 9 Halifaxes (383 aircraft) attacked, but it was a costly raid. Night-fighters caught the bombers over the city itself and shot down 27 Lancasters, 7 per cent of the force.

On the night of 5 January 1944, the main target was changed to Stettin, a round-trip of more than 10 hours for crews of 348 Lancasters and 10 Halifaxes, the first attack on that Baltic city since September 1941. A diversionary raid by 13 Mosquitoes on Berlin and 25 Mosquitoes to four other targets fooled the German night-fighters. RAF losses were only 16 aircraft, still it was 4.5 per cent of the force.

These major raids were to continue throughout January and February and on into March with air armadas that included from 400 to over 620 Lancasters. On one trip to Leipzig, 46 out of 561 aircraft were lost but, while there were even greater losses to come, the aircrew were certainly fighting back.

Stan Bradford DFM, air gunner:

'In January 1944 I had done a Berlin job, and another German fighter thought he had an easy kill as we were going in to the target. I think it was a Heinkel. I had said to my pilot, "When I say go, dive to the port," and he flipped the controls a little bit too hard and he turned the Lancaster completely upside down!

'We were bombed up, and we lost 16,000ft (4,876m) before he got it right way up again. Our engineer was a bloke called Fred Simmons and he used to walk around the squadron singing "Upsidedown Simmons they call me."

'I loved flying a Lancaster. As mid-upper gunner, I could see what was happening all about me. I could see everything all the way around, from the hydraulic turret, powered off the port inner engine. Without external power, I had a handle that I wound around. It was often very cold. Sometimes you couldn't speak because your microphone was frozen up. There were icicles hanging anything up to six inches around your chest. The heated suit, when it worked, was all right, but fairly often it didn't work.'

Tony Hiscock, pilot, 156 PFF Squadron:

'There was one night when we reckoned we shot down a fighter. The rear gunner shouted "Enemy fighter! Pilot, starboard. . . Go!" and I corkscrewed to the right. I could see tracer that was being fired at us but I couldn't see what was happening. It seemed to be flying around, and fortunately not very close. Then the mid-upper gunner called and said, I have checked and there's nothing else, so he started firing at what we thought was a FW190. These were ferocious aircraft, single-seaters, and we saw it catch fire as it dived away

'That FW190 was the closest we came to being chased by a fighter. I saw evidence of other fighters, but not really close. I know we were coned a couple of times. I threw the aircraft all over the sky and succeeded in losing them, and I was confident the Lancaster could take all that rough treatment. I had previously seen aircraft that had been coned and they didn't do anything, just flew along straight, and of course the flak is directed at the coned aircraft. If the flak stopped, the fighters picked you up. Each time I was coned I went mad, we were hit by bits of flak but not much and I was able to get away. It was no trouble to throw her around, the Lancaster was so good anyway.'

Two days later, Berlin once more, hit on the night of 30 January 1944, with 440 Lancasters, 82 Halifaxes, and 12 Mosquitoes (534 aircraft) to pound the city. RAF losses were 33 aircraft, 6.2 per cent of the total. It was becoming apparent to some analysts that, no matter how much damage was being caused, the loss of skilled young bomber crews was too high to continue this forever until Berlin was rubble from horizon to horizon. In fact, there was another two months to go, though there was now a two-week lull.

The end of Harris's obsessive campaign to destroy Berlin solely by bombing was now close. There was a pause of more than five weeks between the middle of February and 24 March when the bombers concentrated on other big German cities like Schweinfurt, Augsburg and Stuttgart, before Harris chose to return to

Berlin with a force that included 577 Lancasters. No less than 46 were lost, a rate of 8 per cent. The Bomber stream was scattered and those which reached Berlin bombed well to the south-west of the city. There was a *total* RAF force of 809 bombers, of which 72 were lost, 8.9 per cent total loss rate.

Harris's campaign ended in what the Luftwaffe soon called the 'Night of the Long Knives', on the night of 30 March 1944. The target was Nuremburg, attacked by 572 Lancasters, 214 Halifaxes and 9 Mosquitoes (795 aircraft). The first German fighters appeared just before the bombers reached the Belgian border and over the next hour 82 RAF bombers were lost on the approaches to Nuremburg. One reason was a rare weather condition. Bombers did not usually create a vapour trail below 25,000ft (7,622m), and for this raid they flew below that height, some as low as 16,000ft (4,878m). For whatever meteorological reason the aircraft gave off vapour trails, clearly indicating to German fighter pilots where they were.

Another 13 RAF bombers were shot down by the Germans on the return flight. In all the RAF lost 11.9 per cent of the force dispatched that night, 64 Lancasters and 31 Halifaxes, 670 men. By comparison, RAF Fighter Command lost 515 pilots during the whole of the Battle of Britain in 1940.

Nuremburg was the biggest Bomber Command loss of the war and ended the Battle of Berlin.

Major Lancaster Raids on Germany – Mid-January to March 1944

Date	Target	Lancasters	Losses	Percentage
21/21 Jan	Berlin	496	27	5.4
21/22 Jan	Magdeburg	421	22	5.2
27/28 Jan	Berlin	515	34	6.6
28/29 Jan	Berlin	432	18	4.1
30/31 Jan	Berlin	446	33	7.4
15/16 Feb	Berlin	561	27	4.8
19/20 Feb	Leipzig	561	46	8.2
21/22 Feb	Stuttgart	460	8	1.7
24/25 Feb	Schweinfurt	554	29	5.1
25/26 Feb	Augsburg	463	17	3.7
01/02 Mar	Stuttgart	414	3	0.7
15/16 Mar	Stuttgart	616	29	4.7
18/19 Mar	Frankfurt	621	11	1.8
22/23 Mar	Frankfurt	620	28	4.5
24/25 Mar	Berlin	577	46	8.0
26/27 Mar	Essen	476	5	1.1
30/31 Mar	Nuremburg	569	73	12.8

Total Lancaster sorties (all operations) this period	8,842
Total Lancaster losses (all operations) this period	443
Overall Lancaster loss rate (all operations) this period	4.9%
Total Lancaster replacements/ deliveries this period	651

The human costs on both sides were terrible. In the Battle of Berlin, RAF Bomber Command lost 2,690 airmen killed, and had nearly 1,000 made prisoners of war. A total of 499 aircraft of all types were lost (5.8 per cent), and a further 1,682 were damaged. As the table shows, the percentage loss rate for Lancasters was slightly lower than the grand total – at 4.9 per cent for the first three months of 1944 – and the losses of 433 Lancasters was more than made up for with replacement aircraft.

Using four separate sources to add up the German losses, it was calculated that a total of 7,480 Berlin residents were killed in the Battle of Berlin, with an additional 2,194 missing. The injuries were calculated at 17,092, with 817,730 made homeless.

Noble Frankland, an RAF navigator in Bomber Command, and later its official historian, made the judgement that the Battle of Berlin was a failure, because it was not the knock-out blow that Harris had predicted.

German civilian morale did not break, the city's defences and essential services were maintained, and war production in greater Berlin did not fall.

In fact, said Frankland, German war production continued to rise until the end of 1944, and area bombing did not succeed in Harris's – and Cherwell's – aim, of bombing Germany until its economy and civilian morale collapsed.

There is still controversy about this judgement today. A future Marshal of the Royal Air Force, Sir Michael Beetham, flew 10 operations against Berlin as a twenty-year-old at the height of this battle. He disagrees strongly, as did thousands of the aircrew involved in it, that the Battle of Berlin was a 'failure'.

Sir Michael believes that a later historian, Denis Richards, writing with more records and other information available, gives a more realistic and accurate summing up of the Battle in his book *The Hardest Victory*.

'If the Battle of Berlin cannot be listed with those of the Ruhr and Hamburg as an outright victory for Bomber Command,' writes Richards, 'it nevertheless played its part in the grim business of "progressively" weakening Germany.'

Sir Michael says today: 'We did a lot of damage to Berlin, and we might have gone on to win it if Harris had had more aircraft, as he demanded. But we had to divert a lot of effort from April 1944 into Normandy and the invasion, as priorities changed.'

Harris was taken away from his single-minded battle anyway, to come under the command of America's Dwight Eisenhower heading the Normandy invasion forces, and Lancasters were set to play a major role in softening up the German forces ranged along and behind the D-Day beaches.

CHAPTER FIFTEEN

Morale, Courage and Air Warfare

Friends ain't s'posed to die
'Til they're old;
And friends ain't s'posed to die
In pain;
No one should die alone
When he is twenty-one
And livin' shouldn't make you feel ashamed.

John Gray, 'Billy Bishop
Goes To War'

'The whole squadron was formed into a square and this sergeant-pilot was brought in under guard, the verdict read, "Cowardice in the face of the enemy", and his rank badges were ripped off him there and then by the flight-sergeant, and he was literally drummed out. I thought that was an awful thing. I have got to admit that I would have sooner got killed than have gone through that.'

Unknown

This is a famous and poignant passage that crops up, word for word, in more than one account of the war, and it may, in isolation, be true. But I served throughout the whole war, from day one until it ended. I knew hundreds of RAF aircrew personally and since then, eventually as Chairman of the RAF Bomber Command Association. I have met thousands. Not one of the men I have met could testify to having experienced that which is described above.

It has been offered as a passage to justify the view that RAF Bomber Command – like the British Army was alleged to have behaved at the Somme in 1916 and Passchendaele in 1917 – were 'Lions led by Donkeys'. This phrase was made famous by the historian and politician Alan Clark, who attributed it to a German general called Hoffman, but its real source was not Hoffman at all and may have been spoken by a Russian General in the Crimean War, when it had some validity.

Moving the allegation to the First World War was, according to the modern historian Gordon Corrigan, an invention of Alan Clark's. Corrigan says Clark admitted that he had made it up.

There are similar mythical inventions about how discipline was enforced in the RAF in World War Two. One such myth is that many more RAF aircrew suffered from LMF – Lack of Moral Fibre, the official jargon for cowardice – than has been generally acknowledged.

The author and historian Max Hastings caused great offence among surviving aircrew of RAF Bomber Command with his contention in his book *Bomber Command*, that *one man in seven* 'was lost to operational aircrew at some point between OTU and completing his tour, for morale or medical reasons'. Hastings seems to have come to this opinion merely because of personal interviews with 100 aircrew, justifying his assertion from observing that they almost all 'lost one member of their crew at some time, for some reason.'

He published his assertions in 1980. A medical study called 'Courage and Air Warfare' by Mark K. Wells on the subject 15 years later, the result of analysis of official records, came to a quite different conclusion. Published in 1995, it made direct comparisons at all stages of the war between the RAF and the USAAF. Wells claimed that in Bomber Command in the early war years, the incidence of neuropsychiatric disorder – 'nervous breakdown' – was at least 2 per cent. By 1942 it was 5 per cent. British doctors found that air gunners made up the majority of the cases, closely followed by pilots. Wells wrote that sergeants 'did not last the pace as well as officers.'

But statistically, from the cull of official records, Wells found that instead of 143 airmen out of every thousand classified as LMF – the Hastings claim of one airman in seven *lacking moral fibre* – 'slightly less than 0.4 per cent of bomber crews have been classified LMF.'

That is, four men in a thousand.

No in-depth and contemporary sociological studies of British airmen during the Second World War exist. The British could spare neither the time nor resources on an exhaustive collection of human factors data. But the prevailing philosophy in Britain during the whole of the war was that soldiers or airmen who broke in battle were innately weak or cowardly.

The flying and fighting environment in Bomber Command was often overwhelmingly life-threatening, physical challenges seemed intolerable and the pressure to perform was relentless. For many, the only tangible reward was survival, yet statistics frequently showed this to be mathematically unlikely.

Two of the most potent causes of stress in aircraft were fatigue and fear; the frostbite rate for bomber aircrew was considerable and men simply could not function efficiently in the icy night cold. Yet at no time did the number of emotional casualties – LMF – ever seriously jeopardise the RAF's operational capability

The greatest tension was between briefing times and actual take-off, where it was common for aircrew to suffer cold sweats, pounding hearts or 'butterflies' as before a big sporting event. Nausea and vomiting were not uncommon.

In the RAF there were two fundamental beliefs about coping with combat stress. The first, defined by Churchill's private doctor, Lord Moran, was that 'courage was a function of character.'

'I contend that fortitude in war has its roots in morality; that selection is a search for character, and that war itself is but one more test – the supreme and final test, if you will – of character. Courage can be judged apart from danger only if the social significance and meaning of courage is known to us, namely that a man of character in peace becomes a man of courage in war.'

Lord Moran wrote a famous treatise called 'Anatomy of Courage' about how men coped in the trenches of the Western Front in World War One, and, along with character – which used to be known as 'grit' – Moran linked the whole idea of courage with morality:

'How is courage spent in war? Courage is will-power, whereof no man has an unlimited stock; and when in war it is used up he is finished. A man's courage is his capital, and he is always spending.'

The second fundamental belief about coping with combat stress was that LMF – the euphemism for cowardice – was contagious. It was felt better to misjudge the unfortunate few than allow the slow decay and subsequent collapse of the entire crew force.

Even as brilliant and sympathetic a leader as Cheshire VC was of this view:

'I was ruthless with "moral fibre cases." I had to be. We were airmen not psychiatrists. Of course we had concern for any individual whose internal tensions meant that he could no longer go on but there was the worry that one really frightened man could affect others around him. There was no time to be as compassionate as I would like to have been. I was flying too, and we had to get on with the war.'

The RAF never widely deployed psychiatric testing to select aircrew. It was considered too time-consuming, too costly, and the necessary number of training specialists was not available. In addition, the authorities frequently doubted psychiatrists and deeply distrusted their motivations. The RAF succeeded, never-theless, in selecting high quality candidates to serve as aircrew.

British medical men placed more emphasis on predisposition – broadly char-acter – than they did on the views of a 'trick cyclist.' They saw neurosis as an 'infectious disease', and capable through character of being overcome. The simple medical goal was to return as many men as possible to flying duty… one third of all emotional casualties were eventually returned to combat. It was felt that the period between the fifth and the fourteenth operation were the most stressful. Many even finished their tours.

There were emotional breakdowns in some British crews, including crews who had not even started operations – 'the fear of fear itself' – and among a surprising 8 per cent who had not flown at all. But despite worsening states of health during their tour of operations, aircrew were actually less inclined to report themselves sick. Most wanted to get through the operations and be done with their tour.

Class

I think it necessary to touch on social class in the 1940s, and its possible effect on the forces binding together one to another in wartime Britain. Lord Moran again:

> 'Britain in the 1940's was still a society where class counted for much. Despite the fact that very many officers in the RAF and Bomber Command were not necessarily public school trained, much of the philosophy of the upper classes permeated the service. From this group a pattern of leadership could be seen which reflected a gentle civility and occasionally a paternal attitude towards NCO's and enlisted men. Faltering airmen were admonished "not to let the side down", or "let's get on with it, chaps", in the same manner as a cricket or rugby team might be encouraged. Understatement, restraint and humility were virtues of leadership. Bragging or showing emotion was eschewed. It was especially important not to admit weakness. Maintaining "a stiff upper lip" was more than a wartime cliché.'

As we noted earlier in this account, as late as June 1942 Kings Regulations and Air Council instructions precluded non-commissioned officers being designated captains of aircraft. Faced with mixed crews, regulations put the senior officer in charge, absolutely impossible to enforce, yet it lasted through the first three years of warfare. Comparing British and American aircrew selection methods, Mark Wells felt the Americans tried to identify the best of the volunteers, while the Brit-ish tried to eliminate the worst. In choosing airmen, British recruiters looked for characteristics associated with sportsmen, hunters or cavalrymen, traditional traits of the ruling class.

It has to be said that all decisions inviting young candidates to risk their lives – then in Bomber Command, now in Afghanistan – take advantage of the peculiar notion that young men have about their own invulnerability in the face of danger. As one ex-air gunner put it:

> 'When I look back on those casualty figures today it seems incredible that I survived, but at the time I never measured the odds. Such faith belongs to the young and without it, I suppose, few would have flown. Viewed today it smacks of arrogance, conceit and stupidity. I can only admit that as I flew more and more raids, I grew more and more contemptuous of the dangers.'

Eagerness counted for much in selection, as did youth, resolution, tenacity and a willingness to take risks. The three most important qualities sought for RAF aircrew were 'courage, confidence and character.' Tests involved detailed questions about family history, schooling, health, hobbies and employment.

The British goal was to find as many public schoolboys as possible, and all three fighting services competed to recruit the same type of officer. There was heavy emphasis on leadership and sportsmanship.

'Breeding is of great importance,' said one Medical officer. 'It is unlikely that the son of a coward would himself become a hero, for it is remarkable how heroism often runs in families.'

In choosing officers, the pre-war RAF was a 'very small, elite service manned by regulars.' As one warrant officer put it, 'You have to be a Gentleman to fly, my lad!' The fundamental benchmark for commissioning during those years had been leadership, 'displaying officer-like qualities' and showing 'character, intelligence and the ability to set a good example – in short, the public school ethos.'

The Selection Board asked questions like 'Can you drive a car?' And 'can you drive a motorbike, or ride a horse?' Few English boys with a working class background could do any of these things in 1941, if only because they did not have the money.

One aircrew candidate reported that there were two cars in his street of about 100 houses – one car was owned by a retired publican, the other by an insurance man. 'I clearly wasn't the traditional type to make pilot, but they took me on just the same. Standards after 1942 were much lower than they had been before the war.' He meant this in terms of social class, not competence.

Another pilot commented that of the 43 pilots who finally completed their training, only 11 were granted commissions. All of these had been to public schools. 'We others were given the rank of Sergeant.'

In 617 Squadron, my experience was that we had a majority of officer pilots, perhaps because of the way we were selected, but 65 per cent of Bomber Command's aircraft were flown by N.C.O. pilots. In any case, by 1942, such was the rate of attrition within Bomber Command, it was to fall to a young group of 'volunteers for the duration', mainly in their early twenties, but some younger, to fight the bulk of the Command's battles.

Senior officers in the RAF went to some lengths not to over-glamourise aircrew, resisting the temptation to encourage publicity about aces. Despite great pressure to do so, the RAF never substantially increased the number of combat flying awards and only reluctantly gave way to the public demand for heroes. There was no RAF equivalent of the American Air Medal, and US awards per 1,000 battle deaths were three times that of the British. In British pubs it was not uncommon to hear cynics say that Americans got bravery awards for 'eating Brussels sprouts.'

It was my personal experience on a liner travelling from the United States to Britain in 1943 that some American soldiers, when they passed the halfway point in the Atlantic, put up the first of their 'ribbons' to show they had experience in the 'European Combat Zone.'

Only 20,354 DFCs were awarded through the whole RAF, along with 1,592 bars. Non-commissioned officers would usually receive the DFM; just over 6,000 DFM's were awarded, though non-coms flew in greater numbers than commissioned officers. The historian Richard Holmes commented that 'the monstrously inadequate distribution of awards to "other ranks" was a flaw in the British system and… regretted that there had not been enough awards for the brave men they led.'

For hundreds of thousands of us facing total war, our view of what was right and wrong, which underlined our determination to 'do the right thing' and 'be fair', was typically built around institutions like Greyfriar's School in the 'Magnet' Comic. These stories are known now for its chief 'character', the fat, greedy, dishonest Billy Bunter, but the values of the school were not Bunter's.

Many of us admired chaps like Harry Wharton, Captain of school, strong-willed, stubborn and a natural leader; Frank Nugent, loyal and self-effacing; Bob Cherry, cheerful, energetic and robust; Johnny Bull, Yorkshire-bred, stubborn yet thoughtful. We carried those models into the Sergeant's and Officers Messes of the RAF and stuck by them.

For us, morale was maintained by patriotism, 'desire to do our bit', even love of flying. We were sustained by self-esteem, supported by group cohesion, the strength of which depended to a great deal on the quality of our equipment, the length of time we were kept in combat, the results we obtained and the rate of attrition. A flying career was seen by me, and by many young men, as the best way 'to get back at the Hun.'

To add from my own experience at how class was perceived in the RAF, I was 21 years old in 1941, a sergeant instructor. One of my pupils was an American –

six years older than me – called Robert S. Raymond. He was an Anglophile and curious about England. I happened to be friends with one of the famous pottery families, the Aynsleys, who lived near the airfield. They were 'old money', and had a daughter called Cynthia, 16 years old and very, very pretty. She invited me to her home for a Sunday lunch, and I said, could I bring my American pupil? I thought I would let Robert Raymond see how another half of England lived. He was impressed, went on to complete a full tour of operations as an RAF flight lieutenant pilot on Lancasters, and won a DFC before being transferred to the USAAF. Raymond later wrote a book called *A Yank in Bomber Command* in which he commented on the class system:

'Unlike the USAAF, commissioned rank is not conferred on all. Ordinarily commissions are granted only to those with the Old School tie and/or those who play rugger. Seriously, the situation is just that. Some day I'll try and explain how such a system works, practically, in this great stronghold of democracy...'

And again, later in the war:

'About half my companions are from New Zealand and Canada, and among the latter are about half a dozen of my own countrymen. All of them are unanimous in their dislike of this country. To them the bread tastes like sawdust, they can't get a cuppa cawfee, the tea is usually unsweetened, there's no candy, fruit or milk and only boiled vegetables, there are few cigarettes and they are always hungry. Above all they dislike RAF officers and take few pains to disguise their feelings. "Little tin Gods on wheels" is their favourite expression. The officers are really in a tough spot. They can't help treating everyone of lesser rank like poor relatives, most of them being the result of the class-conscious training they have received, nor can they afford to antagonise these valuable volunteers, for fear of unfavourable reactions when the boys write home. Today the men from the Dominions demanded more blankets – they are unable to sleep with just four – and got them. We were asked to volunteer in class today for instructors. The Canadians stood up in a body. The officer suspected some trick, for no one ever wants these jobs. One of them spoke for the group: "We'll all volunteer if we can instruct in Canada". There's never any outright insubordination, just incidents like that. Too bad they feel that way, for they are all fine, big, carefree, intelligent fellows.'

Statistics

In coming to a view of what Bomber Command crews went through, take a number of random statistics.

Between 1939 and 1945, Bomber Command lost 8,953 aircraft as a direct result of enemy action. Another 1,368 (13 per cent) were written off in operational accidents. Compare this with USAAF, which lost 4,200 aircraft in battle losses between 1942 and 1945 but lost more than 6,000 in accidents.

RAF records show 2,681 accidents involving casualties in Bomber Command between the start of 1943 and the end of 1944. Almost 6,000 airmen were killed and a further 4,400 were injured in these mishaps. Close to one in seven of Bomber Command's losses came in training.

Between January 1943 and January 1944 in Bomber Command's 1 Group, all flying Lancasters, 813 crews started a first or second tour of 30 ops.

Of these, 455 crews, approximately 3,185 men, went missing, either killed or captured.

Only 207 crews survived to complete their tours.

Mark Wells asserted that inferior crews had less of a chance than the competent of surviving in an emergency. These crews could be spotted by their lack of discipline, lack of knowledge of the aircraft sub-systems, or their air of bravado. Some aircrew seemed to be marked out for death in the air they had about them, and other aircrew seemed to know they were doomed.

In a letter to Charles Portal in January 1943, Arthur Harris wrote:

'It is inevitable in war that the best are the keenest to go back on operations and they are the ones who, when they get there, hit the target. There are perhaps 20-25 in each 100 who can be classed as the best and the remaining 75-80 divert the enemy effort from the destruction of the best, and receive a certain number of casualties, so saving the best from being picked off by the enemy... This is true in any service in any war and in any operation. In the infantry there are a certain number of the not-so-good who confuse the enemy and make it difficult for him to pick off the best men only.'

It was found, said Wells, that a significant proportion of British bombers were damaged by 'friendly fire', that is, other British bombers firing into the night. Some RAF pilots became convinced that air gunners – mid-upper turret and rear gunner – were useless, and too great a readiness to open fire actually increased the risk of attack by German fighters.

Fear could strike anywhere, often when there was no enemy around at all, and dithering over a decision could easily be fatal. Last Witness Michael Beetham:

'We were doing fighter affiliation with a Hurricane. The system we used was one full crew – my crew – plus another pilot and his two gunners. I had done my fighter affiliation and the other pilot took over the controls, the gunners got out of their seats, and the second crew got on with it.

'I was relaxing down in the nose when the pilot said, "Fire in the port outer engine!"

'I thought, "Oh, Christ!"'

'He couldn't get it feathered so he said, "Abandon aircraft." I went out through the front, undid the hatch, jettisoned it, and got out. We were at least 10,000ft (3,300m) up.

'There were ten people on board, and eight out of the ten got out. Two didn't make it out of the back, the flight engineer and one gunner, both of my crew. The chap in the pilot's seat had the responsibility. He did his best and as far as he knew, everyone had got out. By the time he left the aeroplane was now out of control.

'Afterwards we asked my wireless operator what had happened down at the back end. He said the mid-upper gunner, who had gone first, jumped instead of diving head down, and he got caught over the tail-plane, his parachute spewed out but he got dragged over and survived (he died of natural causes in 2004). He made it despite going over the tail-plane instead of under it. The wireless operator said the engineer and the rear gunner were watching, and they then waved him out. He thought he was just being waved out, that it was good manners. We now suspect that, seeing what had gone on, those two funked it a bit. You can't say that about dead men, but those two didn't get out.'

Bomber losses varied with defences encountered *en route*, defences at the target, weather, aircraft performance and crew experience. German fighters accounted for most of Bomber Command's losses. Even so, flak was much feared. Experiments conducted in 1942 showed that the chances of an aircraft being hit by flak, whether or not it was taking evasive action, were roughly even. But the widely employed 'corkscrew' manoeuvre, even if only slightly more effective against fighters, gave crews 'something to do' during situations of high stress.

One in every four RAF aircrew was from the Dominions. Mixed crews, airmen from different nationalities, were found to have the best results.

Crewing Up

The real life-and-death decision flying four-engined heavy bombers like the Lancaster, was 'crewing up', selecting who you were going to fly and fight with. It was not a case of 'you, you and you!' but there were hardly any clues on which to make a selection. As an example of the random ways that luck worked, consider those few aircrew who got stuck as what they called 'spare bods', on their own, attached to nobody, not a state of affairs that anyone much liked. Sergeant Jim Norris CGM, a flight engineer with 61 Squadron, was told one day by his squadron leader Skipper that he had to move to another crew. He resented it:

'The reason he was making the changes is that he wouldn't let this flight lieutenant fly as a flight engineer with the other crew, whose skipper was Bill Reid and that was because Bill was a flying officer, a lower rank. The squadron leader said that as the flight lieutenant was a higher grade than Bill Reid, he can't fly with Bill Reid.

'As I was a sergeant, the squadron leader thought it was acceptable for me to fly with Bill. We went to briefing and I was with one of his crew – we had two engineers anyway – and Bill Reid and the boys in his crew were calling me over. Three-quarters of the way through the briefing, I got up from sitting with the squadron leader's crew and went over to Reid's.

'That was the first time I flew with Bill. If the squadron leader had asked me nicely, if he had told me the truth...

'What happened was that Bill Reid's engineer, on a raid the previous night, was screaming over the target. He was panicked, and when he came back he was moved off operations. The squadron leader didn't tell me that. All he said was, you've got to fly with Bill Reid. It was just an order. If he had told me that Bill Reid's flight engineer had cried off, I would have joined with Bill Reid, and stayed with Bill Reid. As it turned out, flying with Bill Reid was wonderful.

'The first trip I did with Bill was to Kastel. We came back, I walked into the briefing room, and the wing commander said to me, "You're late."

'"No I'm not," I said.

'He said, "Where's the squadron leader?"

'I said, "I dunno."

'"What do you mean, you don't know?"

'I said, "I didn't fly with him, I flew with Bill Reid."

'It turned out that the squadron leader was shot down.

'I knew that he wasn't going to last. He wasn't the best pilot, because he was nervous. The whole crew knew that.

Rupert Noye, DFC, rear gunner with 156 PFF Squadron also went through a potentially difficult stage for quite some time of being a 'spare bod':

'I was with a good crew and we had confidence in each other and did a number of operations on Lancasters connected with D-Day, bombing marshalling yards and guns in France. But after D-Day, we had done about 18 trips – I am a flight sergeant by now – I didn't fly one day because I had a cold. The rest of the crew went to Caen in Normandy and had the bad luck to bomb Canadian troops there.

'The two navigators and the pilot were thrown off operations, and the rest of the crew split up. I stayed on at 156 Squadron as a 'spare bod', filling in for whichever crew needed me, mostly as a rear gunner, though I did a couple of trips in the mid-upper turret. I never liked the mid-upper position. You could see too much to start with, and I always felt more at home in the rear turret. Despite the isolation, you get used to it and I survived 19 'spare bod' trips which was a miracle. By now I had done more than 50 operations. I suppose I could have declared a finish to my tour by this time and been allocated to instruct novice gunners, but I did not really want to do that.

'Then Tony Hiscock turned up one day and said, "Would you like to join our crew?"

'I did the last 19 trips with Tony. In all I did 72 operations – against the average of 21 – so I guess I beat the odds two or three times.'

David Fellowes, air gunner:

'On the train from Crewe to Stafford I met three Australian pilots and we chatted. I discovered that my aunt out in Australia and the mother of one of the pilots were close friends, so we crewed up on the train. We went to Lindholm, the heavy conversion unit from Wellingtons to Halifaxes, and then on to Lancaster finishing school, and there picked up a flight engineer. We were posted to 460 Lancaster Sqdn RAAF at Binbrook, in No 1 Group. The whole Group flew Lancasters. There were other Poms in the squadron, and only two Australians out of seven of us in his aircraft. We were only there to give them Australians a bit of culture.'

Les Munro, Dambuster pilot, RNZAF:

'I got together with my crew at OTU – Operation Training Unit. I have a faint idea that my navigator was allotted to me and we immediately struck up a bond. The air gunners were training in one place and the wireless operators in another place. At the end of our training we were asked to pick our own crews from this collection of gunners and wireless operators. It was a bit difficult. I ended up being beaten to one or two blokes that I wanted to pick at that stage, and I selected a couple of blokes sitting on the fringe. I said, OK for you guys to fly with me? They didn't know me from Adam. It was a bit like a lottery. You took your chances on this bloke, or that bloke. If they turned out to be wrong 'uns, you had to accept that. None of them did turn out wrong, except for the bomb aimer who would pass out at high altitude.

John Bell, bomb aimer for one of 617's most eminent pilots Bobby Knights:

'We were at 40 OTU and assembled in a hangar and told to form up as crews. We had a rear gunner much older than we were, he was 29 with a family, we were all 20 or 21 years old. He went around gathering people together. He was determined to survive the war and chose what he thought were the best crew. Bobby Knights was a very good pilot and it was thanks to him that we survived the war... also to a great amount of luck, of course. Bobby was an excellent pilot and was continually weaving about. He used to tell a lovely story, that someone had found out that he had had a crash at OTU, and said to him, perhaps you learned something from that, you'll be a bit more careful next time, so we'll fly with you.'

To balance the experience, Mark Wells found some dissatisfaction in an air gunner who clearly survived the war:

> 'I don't know why we were not cohesive. For my part I didn't like the cocky bomb-aimer who thought he knew everything, and I didn't like the Welsh gunner who was clearly disinterested. Who wants a disinterested tail gunner? The wireless operator and navigator hung together, being married men. The pilot and bomb-aimer stayed together because the bomb-aimer tended to take charge and the pilot was a quiet chap. That left we two gunners as mates, a situation in which I wasn't very happy'.

In six years of war, of 125,000 Bomber Command aircrew, 55,573 were killed, 8,400 injured, and a further 11,000 were missing or were held as PoWs. Out of any 100 men who joined an OTU, 51 would be killed in combat operations, 12 more would be killed or injured in non-operation accidents, 12 would become PoW's. Only 24 of the original 100 would survive unscathed.

I was lucky enough to be one of them.

CHAPTER SIXTEEN

German Defences

'The rate of night losses was highest in 1942, before our tactics and countermeasures were properly developed,' said Air Chief Marshal Sir Norman Bottomley after the war. 'The loss rate in 1942 was 4.1 per cent. I often wonder if the significance of a loss rate of 4.1 per cent is generally realised. The normal operational tour of bomber crews was 30 sorties. If they survived, they were then withdrawn for a change of operation – say, for six months – before a second tour. A loss rate of 4 per cent meant, therefore, that the chances were against completing the first operational tour, and it meant that on an average there was a complete turnover of aircrews in squadrons in about four months, due to casualties.

'It is a matter of pride that morale in the heavy bomber forces remained so high in the face of these casualty rates. The loss rate fell to 3.7 per cent in 1943 and in 1944 it amounted to 1.7 per cent. In the last months of the war in 1945 it was less than 1 per cent.'

On 21 February 1945, an RAF navigator arriving late in an attack by 514 Lancasters on the Dortmund-Ems Canal had no work to do when his aircraft headed for home; his pilot could find his way by following the blazing wrecks of Lancasters which went before them.

The greatest of all night-fighter aces, Major Heinz-Wolfgang Schnaufer, flying a Heinkel He219, took just 20 minutes that day, between 20.43 and 21.03 hours, to shoot down *seven Lancasters*, an average of one every three minutes. He was using 'Schräge Musik', the lethal upward-firing cannon, and he had already destroyed two Lancasters that morning before his rest period.

This was just 10 weeks before the end of the war.

On that raid and on two raids the following night to Duisburg by 362 Lancasters, and Gravenhorst by 166, the Lancasters had been guided accurately to their targets. They were where they were supposed to be. Yet, along with Heinz-Wolfgang Schnaufer, his Luftwaffe colleagues Heinz Rokker shot down six Lancasters, Gerhard Behr destroyed seven and Johannes Hager shot down eight.

Those four pilots between them destroyed 30 of the 39 Lancasters lost by RAF Bomber Command in those three raids. The Luftwaffe night-fighter pilot's weapon of choice in the last years of the war was, overwhelmingly, Schräge Musik, even now a word and weapon virtually unknown to the wider public and hardly known by many RAF veterans.

In the RAF we gave the German Air Force far more 'trade' than they gave us, after the initial horrors of the Luftwaffe Blitz in 1940/41. Back then, there were virtually no night-fighter weapons beyond the Mark One Eyeball to find German bombers.

By 1944, German attacks on Britain were mainly confined to V-1 'Doodle Bugs' and V-2 rockets. Yet, virtually every night, thousands of RAF aircrew were over German soil in Lancasters, preyed upon by a group of Luftwaffe night-fighter pilots whom aviation author Francis K. Mason calls 'The Old Hands' and who had fantastic successes. Statistically, Bomber Command losses had fallen below 2 per cent on every operation, but there were exceptions. Mason cites several other examples of Luftwaffe successes. In an attack on Ladbergen, on the infamous Dortmund-Ems canal, on the night of 7 February 1945, 24-year old Hauptmann Gerhard Raht flying a Ju88 with Schräge Musik, penetrated the bomber stream and destroyed *all five Lancasters* lost that night, as well as a Halifax.

Only Martin Becker would 'improve' on these figures. On 14 March 1945 he caught a bomber stream approaching Lutzendorf, shooting down eight Lancasters and a Halifax. Becker said flying an He219 and using Schräge Musik against Lancasters was 'like shooting geese.'

Major Heinz-Wolfgang Schnaufer, with 121 kills, of which 114 were RAF 4-engined bombers, was the most successful night-fighter pilot of all time. He was awarded the German equivalent to a VC, Diamonds to a Knight's Cross – the Blue Max (he was killed in a car accident five years after the end of the war).

These were the top ten German night-fighters:

Major Heinz-Wolfgang Schnaufer	121 kills
Lt Col Helmut Lent	113 kills
Major Prince Sayn-Wittgenstein	83 kills
Col Werner Streib	68 kills
Maj Rudolf Schoenert	65 kills (inventor of *Schräge Musik*)
Capt Manfred Meurer	65 kills (died when a bomber fell on him)
Col Gunther Radusch	65 kills
Capt Heinz Rokker	65 kills
Major Paul Zorner	59 kills
Capt Martin Becker	58 kills

Compare these astonishing kill-rates with those of the RAF's top night-fighter pilot, Group Captain John 'Cats Eyes' Cunningham, credited with 20 kills, 19 at night, who was awarded three DSOs and two DFCs in recognition of his skill.

The Luftwaffe had come a long way since the beginning of the war in 1939 when their night-fighter force was precisely zero. Despite his empty boast that no enemy aircraft would ever bomb the Ruhr, in May 1940 Hermann Goering appointed Oberst (Group Captain) Joseph Kammhuber to set up a night-fighter operation. British bombers were starting to conduct operations over Germany, although claims were already being made that began to look doubtful.

Before the war RAF crews had simply not flown in bad weather at night, because it was too dangerous. The only navigation exercises at night had been either DR – dead reckoning – or by star shots. DR depended on knowing the wind strengths throughout the flight, on accurate measuring instruments for the aircraft's speed and height, so for at least two years very few British bombs fell within five miles of the intended target.

British night bombing raids in 1940 were undertaken at heights between 8,000 and 12,000ft – the Whitleys, Wellingtons and Hampdens which conducted the attacks could not carry much of a bomb load anyway, never mind at heights above that. These were just the heights at which the German gun defences were most efficient. The genuine airspeed achieved by, say, a Hampden with a full load of 4,500lbs, was 165mph, which meant that every German 88-mm flak gun it flew over had it in range for more than two minutes. German marksmanship was very good and got a lot better. But night-fighters were still needed.

Oberst Kammhuber used single-engine Me 109s to begin with, fast but cramped, and not really suitable to search the skies at night. They needed full outside guidance to get to their targets. To achieve that guidance, Kammhuber introduced two different types of radar, Freya, with a maximum range of 100 miles, and Giant Wurzburg, precision tracking under 50 miles. A pair of Giant Wurzburgs and one Freya station formed what was called the 'Himmelbett System.' After Freya picked up a possible target, one Giant Wurzburg tracked the target while a second Giant Wurzburg tracked the fighter, putting it on track to reach the target bomber and get a visual sighting.

After they swept through northern Europe, the Germans set up a line of Himmelbett stations, each separated by 20 miles in an 'inverted sickle' with its handle in Denmark, the sickle curving through northern Germany, Holland, Belgium and eastern France to the Swiss frontier. It was known as the 'Kammhuber Line'. One fault with it was that each Luftwaffe fighter station could control only one interception at a time, or six per hour.

In 1942, the Germans fitted an early form of interception radar, known as Lichtenstein, to their night-fighters, favouring the twin-engined Me110. The RAF countered by overwhelming the Freya and Giant Wurzburg radar stations, introducing 'bomber streams' with hundreds of bombers heading for a single target, all packed together to get through the radar belt at speed. The Germans added more stations to thicken the defence.

In the Spring of 1943, a German major, Hajo Hermann, argued for single-engine fighters to be involved over targets against RAF bombers. He said that flak shells should be fused to explode below 18,000ft and bombers above this level were highlighted from below by fires, and could be downed by higher-flying fighters. On 3 July Hermann was authorised to start his 'Wild Boar' tactics with six Me109 fighters. When his section shot down six British bombers, he was authorised to expand his single-engined night-fighter units to a 90-aircraft Geschwader. From a German point of view, not before time.

The most fearsome of German ground weapons was the Krupps-built 88mm anti-aircraft gun. There were 900,000 anti-aircraft gunners in Germany in 1944, firing 14,250 heavy guns – 88mm to 128mm – and 35,000 lighter weapons, 20mm and 37mm. Seventy per cent of German flak guns were 88mm, typically firing 15 to 20 high-explosive 20lb shells every minute, and 20,000ft was the optimum effective height. Exploding shells sent 1,500 steel shards through a radius of 20 yards. A direct hit was enough to destroy a bomber. One estimate says that German flak batteries could fire 5,000 tons of explosive every 60 seconds.

The 88mm gun was an effective anti-aircraft weapon, but it was also a deadly destroyer of tanks and lethal against advancing infantry. These weapons, devoted to downing Lancasters, would have done much to bolster German anti-tank defences on the Russian front. To man them the flak regiments in Germany required not only 900,000 fit personnel, but a further one million people deployed in clearing up and repairing the vast bomb damage caused by the RAF attacks.

By 1944 the bombing offensive, RAF and USAAF, was costing Germany 30 per cent of all artillery production, 20 per cent of heavy shells, 33 per cent of the output of the optical industry for sights and aiming devices – the Zeiss factory in Dresden produced those – and 50 per cent of the country's electro-technical output which had to be diverted to the anti-aircraft role.

The new, improved air-defence system the Germans had built was countered on 24 July 1943 by RAF Bomber Command opening the Battle of Hamburg, attacking that port city with 791 bombers – 354 of them Lancasters – all using Window, which saturated the defence. Instead of the standard loss of 4 per cent, 30 aircraft, only 12 aircraft were lost, 1.6 per cent. New harrying tactics by the RAF which led to the formation of 100 Group later in the year also turned the tide against the Germans.

As a direct result, Kammhuber was sacked and his replacement, Joseph Schmid, revamped tactics. The Germans re-organised the whole Himmelbett system, and more resources were given to the Wild Boar units. Not using airborne radar, just visual means, as well as being guided by a running commentary from ground stations, they could not be jammed. Two more Wild Boar Geschwaders were planned. Previously, night-fighters took off and circled, waiting for a controlled one-to-one interception, never outside the 50-mile range of the Giant Wurzburg radar. In the new system, hunting packs of night fighters took off as the bomber stream came in, and the packs were directed from beacon to beacon to bring them near to the bomber stream, after which they stepped off searching for targets visually and with radar. The idea was to have long-running battles throughout the time the bombers were over German-occupied territory.

In the Autumn of 1943, the Luftwaffe was issued with new SN-2 radar with a 4-mile range operating on a longer wavelength than the earlier sets, which meant Window had little effect in jamming them.

RAF Lancasters and Halifaxes were also betraying themselves because the Luftwaffe could track emissions from two sources on a bomber, H2S ground-mapping radar, and the Monica tail-warning radar. Naxos homed in on H2S, and Flensburg on Monica.

One of the Luftwaffe aces, Martin Becker on night-fighter Geschwader 6, shot down six British bombers in one night – 22 March 1944 – among a total of 58 by the end of the war.

To appreciate the magnitude of the RAF losses, go through a list of 20 Lancasters produced consecutively in a huge batch of 550 by Avro between June and December 1943:

JA923, 97 Squadron, Peenemunde 17.8.43, Berlin 3.9.43, Manheim 23.9.43. MISSING Frankfurt, 5.10.43.

JA924, 83 Squadron, no key raids. 405 RCAF Squadron, MISSING Berlin, 30.1.44.

JA925, 156 Squadron, Peenemunde 17.8.43, Berlin 3.9.43, Berlin 18.11.43, Berlin 22.11.43, Berlin 26.11.43, Berlin 2.12.43, Berlin 16.12.43, Berlin 23.12.43, Berlin 29.12.43 MISSING Berlin 1.2.44

JA926, 101 Squadron, Hamburg 27.7.43, Hamburg 2.8.43 (aborted), Peenemunde 17.8.43, Berlin 3.9.43, MISSING Mannheim 5.9.43.

JA927, 83 Squadron, Peenemunde 17.8.43, MISSING Berlin 23.8.43.

JA928, 101 Squadron, no key raids. 83 Squadron Peenemunde 17.8.43, Berlin 3.9.43, Hanover 18.10.43, Berlin 18.11.43, Berlin 22.11.43, Berlin 23.11.43, Berlin 2.12.43. Berlin 16.12.43 (abortive), Berlin 29.12.43, Berlin 1.1.44, Berlin 2.1.44, Brunswick 14.1.44, Berlin 30.1.44, Berlin 15.2.44, Berlin 24.3.44, Nuremburg 30.3.44, MISSING Schweinfurt 26.4.44.

JA929, 7 Squadron, MISSING Berlin 3.9.43

JA930, 100 Squadron, Hamburg 27.7.43, Hamburg 2.8.43, Peenemunde 17.8.43, MISSING Berlin 3.9.43

JA931, 7 Squadron Aircraft abandoned by crew when short of fuel 10 miles NE of Canterbury, Kent, on return from Nuremburg 10.8.43

JA932, 7 Squadron, Peenemunde 17.8.43, Hanover 18.10.43, Berlin 22.11.43, MISSING Berlin 23.11.43

JA933, 7 Squadron, Peenemunde 17.8.43, Berlin 3.9.43, Hanover 18.10.43, Berlin 26.11.43, Berlin 2.12.43, Berlin 16.12.43, Berlin 23.12.43, Berlin 29.12.43, Berlin 1.1.44, Brunswick 14.1.44, Berlin 27.1.44. Transfer 582 Squadron MISSING Laon, France 23.4.44

JA934, 100 Squadron...shot down over Berlin 15.2.44 on its 15th operation.

JA935, 7 Squadron…shot down over Brunswick 14.1.44 on its 12th operation.

JA936, 7 Squadron…shot down over Munchen Gladbach 30.8.43 on its 2nd trip.

JA937, 7 Squadron…shot down over Munchen Gladbach 30.8.43 on its 1st trip.

JA938 sent to Farnborough to become instructing machine, Struck off charge 4.2.47

JA939, 97 Squadron…shot down over Nuremburg 10.8.43 on 1st operation.

JA940, 83 Squadron…crash landed in England on return from Berlin with two engines shot out 29.1.44

JA941, 156 Squadron…shot down over Augsburg 25.2.44 on 11th operation, 8 to Berlin.

JA957 (next on line), 103 Squadron…shot down over St Leu d'Esserent 7.7.44 after 10 trips over Germany, 8 of them to Berlin.

Of these 20 consecutive Lancasters off the Avro production line in Manchester, producing 21 per week between June/December 1943, only one was SOC (Struck off Charge) after the war. One was abandoned short of fuel, a second crash-landed with two engines shot away over Berlin, and the other 17 Lancasters, each with crews of 7, were shot down. At an average escape rate for Lancasters of just 15 per cent, 18 of those 119 aircrew might have survived.

By 30 March 1944, German night-fighter defences were at peak efficiency. Of a force of 569 Lancasters attacking Nuremburg, 69 were lost with 55 attributed to night-fighter attacks. The decision by Sir Arthur Harris, under orders, to move away from the cities he had been attacking to targets in France ahead of D-Day meant Bomber Command losses fell, but the Germans had every reason to believe they had put an end to the nightly aerial attacks over Germany.

Mosquito intruders were not able to cope adequately with the new German defences, especially their night-fighter radar, and it was feared that the Germans had discovered a fearsome weapon, against which there seemed to be little defence. We now know it was an upward-firing cannon.

One German estimate suggested that Schräge Musik accounted for almost 80 per cent of the British bomber losses through the whole of 1944 and the four war months of 1945. How did it come into being?

Schräge Musik

During the First World War, forward-firing Lewis guns were often mounted on the top-plane of a biplane to fire over the propeller, because it was difficult to synchronise this type of weapon to fire through the propeller arc without hitting the propellers themselves. The Lewis gun had to be tilted back to change ammunition drums, so it could also be fired upwards at an angle. The guns of the French-built Nieuport fighters in British service, along with the British-built S.E.5A were often used in this way to attack enemy bomber or reconnaissance aircraft from the 'blind spot' below the tail. Albert Ball VC, with 40 kills, championed the technique.

Prior to the introduction of Schräge Musik in 1943, German night-fighters were normally twin-engined heavy fighters equipped with radar in the nose. To score a kill, the fighter pilot stalked his victim, approaching from behind and killing the rear gunner as quickly as possible before knocking the bomber down. But the bomber's profile was small, and most rear-gunners were alert and aggressive. Aside from firing his four turret-guns, the rear-gunner could also call out corkscrew turns to his pilot, which, well-executed by a pilot flying for his life, would often remove the bomber from the fighter's radar.

Another tactic was to approach the bomber from below, then pull up sharply, almost in a stall, and get in a quick two-second burst. This often worked, but was difficult to perform and it could lead to a collision. It was targeted on the bigger target of the fuselage rather than the wing, but if the bomb load in the fuselage was hit, the explosion would knock down both aircraft.

Oberleutnant Rudolf Schonert was, in 1941, a 'two-pipper', the equivalent of a Flying Officer in the RAF, quite a junior rank. When he began experiments that year with upward-firing guns, most of his colleagues thought he was daft and laughed at him. He did not impress his senior officers either. There was an attempt to put such an arrangement on a Dornier 17 that was equipped with the early version of Lichtenstein radar, but the tests were not successful and the idea dropped.

Rudolf Schonert, a determined young man, was made a Squadron Commander in 1942, and he and his armourer, a corporal called Paul Mahle ignored the ridicule and fitted a pair of upward-firing 20mm cannons to the Squadron's Me110s. Experiments were carried out by the Luftwaffe weapons testing centre at Tarnewitz for the rest of the year, and an angle of between 60 and 75° was thought to give best results.

Schonert used this aircraft to shoot down a bomber in May 1943, months before the officially recognised introduction of Schräge Musik – German slang for Jazz Music – at Peenemunde on 17 August. From June 1943 an official Schräge Musik conversion kit was produced for the night-fighters. The upward-firing cannon spread across all the Luftwaffe night-fighter squadrons by the end of 1943, but for some curious reason it was not picked up by British Intelligence. This was partially because German night-fighters shot down by Mosquito intruders were falling in occupied Europe. By 1944 a third of all German night-fighters carried upward-firing guns, their gun-sights modified to allow the reflector to be placed above the pilot's head, while the sight itself was further to the rear. Some of them, such as those fitted to the He219, used the very powerful 30mm cannon. Just one shell from a range of less than 100ft (30.5), virtually a certain hit (in Lancasters, we must have looked as big as a barn door) could easily be fatal.

There were different configurations for Schräge Musik, it wasn't as simple as just fitting a few angled-up cannon, usually MG 151/20 or MK 108. They were housed in the rear of the cockpit of the Me110, in the aft fuselage of the He219, and behind the cockpit of the Ju88 and Do217. On an Me110 the 20mm MG151 cannon carried 200 shells, while the 20mm MG FF cannon had 60-round drums, manually changed.

The cannon had varied angles to the aircraft's fuselage, mostly between 70° and 78°. Some Ju88s had a pair of monster 30mm MK108 cannons, each fed by a large 180-round tank, angled at either 65° or 72°.

It was important to attack undetected so tracers were not used. Special ammunition with a faint glowing trail replaced them, and the guns were given flash reducers. The attack from below had the advantage that the night-fighter crew could identify the silhouette of the aircraft before they attacked. At the same time the bomber crew could not see the night-fighter against the dark ground, nor defend itself.

Belly turrets had been experimented with on British bombers, but had been removed to reduce drag and because of their limited effectiveness. The night-fighter usually aimed for the fuel tanks in the Lancaster's left wing, not for the fuselage, because of the risk that exploding bombs would damage the attacker. One other advantage of Schräge Musik was that it did not blind the pilot in the way that forward-firing guns did.

Last Witness Desmond Selley DFC, then 21 years old and a pilot with 156 Pathfinder Squadron, was the recipient of one of these attacks:

'We were on a diversionary raid on 13 February 1945. The idea was to take the fighters off the main raid that night. We must have been rather successful, because we were bombing a munitions factory – not far from Cologne – and were actually on our bombing run at 18,000ft (5,940m) when an Me110 got underneath us with Schräge Musik guns. The

ROLLS-ROYCE MERLIN II
First produced in 1937

More than 150,000 Rolls Royce Merlin engines were built, to be used in aircraft as diverse as the Spitfire, Hurricane, Mustang, Mosquito, Halifax and Lancaster. Initially the 27-litre engine developed 1,000 hp, but by the end of the war that had increased to 1,600 hp.

Lancaster being loaded with mines for a mine-laying operation known as 'Gardening'. Parachutes at one end of the mines opened as they were dropped over the sea. Note the Avro Manchester in background.

Lancasters of 44 Squadron, based at Waddington, Lincolnshire, pictured in September 1942. They are flown by Sergeant Colin Watt, Royal Australian Air Force; Pilot Officer T G Hackney, who was later killed while serving with 83 Squadron; and Pilot Officer J D V S Stephens DFM, who was killed with his crew two nights later during a raid on Wismar.

Loading a 'cookie', a 4,000lb 'blockbuster' bomb, with no stabilising fins and a thin skin, designed to blow the roofs off buildings so that incendiaries dropped with them would cause fires. Some later 'cookies' weighed 12,000lbs and could only be carried by Lancasters.

Guy Gibson's 'Dambuster' Lancaster, G-George, fitted with Barnes Wallis's bouncing bomb for the Dams Raid. Note calliper arms that enabled Gibson's flight engineer Sgt John Pulford to start the bomb spinning before his Australian bomb aimer, F/O 'Spam' Spafford dropped it from 60ft.

Gerald Coulson's famous painting, now hanging in RAF College Cranwell, of the sinking of the *Tirpitz* on 12 November 1944. It was by chance that Coulson chose F-Fox – the author's Lancaster – as the central feature of the picture, dropping the 12,000lb Tallboy bomb.

The 'Grand Slam' Lancaster with no mid-upper or rear turret, fully strengthened main spar to carry the 22,000-pound bomb, strengthened undercarriage and bomb bay. The bomb was so expensive that, if not used in anger, it could not be jettisoned as there were so few of them. The girth of the bomb was so wide that the bomb-bay doors had to be taken off.

Alliot Verdon Roe, founder of the AVRO aircraft company that produced the Lancaster bomber, showing his dexterity on his eightieth birthday by riding a bicycle backwards. He lost two of his four sons serving with the RAF in the Second World War.

The crew of M-Mike immediately after landing in Sumburgh on 12 January 1945 following the Bergen raid. From left, navigator Jack Harrison, flight engineer Desmond 'Taffy' Phillips, the author/pilot, and bomb-aimer Frank Chance. Note the damage to the port fin after Heinz Orlowski's attack. M-Mike never flew again.

Oberleutnant Kurt Schulze, one of our Last Witnesses, was 23 in 1944 and Adjutant to 9 Staffel, III Gruppe, Jagdeschwader 5 (Fighter Wing), the 'Eismeerjaeger'. His unique story of why two of Germany's greatest fighter 'aces' – with 320 kills between them – did not shoot down the 617 and 9 Squadron Lancasters, on the third *Tirpitz* raid, is told in Chapter 19.

The Avro Lincoln, the larger, more powerful successor to the Lancaster. More than 600 were built, although it came too late for war service. It was the last piston-engined bomber ordered by the RAF. The author flew a Lincoln from England to Argentina in 1947, to deliver it to the Argentine Air Force.

Avro Lancastrian, civilian version of the Lancaster, fitted with two Rolls Royce Nene turbojets in October, 1945. In September, 1946 this aircraft made three flights carrying journalists to claim to be the 'first jet airliner'.

Pictured during one of ten refuellings to take place on 7 August 1949 over Bristol, Devon and Dungeness, one of Sir Alan Cobham's Flight Re-Fuelling Lancastrians (flown by Tom Marks) helps a Meteor 3 jet fighter (flown by Pat Hornidge) to become the first jet aircraft to make a non-stop flight of more than 12 hours (+1 minute!)

One of 30 Lancastrian 15-seat airliners delivered to BOAC in 1945. On a demonstration flight G-ALGF flew 13,500 miles from England to Auckland, NZ, in 3 days, 14 hours, at an average speed of 220 mph. Mostly suited for mail and VIP passengers, Lancastrians flew until the 1960s. The author flew this particular aicraft between the Middle East and the UK.

The Avro Shackleton, grandson of the Lancaster through the Avro Lincoln, was employed by the RAF on maritime reconnaissance. A total of 185 Shackletons, fitted with tricycle undercarriages, were built and served with the RAF and the South African Air Force. The last RAF Shackleton retired in 1990. It has been described as 'a hundred thousand rivets flying in close formation.'

The Battle of Britain Memorial Flight – Spitfire, Lancaster and Hurricane – over Buckingham Palace on 8 May, 2005, the 60th anniversary of the end of the war in Europe.

shells went right across our petrol tanks. Why he didn't hit any of our bombs remains a mystery. He set fire to our petrol tanks. I expected the aircraft to blow up so I told the crew to get out, which they did. We lost three, two through parachuting accidents.

'My rear gunner was killed in the aircraft, the mid-upper gunner panicked in the aircraft and opened the parachute before he jumped; the parachute caught on the tail-plane and he went down with it. I lost my navigator, but I don't think his parachute opened. He may not even have had one on as he went by me on his hands and knees, and I couldn't tell whether he had his parachute on.

'I was sitting on my parachute, and the Lancaster was going around in circles and in flames. When I left we may have been down to 10,000ft (3,300m). I understand that shortly after I left, it blew up. One of my crew who had already got out saw it go. I was lucky to get out. I had dived out of the forward hatch, hoping I would not be hit by anything. I know I counted to 10 before I pulled the rip-cord, and was not hit by falling debris.

'We were east of Cologne when we were shot down, and our armies were still west of Cologne. When I landed safely in a field – my first parachute jump – I bundled up my parachute and put it away. We had little compasses, and I started to walk west in the hope of joining up with our own forces. I walked that night, hid up the next day, and walked again the following night. I was caught then by two German soldiers, more or less asleep by the side of the road.

'When I got back from being a PoW I did go back to the squadron, just to see the ground crew. They were fed up with me for losing their aeroplane.'

The technique for using Schräge Musik meant the fighter had to formate under the aircraft it was attacking, outside of the cone of the Monica backward-looking radar. Luftwaffe pilots talked of being able to see the pale profiles of doomed young Lancaster airmen so close above them, straining into the night in their last few seconds of life. A two-second burst was nearly always enough. This had its dangers, and some fighters were destroyed by the bomber they had just attacked falling on top of them, or the bomb load exploding and destroying both aircraft. Normally bomber crews did not know what had hit them.

Last Witness David Fellowes was a 20-year-old rear gunner with 460 Squadron RAAF who had been so worried that he would not get to fight in the war if he took the 18-month course to qualify as a pilot (because the war would be over) that he signed on as an air-gunner. He was probably being set up for a Schräge Musik attack in 1945:

'On our ninth operation in January 1945, attacking Stuttgart in a Lancaster, we were jumped on the run-out past the target, when we had to fly straight and level and get a photo of the bombs exploding. It was very bright outside. The wireless/op had been looking out of the astrodome and had seen an FW-190 cruise over the top of us, going in our direction but faster. It was flying from port to starboard. I looked out on the port side because I thought something might be happening, and I think he saw us. I got the idea that he was directing a Ju88 on to us.

'As I swung around again, sure enough, we had a Ju88 right on our tail! We both opened fire on each other at much the same time. Our aircraft was hit badly by heavy and light machine-gun fire – fuel tanks pierced, holes in the fuselage, mid-upper gunner got hit in the neck (he survived) – but I hit the Ju88. We were sure, I put a claim in and I did find out subsequently that the Ju88 was destroyed, though I heard nothing more from the authorities.

'I knew I had hit it because all of a sudden it flipped right over on his side, on his wing-tips and fell straight down. I followed him in my gyro-gun-sight and saw no recovery. The combat took place at around 20,000ft (6,600m) and Ju88s had a three-man crew – pilot, wireless operator and gunner. It had all the radar junk on the nose of the aircraft. I saw his bullets whizzing past me and my bullets whizzing into him. The whole affair lasted only seconds, and I gave the order to "corkscrew port – go!" and then he fell away. We got back to our own base at Binbrook despite the damage, and landed safely.'

When it was introduced, Schräge Musik was not popular among older Luftwaffe pilots who had trained with, and become accustomed to, forward-firing guns. But young pilots liked it because kills were so certain, and they had often a young man's habit of opening fire too early with conventional guns, beyond their maximum range. This gave their position away and the RAF rear gunner got upset and fired back. Using Schräge Musik was also not all that easy, especially trying to draw a bead below a bomber taking evasive action such as corkscrewing. Schräge Musik proved to be most successful on the Ju88 G-6, which was both fast and nippy. One had to be quick and accurate to use this fearsome weapon.

Not getting away quickly enough killed one of the Luftwaffe's top scorers. Manfred Meurer, credited with 65 night kills, died on the night of 21 January 1944 when a Halifax bomber he had just attacked fell on his He219.

This almost happened to Last Witness Rolf Ebhardt, then 20 years old and operating an Me110 with Schräge Musik looking for his first kill:

'My first victory was shooting down a Lancaster on 26 April 1944, which I marked in my log book with a small RAF roundel. I must say we were not actually taught how to shoot down bombers at night. We were left alone to do it whatever way we could. The squadron leader told us occasionally – this was informally, in the officer's mess – do this, that and the other, but we were not taught formally. We had to find out ourselves. The more experienced pilots would talk about their techniques in the mess and we younger pilots would listen in. But of course, they were keen on maintaining their status as top scorers, so they never addressed us personally.

'They were interested in their own "scores" first, rather than teaching us. There were only a few commanders who really looked after the new flyers. Major Schonert who actually invented Schräge Musik, he was very good. But others were just the opposite, especially my commander – Major Prinz zur Lippe Weissenfeld, who had 51 kills – he was a very arrogant character and he would teach us nothing. We were learning by doing.

'Yet that night I forgot everything I learned. I just saw the target and went after it. I pulled the trigger myself.

'That Lancaster was detected by my wireless operator by radar, he came fairly quickly in the air. Our paths crossed, he was on my right side. I saw him for the first time when I looked up. I was about 100 yards away, the first time I had seen an enemy bomber at night. I was out of my mind with excitement, my first contact with the enemy monster above me.

'The only thing I knew about a Lancaster was where the fuel tanks were and where the rear gunner was. We did a lot of aircraft recognition, but it was only silhouettes on the ceiling. I think, on that first Lancaster, I had a direct hit on the bomb bay with two 30mm cannon. One 30mm cannon shell on the right spot was enough to kill a Lancaster anyway.

'I was shaking like hell.

'I positioned myself beneath his belly, with my Schräge Musik cannon pointing upwards – 30mm shells – and fired just two cannon shells.

'I had forgotten that he would still have his bombs on board and he exploded immediately, right above me.

'I was blinded by this white light and could not see anything except a large red point in front of my eyes. I was not able to react to my flying instruments and I dived away. My wireless operator took his torch and told me what my speed was and what the aircraft was doing. After five minutes I slowly started to see again, but it was still red spots . My target must have been a Pathfinder. There were lots of target indicator flares that dropped from it and fell to the ground, burning. It must have been on its way to bomb, because it would not have had that load on the way back.

'He would not have known what hit him.

'Of course, we were very excited with our first victory, and we went home almost immediately afterwards because our radio communication was gone. After we landed safely my mechanic came up to me and said, Herr Lieutenant, what have you done with your aeroplane? He showed me and we counted 69 holes from the explosion. The two biggest ones, left and right of me in the wings, next to the fuselage, were 2ft (70cm) across. I had been too excited to notice it. I had to have a new aeroplane.'

A myth grew up that the Germans had invented a new weapon to scare RAF pilots, and it was given the name Scarecrow. Bomber Command crews reported seeing tremendous explosions in the air, which happened suddenly with no flak or tracer. There was no evidence of a fight, just a quiet sky and then suddenly a huge explosion. German anti-aircraft guns were, it was said, using this device to pretend there were more bombers shot down than was actually happening. Sadly, there is no evidence that this story was true, and Scarecrows were usually evidence of German fighters using Schräge Musik with their non-tracer shells.

Freeman Dyson, a brilliant analyst who had joined Bomber Command in the Second World War at the age of 19, and – still alive in 2009 – has some pungent things to say about what he saw as faults in the Lancaster, confirmed the potency of Schräge Musik:

'It killed novice and expert crews impartially, a result that contradicted the official dogma that the more experienced you were, the more likely you were to survive a tour of operations. I blame the Operational Research Section to which I belonged, and I blame myself in particular, for not taking this result seriously enough... If we had taken the evidence more seriously, we might have discovered Schräge Musik in time to respond with effective countermeasures.'

The capture on 13 July 1944 of the Ju88 which landed at the RAF airfield in Woodbridge, Suffolk, was a killing blow to the Luftwaffe, and revealed secrets which had caused most of the serious Bomber Command losses. Examination of the aircraft revealed Germany's secret progress. New metal strips, called 'Rope' and not 'Window' were devised to confuse the SN-2 radar. Monica radar was removed from RAF aircraft, and soon afterwards H2S was restricted.

It was the first of four major losses by the Germans. The second loss was the formation of 100 Group, which consisted of 260 aircraft, the majority Mosquitoes, half of them jamming the German radar network, the other half harassing German night-fighters.

The third loss was the speed of the advance of the allies through France, causing a huge gap in the German radar net and severely reducing their early warning capacity.

Last Witness Rolf Ebhardt, was credited with eight kills in his Me110, four Lancasters and four Halifaxes, three of the latter in one night. This is his account of how Luftwaffe aircrew coped with their reverses:

'Unlike some of the portraits you see on the cinema screen about the last months of the war, there was not a lot of drinking being done. We behaved as soldiers, correctly. There was no Götterdämmerung. We didn't drink at all, but again, we had no time to drink. At night we were in a state of readiness, and in the day we had to sleep, especially in the winter time when readiness started at four o'clock in the afternoon. In contrast to your bomber crews, we had to fly every night with no exception.

'Morale was good. Of course, underneath, we expected to die, that fear was always present. Maybe we put it to the back of our minds and didn't think of it. At that time we knew the war was lost. That was a terrible thing for us, to know that whatever you do, there's no sense in it. You risk your life, you have to go up in terrible conditions, and sooner or later the war is over and we have lost. To know that every night to risk your life, that was not a good thing. For you British, you knew you would be the victors, there was sense in what you did, but we knew the war had gone down the drain. We did not speak about it, not even amongst the officers, everybody continued to do their duty. We knew what was coming, that it was terrible, and so we tried to act like good soldiers. If we spoke what we thought, that the war might be lost, we risked prosecution by the political state police, and we hoped till the bitter end that the Vengeance Weapons would turn the tide, as always promised by our political leaders.'

The fourth Luftwaffe loss, most serious of all, was that in June, July and August of 1944, day and night bombers concentrated on the German oil industry. Monthly production of aviation fuel slumped from 175,000 tons in April to 34,700 tons in July, 17,000 tons in August and to 7,000 tons in September. Luftwaffe consumption in April 1944 had been 165,000 tons. Harris had previously opposed the 'Oily Boys', those advocating sustained attacks against German oil targets, and felt he had been dragged into bombing oilfields rather than cities, but the oil offensive was very effective. As a result of the fuel starvation, priority was given to day fighter squadrons of the Luftwaffe, most bomber units were disbanded, aerial reconnaissance was limited, and the blitzkrieg operations in support of the German Army were only rarely permitted.

In the final seven months of the war the German night-fighter force was worn down.

In the whole of January 1945, Bomber Command carried out 25 major night attacks against targets in Germany, involving 6,572 sorties, and lost 99 aircraft to all causes, 1.4 per cent of the total. Despite the incredible success of 'Old Hands' like Schnaufer and Schoenert on individual raids in February, monthly Bomber Command losses would remain at this sustainable level until the end of the war. It was during this period that the last of the 10 Lancaster Victoria Crosses was won.

George Thompson, VC (posthumous) Flight Sgt RAFVR, wireless operator with 9 Squadron. 1 January 1945:

'This airman was the wireless operator in a Lancaster aircraft which attacked the Dortmund-Ems Canal in daylight. The bombs had just been released when a heavy shell hit the aircraft in front of the mid-upper turret. Fire broke out and dense smoke filled the fuselage. The nose of the aircraft was then hit and an inrush of air, clearing the smoke, revealed a scene of utter devastation. Most of the Perspex screen of the nose compartment had been shot away, gaping holes had been torn in the canopy above the pilot's head, the intercommunication wiring had severed, and there was a large hole in the floor of the aircraft. Bedding and other equipment were badly damaged or alight; one of the engines was on fire.

'Flight Sergeant Thompson saw that the gunner was unconscious in the blazing mid-upper turret. Without hesitation he went down the fuselage into the fire and the exploding ammunition. He pulled the gunner from his turret and, edging his way around the hole in the floor, carried him away from the flames. With his bare hands he extinguished the gunner's burning clothing. He himself sustained serious burns to his face, hands and legs.

'Flight Sergeant Thompson then noticed that the rear gun turret was also on fire. Despite his own severe injuries he moved painfully to the rear of the fuselage where he found the rear gunner with his clothing alight, overcome by flames and fumes. A second time Flight Sergeant Thompson braved the flames. With great difficulty he extricated the helpless gunner and carried him clear. Again, he used his bare hands, already burnt, to beat out the flames on his comrade's clothing.

'Flight Sergeant Thompson, by now almost fully exhausted, felt that his duty was not yet done. He must report the fate of the crew to the captain. He made the perilous journey back through the burning fuselage, clinging to the side with his burnt hands to get across the hole in the floor. The flow of cold air caused him intense pain and frostbite developed. So pitiful was his condition that the captain failed to recognise him. Still, his only concern was for the two gunners he had left in the rear of the aircraft. He was given such attention as was possible until a crash landing was made 40 minutes later.

'When the aircraft was hit, Flight Sergeant Thompson might have devoted his efforts to quelling the fire and so have contributed to his own safety. He preferred to go through the fire to succour his comrades. He knew that he would then be in no position to hear or heed any order which might be given to abandon the aircraft. He hazarded his own life in order to save the lives of others. Young in years and experience, his actions were those of a veteran.

'Flight Sergeant Thompson's Lancaster was successfully crash-landed at Grolder in Holland. The mid-upper gunner, Sergeant E.J.Potts, died almost immediately, while Flight Sergeant Thompson died on 23 January 1945 in a British Army hospital. The second gunner, Sgt 'Taffy' Price owes his life to the superb gallantry of Thompson.'

He was 24 years old.

The Germans could always bite, and not just individually. On 4 March 1945, more than 100 German night-fighters raced after 450 Lancasters, Halifaxes and Mosquitoes after they had bombed Kamen and Ladbergen, and shot down 20 RAF bombers over East Anglia. Twenty-seven RAF airfields in Norfolk, Suffolk, Lincolnshire and Yorkshire came under attack from cannons and small bombs.

As seven RAF bombers had been lost over Germany, we had a total loss that night of 27, the largest for several weeks, 6 per cent.

While they had the fuel and the ammunition to fly, the Luftwaffe continued to fight to the last day. Last Witness Rolf Ebhardt:

'We knew there was something terrible in front of us. But what it was exactly we didn't know. We knew, after that, after all the millions of deaths....what happened in the concentration camps, we didn't know anything about that. We knew the Allies would probably keep us down for years, even decades, that something terrible must come when it ends...'

CHAPTER SEVENTEEN

Last Year of the War and Special Ops

The year 1944 was when my personal relationship with the Lancaster bomber began, after I arrived back in Britain from an instructor's job in Rhodesia and went to Scotland. I was expecting to become a fighter pilot again, flying Spitfires as I had done so modestly in the Battle of Britain. But there was a much higher demand in 1944 for new bomber pilots, so I was persuaded to train as a pilot on Wellingtons then Stirlings and eventually Lancasters, expecting to form 49 Squadron.

The day I was clearing up my paperwork ahead of that posting I was asked to volunteer for 617 Squadron!

This was the first-ever invitation from such a prestigious squadron to a pilot without previous operational experience on bombers, it was at the personal invitation of the great Leonard Cheshire and without hesitation I said yes. My crew came with me and I was sent to 'A' Flight, where David Shannon, a squadron leader and my flight commander, greeted me thus: 'What are they sending us now? Bloody sprogs like you, never done a bombing trip? They'll have you for breakfast.'

He was 22 years old, I was 24, but he had a DSO and bar, and a DFC and bar, while I had just my single service ribbon. As I joined the squadron, Cheshire was stood down, as were the other 'originals' from the Dams Raid, Shannon himself, Joe McCarthy, Les Munro and Mick Martin. It was like that back then in the RAF. A bloke was there one day and gone the next, either dead or alive. If you were alive you didn't have a week of saying goodbye, you just went. Cheshire had done 100 operations and was soon awarded the Victoria Cross.

Geoffrey Leonard Cheshire, DSO and 2 bars, DFC, RAFVR, 617 Squadron.
8 September 1944:

'This officer began his operational career in June 1940. Against strongly defended targets, he soon displayed the courage and determination of an exceptional leader. He was always ready to accept extra risks to ensure success. Defying the formidable Ruhr defences, he frequently released his bombs from below 20,000ft (6,600m). Over Cologne in November

1940, a shell burst inside his aircraft, blowing out one side and starting a fire; undeterred, he went on to bomb the target. At about this time he carried out a number of convoy patrols in addition to his bombing sessions.

'At the end of his first tour of operational duty in January 1941, he immediately volunteered for a second. Again, he pressed home his attacks with the utmost gallantry. Berlin, Bremen, Duisberg, Essen and Keïl were among the heavily defended targets he attacked. When he was posted for instructional duties in January 1942, he undertook four more operational missions.

'He started his third tour in August 1942, when he was given command of a squadron. He led the squadron with outstanding skill on a number of missions before being appointed in March 1943, as a station commander.

'In October 1943, he undertook a fourth operational tour, relinquishing the rank of Group Captain at his own request so that he could take part in operations. He immediately set to work as the pioneer of a new method of marking enemy targets involving very low flying.

'In June 1944 when marking a target in the harbour of Le Havre in broad daylight and without cloud cover, he dived well below the range of the light batteries before releasing his marker bombs, and he came very near to being destroyed by the strong barrage which concentrated on him.

'During the fourth tour which ended in July 1944, Wing Commander Cheshire led his squadron personally on every occasion, always undertaking the most dangerous and difficult task of marking the target alone from a low level in the face of strong defences.

'Wing Commander Cheshire's cold and calculated acceptance of risks is exemplified by his conduct in an attack on Munich in April 1944. This was an experimental attack to test out the new method of marking at low level against a heavily-defended target situated deep in the Reich territory. Munich was selected, at Wing Commander Cheshire's request, because of the formidable nature of its light anti-aircraft and searchlight defences. He was obliged to follow, in bad weather, a direct route which took him over the defences of Augsburg and thereafter he was continuously under fire. As he reached the target, flares were being released from our high-flying aircraft. He was illuminated from above and below. All guns within range opened fire on him. Diving to 700ft (230m), he dropped his markers with great precision and began to climb away. So blinding were the searchlights that he almost lost control. He then flew over the city at 1,000ft (330m) to assess the accuracy of his work and direct other aircraft. His own aircraft was badly damaged by shell fragments but he continued to fly over the target area until he was satisfied that he had done all in his power to ensure success. Eventually, when he set course for base, the task of disengaging himself from the defences proved even more hazardous than the approach. For a full 12 minutes after leaving the target area he was under withering fire, but he came safely through.

'Wing Commander Cheshire has now completed a total of 100 missions. In four years of fighting against the bitterest opposition he has maintained a record of outstanding personal achievement, placing himself invariably in the forefront of the battle. What he did in the Munich operation was typical of the careful planning, brilliant execution and contempt for danger which has established for Wing Commander Cheshire a reputation second to none in Bomber Command.'

The new 617 Squadron commander was Wing Commander James Tait, known as 'Willie'. He already had three DSOs and a DFC. I over-lapped with the 'originals' over 10 days or so. It was the first time I met those men, some of whom were to become my friends for life. I was a new boy, not part of their inner circle, but there was no problem. I had my time in 617 ahead of me to earn whatever reputation I could, while that time was behind them.

The nature of the air war changed in its final year. Lancasters were now the dominant British heavy bomber, Harris running 51 squadrons and a total of 1,191 Lancasters on operational strength. He directed his forces at targets in France in the lead up to the Invasion in June 1944, in which precise locations were aimed at and mostly hit. There was the constant risk of killing French civilians and one very unpopular policy was ordered. Last Witness Tony Hiscock, pilot, 156 Pathfinder Squadron:

'There was a great outcry when Harris decided, or Bomber Command decided that, compared to Germany where 30 operations was enough for a tour, bombing German-occupied France was 'easier' and so each operation was worth a third of a trip to Germany. They seemed to forget that the Germans were still shooting at us. France could be more difficult because, whereas over a German city, going in with Oboe to guide us, even if we didn't actually hit the target we were hitting something German. In France, if we were going for marshalling yards, we didn't want to kill civilians and we had to be a great deal more accurate. They scrapped the whole idea after the outcry, but I remember how furious we were about it.'

The huge raids to pound German cities into rubble were much less frequent in the summer months, but Germany was re-targeted with new vigour in the late autumn, though Harris had kept paying enough visits to his familiar targets to ensure the fighter forces assembled there did not all pack up and head West to contribute more closely to stopping the Allies spreading out from their Normandy bridgeheads. It was during this build-up that another Victoria Cross was won by a Lancaster crewman.
Norman Cyril Jackson, Sgt, 106 Squadron, RAFVR. 26 April 1944:

'This airman was the flight engineer in a Lancaster detailed to attack Schweinfurt. Bombs were dropped successfully and the aircraft was climbing out of the target area. Suddenly it was attacked by a fighter at 20,000ft (6,600m). The captain,

Flying Officer Fred Mifflin, took evading action at once, but the enemy secured many hits. A fire started near the petrol tank on the upper surface of the starboard wing, between the fuselage and the inner engine. Sgt Jackson was thrown to the floor during the engagement; wounds which he received from shell splinters in the right leg and shoulder were probably sustained at that time. Recovering himself, he remarked that he could deal with the fire on the wing and obtained Mifflin's permission to try and put out the flames.

'Pushing a hand fire extinguisher into the top of his life-saving jacket and clipping on his parachute pack, Sgt Jackson jettisoned the escape hatch about the pilot's head. He then started to climb out of the cockpit and back along the top of the fuselage to the starboard wing. Before he could leave the fuselage his parachute pack opened and the whole canopy and rigging lines spilled into the cockpit. Undeterred, Sgt Jackson continued. The pilot, bomb aimer and navigator gathered the parachute together and held on to the rigging lines, paying them out as Jackson crawled aft. Eventually he slipped and, falling from the fuselage to the starboard wing, grasped an air intake on the leading edge. He succeeded in clinging on but lost the extinguisher, which was blown away in the 240mph air-stream.

'By this time the fire had spread rapidly, and Sgt Jackson's face, hands and clothing were severely burnt. Unable to retain his hold he was swept through the flames and over the trailing edge of the wing, dragging his parachute behind him. When last seen it was only partly inflated and burning in a number of places. Realising that the fire could not be controlled, the captain gave the order to abandon the aircraft. Four of the remaining members of the crew baled out and landed safely. Fred Mifflin, and rear gunner, Flight Sgt Hugh Johnson, have not been accounted for.

'Sergeant Jackson was unable to control his descent and landed heavily. He sustained a broken ankle, his right eye was closed through burns and his hands were useless. These injuries, together with the wounds received earlier, reduced him to a pitiable state. At daybreak he crawled to the nearest village, where he was taken prisoner... (he later escaped and reached the oncoming American lines!)

'This airman's attempt to extinguish the fire and save the aircraft and its crew from falling into enemy hands was an act of outstanding gallantry. To venture outside, when travelling at 200 miles an hour, at a great height and in intense cold, was an almost incredible feat. Had he succeeded in subduing the flames, there was little or no prospect of his gaining the cockpit. The spilling of his parachute and the risk of grave damage to its canopy reduced his chances of survival to a minimum. By his ready willingness to face these dangers he set an example of self-sacrifice which will ever be remembered'.

Bomber Command pilots were required to hit five principal targets in support of the Normandy Invasion forces. These were V-1 'buzz-bomb' and V-2 rocket sites; road, rail and canal communication, including that fateful deadly target the Dortmund-Ems Canal; fuel depots; German troops and armour, including the

'Das Reich' Division of Panzer tanks struggling up from the South of France; and designated military targets called for by commanders on the ground. People were beginning to believe there was hope of winning the war in a finite time, but great sacrifices were still demanded.

Andrew Charles Mynarski, (Posthumous VC) Pilot Officer, RCAF, 419 Squadron. 12/13 June, 1944:

'Pilot Officer Mynarski was the mid-upper gunner of a Lancaster aircraft, detailed to attack a target at Cambrai in France. The aircraft was attacked from below and astern by an enemy fighter and ultimately came down in flames. As an immediate result of the attack, both port engines failed. Fire broke out between the mid-upper turret and the rear turret, as well as in the port wing. The flames soon became fierce and the Captain ordered the crew to abandon the aircraft. Mynarski left his turret and went towards the escape hatch. He then saw that the rear gunner was still in his turret and apparently unable to leave it. The turret was, in fact, immovable, since the hydraulic gear had been put out of action when the port engines failed and the manual gear had been broken by the gunner in his attempts to escape. Without hesitation, Mynarski made his way through the flames in an endeavour to reach the rear turret and release the gunner. Whilst doing so, his parachute and his clothing up to his waist were set on fire. All his efforts to move the turret and release the gunner were in vain. Eventually the rear gunner indicated to him that there was nothing more he could do and he should try and save his own life. Mynarski reluctantly went back through the flames to the escape hatch. There, as a last gesture to the trapped gunner, he turned towards him, stood to attention in his flaming clothing and saluted before he jumped out of the aircraft. Mynarski's descent was seen by French people on the ground. Both his parachute and his clothing were on fire. He was found eventually by the French but was so severely burnt that he died from his injuries. The rear gunner, George Brophy, had a miraculous escape when the aircraft crashed, and was able to evade capture and return to his unit. Brophy subsequently testified that, had Mynarski not attempted to save his comrade's life, he could have left the aircraft in safety and would doubtless have escaped death. Mynarski must have been fully aware that in trying to free the rear gunner he was almost certain to lose his own life. Despite this, with outstanding courage and complete disregard for his own safety, he went to the rescue.'

Lancasters were pouring off the production lines in their thousands. Vickers Armstrong had an order for 200 Lancaster Mark IIs – with the radial engine – changed to Mark IIIs on 13 February 1943. Deliveries started in December 1943 and were completed in February 1945. Avro itself had an order for 550 Lancasters, starting in June 1943 and ending in December that year. Victory Aircraft in Canada started a production run of 300 Lancaster X's in September 1943, and at about four a week, rolled on to March 1945. This production has fewer of the terrible list of 'Missing', 'Missing', 'Missing', which characterised the fate of the big Avro order in Manchester of 550 Lancasters thrown into the Battle of Berlin. More Lancasters were getting through to the end of the war. It was, as ever, a matter of good luck.

I was lucky to go to 617 Squadron, despite dark rumours about it being a 'Suicide Squadron.' Of the other 13 pilots with me at Lancaster Finishing School, the only other one left with me at the end of the war was Bob Walker, of 49 Squadron. All the others in that last year were shot down, either killed or missing or prisoners of war. In Main Force at that time of the war, the opposition was really very tough.

I did a 'second dicky' operation on 31 July, 1944 with John Williams – he went on in later life to become a priest – attacking Rilly La Montagne, near Rheims. My crew found individual 'second dicky' places with other 617 aircraft, just to get the feel of it. That was the operation when one of the rare living VCs, Bill Reid, now with 617, flying at 12,000ft, had his aircraft hit by bombs dropped from a Main Force bomber above him at 18,000ft (5,940m). Bill got out safely, as did only one of his crew, to be captured by the Germans and survive the war.

Last Witness John Langston was a 19-year-old sergeant navigator with 630 Lancaster Squadron at East Kirkby, whose first operation was in the middle of 1944:

> 'We used to come home with all sorts of holes in the Lancaster, particularly when we were doing Main Force trips. We did Munich twice, Stuttgart twice, we did Damstadt, all long-distance penetrations, lots of aeroplanes, 500/600 aeroplanes on the target at the time. You were as scared about the bombs on the aircraft above you hitting you, as you were about the Germans. On one operation, a Pas de Calais run on the buzz-bomb sites, when we got back our ground crew counted 400 holes in our Lancaster and then gave up counting. This was flak damage. On another trip to the same area we actually watched a bomb go through the wing of a Lancaster in front of us. It just folded up and went down. Also in daylight, a raid on buzz-bomb sites, the mid-upper gunner went, "Christ!" A bomb had dropped between our main-plane and tail-plane, just came down beside us from the chap on top.'

The threat to shipping in the English Channel from E-boats, and the Atlantic from U-Boats, was another priority. U-Boat pens had huge concrete roofs, thought to be impervious to bombing, but not to Tallboys or to the Grand Slams that 617 Squadron used.

In Le Havre on 14 June two waves of Lancasters attacked the E-Boat facilities in two waves, led in by 22 Lancasters of 617 Squadron with 3 Mosquito marker aircraft. There were several hits on the pens and one bomb penetrated the roof.

On 15 June, 297 aircraft, including 155 Lancasters attacked Boulogne harbour. A French report described the great destruction as the worst raid on Boulogne.

On 5 August 1944, I was the pilot of one of 15 Lancasters of 617 Squadron attacking the U-boat pens at Brest. We scored six direct hits with Tallboys, penetrating the concrete roofs. Subsequent attempts to reinforce other sites with even thicker concrete diverted resources from other projects. One of our Lancasters was shot down by flak. The Canadian pilot, Don Cheney, and three of his crew baled out safely and evaded capture.

We had a number of operations that month against U-Boat pens at Brest, Lorient, La Palice, and St Nazaire on the west coast of France. We intended to give the U-Boat people a hard time, and to drive them out. If they couldn't stay in France, they would have to head back to German bases, which would mean either travelling around the north of Scotland or through the English Channel when they set out for their Atlantic hunting grounds. Either way it made for a much longer and more difficult trip, with better chances of being intercepted than if they operated off the west coast of France. The German submariners held out on their own in that part of France for some time after the Invasion, when the Allies broke out of the Normandy bridgehead. The Americans by-passed them and moved eastwards, and were quite happy to sit outside and besiege these places rather than put in a frontal assault.

The Germans capitulated in Cherbourg and its peninsula on 26 June and I remember seeing a photograph in the *Illustrated London News* of an American officer inside one of the U-Boat pens. He was looking up at a big hole, and all the concrete reinforcement was hanging down as a result of one of our attacks.

Most of the bombing I did with 617 was daylight, rather than the common Bomber Command practice of night bombing. It was the way one part of the war was going attacking the specific targets they gave us. We could be far more accurate by day. The target did not have to be marked, and we used SABS – the Stabilised Automatic Bomb Sight – which marked out the difference in accuracy between those few squadrons, like 617, which had SABS, and other squadrons, such as 9 Squadron, which had to make do with the Mark XIV bomb-sight.

Last Witness John Bell had hands-on experience using SABS as bomb aimer to Bobby Knights, a pilot with 617 Squadron:

'SABS had been in existence since late 1942, but it was in very limited supply because it was hand-made. SABS worked by computing various information, height, aircraft speed, allowing for the wind, temperature, some aspects of what type of bomb you were dropping. There was a disc that you inserted into the bomb sight. It was electrical. Once you set off on the bombing run, which was long, about five minutes, it was a bit hazardous. You got the target in sight, switched on, and there was a graticle which hopefully would stay pointing at the target all the time in the last minute of the bombing run.

'The pilot couldn't see the target over the nose of the Lancaster, so he responded to my instructions. These were "left, left", and "right", or "steady". We always said "left" twice, and "right" once, so even if pilots couldn't hear exactly because of the noise or the flak, they knew two words meant left and one word meant right. The pilot had an instrument in front of him which gave him some idea of the attitude of the aircraft. He could call off the bombing run if he felt it was not accurate enough. The aircraft had to be stable and not slipping sideways. Everything was pertinent. The pilot had to watch his turn and bank indicator, and his artificial horizon, and maintain a steady course with the wings level. Everything had to be absolutely stable when the bomb dropped. The only two people talking to each other during this period were the pilot and the bomb aimer, a combined effort.

'SABS actually released the bomb. The bomb-aimer did not physically press a button. It was a set of electrical contacts. It was always the case that after dropping a bomb, the aircraft had to maintain a steady course for at least eight seconds to capture the photograph of the bomb exploding, though taking the photo was always automatic. The bomb-aimer did not actually release the bomb and then eight seconds later take the photograph. It was all part of the same sequence.

'The issue of flying straight and level to take the photograph was uniform throughout the RAF, regardless of the bomb sight used. If you put any bank on, you would be looking at something that was not the target area.'

We needed that accuracy from the Spring of 1944, not only for precision attacks on Invasion targets in France, where there was constant concern not to kill innocent French men and women, but also to cope with the three main 'Vengeance' weapons that Hitler had promised the German people he would let loose on Britain. Despite the sacrifices made attacking Peenemunde in August 1943, the Germans had succeeded in creating what was, effectively, the first 'Cruise Missile', and had set up sites to launch them at England, initially from fixed sites, but when the RAF bombed them, then mobile sites. Hitler authorised the first attacks in the same month as the Normandy Invasion.

The V-1 Doodlebug

Buzz-bombs, or Doodlebugs as the V-1 came to be known, were 25ft (7.6) long with stubby wings and a pulse-jet engine, capable of carrying a one-ton bomb. They were launched by catapult from sites in northern France along rails 165ft (50m) long; some were later launched from aircraft. Created by the same people who built the STOL Storch aircraft – Fieseler Flugzeugbau – they had enough thrust to fly at 400mph as they passed overhead, making a very distinctive sound.

They usually flew at between 2,000 and 3,000ft (914m), too high for light guns, two low for heavy flak guns. Doodlebugs spent an average of 22 minutes in the air, and were all targeted at Tower Bridge, considered the centre of the capital. Londoners nervously learned to live with them, recognising that, after the engine cut out, there was usually less than a minute to find shelter as the Doodlebug went into a steep dive, hit the ground and exploded.

In the nine months between June 1944 and 29 March 1945, a total of 9,251 V-1 flying bombs were launched against England. Just over a quarter of them, 2,419, made it to their intended targets in Greater London. RAF fighters, including Hawker Tempests, Mosquitoes and even the Gloster Meteor Jet were sent up to knock them down. Spitfire pilots with clipped wings and Griffon engines for greater speed learned that placing the wing tip of their fighter plane underneath the V1's outer wing would often upset the missile, tumble the gyros, and send it crashing out of control into the English countryside. Between June and September 1944, one Tempest wing shot down 638 flying bombs, with No 3 Squadron claiming 305. A Tempest pilot, Squadron Leader Joseph Berry shot down 59 V-1s, and Wing Commander Roland Beaumont destroyed 31. Next most successful at knocking them out of the air were the Mosquito (428), Spitfire XIV (303), and Mustang (232).

In all more than 2,000 of them were shot down or knocked off course by the RAF. An additional 1,971 V1's were shot down by anti-aircraft guns and 278 were snagged by barrage balloons that dotted the approach paths to the south of London. An estimated 6,184 people were killed by these flying bombs even though, by August 1944, only 20 per cent were reaching England.

Robert Owen specialises in 617 Squadron history:

> 'It was Leonard Cheshire and Mick Martin at 617 who pioneered the use of low-level marking using Lancasters which was then adopted within 5 Group and taken over by 627 Squadron, to hit V-weapons. Cheshire and Martin later moved on to faster and more manoeuvrable aircraft, Mosquitoes and even the Mustang. Their pioneering work on Lancasters set the scene and created the template which 5 Group used, in modified form, for marking targets for the rest of the war.
>
> 'Initially, in attacking targets in occupied territory, it saved civilian lives, because the brief there was to knock out a centre of industry or a weapons launching site, and the industrial targets were surrounded by worker's homes. In the run-up to D-Day we were looking at transportation targets, marshalling yards such as the two in Paris at La Chapelle and Juvisy, surrounded by tenement blocks and city dwellings. Precision was absolutely key to accurate marking, and the only way you could mark accurately was at low level. That process was pioneered and developed by Cheshire and the marker section of 617.'

Barnes Wallis's huge Tallboy five-ton bomb was used by 617 Lancaster Squadron attacking 'Vengeance' sites in France. The bombs were very expensive, and used against high-value targets which could not be destroyed by other means. Cheshire led the squadron against the Saumur rail tunnel, to block the movement by rail of panzer divisions coming up from the south of France. Nineteen Tallboy-equipped, and six conventionally-equipped Lancasters of 617 Squadron, attacked on the night of 8/9 June 1944. This was the first use of the Tallboy bomb and the line was destroyed – one Tallboy bored through the hillside and exploded in the tunnel about 60ft below, completely blocking it. No aircraft were lost during the raid.

There was an attack on the Le Blockhaus bunker system on 19 June, and the nearest Tallboy dropped by 617 Squadron landed 50 yards from the target, causing a minor earthquake The bunker was rendered useless.

There was the same effect on 24 June at Wizernes, where several Tallboy hits undermined the foundations but did not penetrate the dome. The bunker was abandoned. The following day the bunkers of Siracourt were subject to three direct hits from Tallboys dropped by 617 Squadron.

On 4 July at St-Leu-d'Esserent 17 Lancasters, 1 Mosquito and 1 Mustang – Cheshire really got to like that Mustang, as I did later – from 617 Squadron used Tallboys in an attempt to collapse the limestone roof of the caves used as a storage dump for V-1s. There was one direct hit, destroying the railway line and sealing the cave entrance, trapping an estimated 800 Germans buried there. This attack was followed up by 5 Group Main Force Lancasters' 1,000lb bombs.

Mimoyecques was hit on 6 July and Wizernes on 17 July, the latter by 16 Lancasters, 1 Mosquito and the Mustang; three Lancasters managed to drop Tallboys, one causing the dome to shift out of alignment, two others blocked the entrance. On 27 July one 617 Squadron Tallboy hit Le Blockhaus but did not penetrate. Canadian ground forces captured it in September.

Sir Arthur Harris claimed that his men had bombed the first launch sites so effectively that the Germans had to abandon them:

> 'It was hopeless of them to rely on anything vulnerable to bombing, especially at so short a distance from bases in England. The bombing of the French railways also had a profound effect on the V-weapons campaign and made largely ineffective the new dispersed sites which sprang up all over the Pas de Calais. When the bombs were eventually launched, the enemy's supply system was thoroughly disorganised and the new sites were ill-adapted to the rapid launching of bombs. Instead of an average of 6,000 flying bombs, the enemy was only able to launch an average of 95 a day between the middle of June and the end of August. Of these only two-thirds made landfall and less than one-third reached Greater London after encountering the fighters and anti-aircraft defences of Southern England. Judge what a bombardment more than 60 times as heavy would have been like!'

The V-2 Rocket

The Germans' V-2 rocket bomb was first used against England on 8 September 1944. The only known defence for a weapon that travelled at four times the speed of sound, and was effectively the first spacecraft, was to bomb everywhere the RAF could find it. Harris sent his Lancasters to target its research laboratories, its production factories, its storehouses, its launch sites, and if he could find them personally in any cluster, its boffins. Two of the boffins they really wanted to take out were Werner von Braun and Walter Riedel, who had lobbied Hitler for money for rocket science in 1936. By 1941, at their base in Peenemunde, they were confident they had solved the three big problems with rockets; coping with supersonic speed, how to guide a rocket, and the method of control.

Hitler did not focus on rockets at that time – he was winning with conventional weapons – and saw a rocket as merely a giant artillery shell. But as the tide of war turned and, having survived the von Stauffenburg assassination attempt on 20 July 1944, he gave the go-ahead for the V-2 attacks.

The Peenemunde Raid in August 1943, had done some damage to German rocket research and put back the rocket programme by up to eight weeks. It also made the Germans move their rocket research to Mittelwerk in Nordhausen, in what was to become East Germany after the war. Two test launches were recovered by the Allies, one by the Polish Resistance on 30 May, 1944, and smuggled to England, the other the so-called Backebo Bomb in Sweden on 13 June, 1944.

The rockets were built by slave labour at the Mittelbau-Dora concentration camp – 20,000 inmates died in their construction, more than 9,000 from exhaustion, while 350 were hanged (including a brave 200 for sabotage) and the remainder shot or died from disease and starvation.

V-2 production:
Up to Sept 1944 – 1,900
15 Sept to 29 Oct, 1944 – 900
29 Oct – 24 Nov 1944 – 600
24 Nov to 15 Jan, 1945 – 1,100
15 Jan to 15 Feb 1945 – 700
Total: 5,200

Because of the ferocity of the bombing attacks on German bunkers housing the V-2 rockets in northwest France, fixed firing sites were dropped in favour of mobile launches. Four main storage dumps had been completed by July 1944, but the missile could be launched practically anywhere, roads running through forests being a particular favourite. The system was so mobile and small that not one 'Meillerwagen' was caught in action by Allied aircraft.

An average of 10 V-2s were reported to have been launched per day, and the capacity existed to launch up to 1,000 V-2s per month, given sufficient supply of the rockets.

On 29 August 1944, Adolf Hitler gave the order for V-2 rocket attacks on London to begin after 5 September. The first landed in Chiswick and killed 63-year-old Mrs Ada Harrison, 3-year old Rosemary Clarke and Sapper Bernard Browning, on leave from the Royal Engineers. The rocket attacks were hushed up. Unlike the Doodlebugs, the public did not see the V-2 coming. The massive explosions in their midst were something of a mystery. The Germans went public on 8 November. Two days later, Churchill confirmed that England had been under rocket attack 'for the last few weeks.'

Over the next few months the number of V-2s fired was at least 3,172. London was hit by 1,358; Norwich by 43, Ipswich by one. A further 1,740 were dropped on towns and cities on the Continent, with Antwerp the main target. The final two V-2s exploded in England on 27 March 1945, and the last British civilian killed was 34-year-old Mrs Ivy Millichamp in her home in Elm Grove, Orpington in south east London.

An estimated 2,754 civilians were killed in London by V-2 attacks with another 6,523 injured. Many of the early V-2s missed London and exploded in the countryside, but later V-2s were much more accurate. The only sound defence was to destroy the launch infrastructure, which could be expensive on Lancasters. The Allied advance ultimately forced the launchers back beyond range.

The V-3 'London Gun'

The third 'Vengeance' weapon, the V-3, was a giant cannon designed to fire shells from its site in the Pas de Calais across the English Channel and hit London. It consisted of three bunkers near the village of Mimoyecques buried under a slab of reinforced concrete 20ft (6.6m) thick, each bunker with a shaft holding five barrels side by side, and each barrel 500ft (165m) long. Because of its target it was known colloquially as the 'London Gun', and the Germans wanted to use it to pour 600 tons of explosive a day into London. As a comparison, this would in a fortnight put as much tonnage of explosive into London as RAF Bomber Command dropped on Berlin in the whole war – Vengeance indeed.

Before it became operational, the V3 was destroyed by 617 Squadron. On 6 July, about three weeks before I flew my first operation with the squadron, specially modified Lancasters dropped several 12,000lb Tallboy bombs on it. One of the Tallboys ripped a corner off the 20ft (6m) thick concrete roof and completely blocked one of the gun shafts. A near-miss collapsed another shaft and made the third shaft unfit to use.

For the rest of the war 617 Squadron was devoted exclusively to specific targets, acting individually as a squadron rather than joining massed raids of 600 Lancasters. We were given special weapons, the 12,000lb Tallboy bomb, which we shared with one other unit, 9 Squadron. Barnes Wallis's 'Grand Slam' bomb, a whopping 22,000lbs, was exclusive to 617. They were used against targets that otherwise would have remained untouched and yet were vital to the war effort. Tallboys were used against U-Boat pens in particular, and against the *Tirpitz*. 'Grand Slam' bombs were used for the first time by 617 Squadron against the Bielefeld and Amsberg viaducts.

Last Witness John Langston was a navigator on 617 Squadron with experience of flying twice with 'Grand Slam' bombs:

'On a long journey carrying a Grand Slam bomb, we didn't have any armament. They took two guns out of the rear turret and most of the ammunition, took the mid-upper out and all its ammunition, the nose-turret and all the ammunition, no H2S or radar, even no wireless sets. All we had were three VHF sets, we didn't even have a wireless operator. One VHF was to work the fighter frequencies, one the bomber control frequency, and one was listening for air traffic control for take-off and return. So we had a crew of a rear gunner, a bomb aimer, flight engineer, pilot and navigator.

'The "Grand Slam" Lancaster was a unique aeroplane. We only got them right at the end of the war. They had a fully strengthened beam on the main spar in order to take the weight of the bomb itself – 22,000lbs – and it had a strengthened Lincoln undercarriage – the Lincoln, direct successor to the Lancaster, was just coming in to service. Another reason for the strengthened undercarriage was that the bomb was so expensive that, if not used in anger, it could not be jettisoned; there were so few of them. We also had a strengthened bomb bay. The girth of the Grand Slam bomb was too wide for the aeroplane so the bomb doors were taken off.

'When we flew back we were virtually naked.

'We had the most powerful version of the Merlin engine at that time. At take-off we needed the full run of Woodhall Spa runway, and were allowed an extra 10 seconds of boost. Once we lifted off, the flight engineer was keen to throttle back because he did not want to burn out the engines.

'The weight of the bomb gave a dihedral to the aeroplane which it did not normally have on the ground. In flight the dihedral was noticeable, the wings really bent upwards. Once you released the bomb the wings went back to normal position and the aircraft leapt up.

'Only 41 Grand Slams were dropped in total and they were all daylight operations. You couldn't have dropped a Grand Slam at night because you wouldn't get the precision run on to the target. Going for precision targets like bridges and viaducts, we needed daylight. Yet you did not have to be completely accurate with the Grand Slam. That was the joy of it, you just had to be somewhere close. The only person who could see where the bombs were actually going was the bomb aimer, who could follow it down.'

Hamburg was bombed regularly up to the last three weeks of the war as a centre of U-Boat construction, including a big raid by 469 aircraft, mostly Lancasters, at the end of March1945, during which German fighters shot down 11 bombers.

One of the last raids was on 9 April 1945, when a force of 57 Lancasters from 5 Group struck, with 40 Lancasters attacking oil-storage tanks, and 17 Lancasters from 617 Squadron hitting the U-boat shelters with Grand Slam bombs and Tall-boys. Two Lancasters were lost from the raid on the oil tanks. Last Witness Flight Lieutenant Benny Goodman, pilot 617 Squadron:

'That was when we had a very strange close shave. We bombed Hamburg and it was the only time we had a hang-up, which meant that our bomb didn't release immediately, despite heated release hooks. So our bomb went into the workers' houses around the port area. There was nothing we could do about it once we pressed the tit, that was it, and that was significant afterwards for this reason.

'We left the target and on the way back, Jock, my flight engineer, he never spoke in the cockpit, never, but this time he nudged me. Having another pair of eyes over the Fatherland was very useful. Jock nudged me and cast his eyes to the right without saying anything. I looked. There was an Me262 jet fighter in close formation with us!

'I nearly had the shits. Don't ask me what he was doing. I think he had run out of ammunition, and he was curious about us. He stayed there, neither of us made a signal, and the gunners couldn't shoot at him, there was no mid-upper turret anyway.

'I thought, is this it? The wireless/op looked and he felt the same way. We thought of doing a corkscrew, but we didn't. The other Lancasters were around but they weren't close. Then I thought, "Christ, they've told him that our bomb has dropped on the dockers' houses in Hamburg, and he's come to shoot the shit out of us."

'What he did, he just broke off. He could have opened up at a thousand yards because our harmonisation range was 400 yards, and he had a big cannon. Absolutely weird.

'I did report it, and they just said, jolly interesting, and that was that.'

Dresden

The most controversial British bomber raid of the war was the attack on Dresden on 13 February 1945, for which 'Bomber' Harris has been loaded with blame and which has in turn been dropped on to the shoulders of my generation of young men, who carried out the operation. There was some deft footwork by politicians afterwards – including Winston Churchill – to imply that it was 'nufink to do with me, guv,' but Harris was too honest and blunt to dodge this issue.

For the RAF aircrew themselves it was just one more mission, although one in which Luftwaffe fighter attacks were lighter than elsewhere. At the time, in the second half of January 1945, Russian forces had made a rapid advance across Poland and into the eastern frontier of Germany. The Germans were fighting hard on two fronts inside their own territory, but the situation in the East was particularly critical. The Allies, as a whole, considered Berlin, Dresden, Leipzig and Chemnitz, all threatened by the Russians, as suitable targets. They were vital communications and supply centres, and no one wanted the Germans moving reinforcements from the West to face the successful Russian advance.

At the Yalta Conference involving Stalin, Roosevelt and Churchill on 4 February, the Russians asked for attacks of this type to take place. RAF Bomber Command was specifically requested by the Air Ministry, with Churchill's encouragement, to carry out heavy raids on Dresden, Chemnitz and Leipzig. The Americans were also asked to help and agreed to do so.

Dresden was the largest German city not to be bombed up to that time, and its population of 650,000 had been swelled by refugees. The campaign should have begun with an American raid on Dresden on 13 February but bad weather over Europe prevented it, so the RAF carried out the first raid.

A force of 796 Lancasters and 9 Mosquitoes was sent in two separate raids. They dropped 1,478 tons of high explosive and 1,182 tons of incendiary bombs. The first attack was carried out entirely by 5 Group, using our own low-level mark-ing methods. The raid, in which 244 Lancasters dropped more than 800 tons of bombs, was only moderately successful.

The second raid three hours later was an all-Lancaster attack by aircraft of all the other RAF Groups. The weather, cloudy before, was now clear and 529 Lancas-ters dropped more than 1,800 tons of bombs with great accuracy.

Much has been written about the fearful effects of this raid. A firestorm similar to the one experienced in Hamburg in July 1943 – and Coventry in November 1940 – was created and large areas of the city were burnt out.

Six Lancasters were lost in the attack, two more crashed in France and one back at home in England.

The USAAF sent 311 B-17s to drop 771 tons of bombs on Dresden the next day, with the railway yards as their aiming point. Part of the American Mustang fighter escort was ordered to strafe traffic on the roads around Dresden to increase chaos and disruption. The Americans bombed Dresden again on 2 March, although it is generally accepted that it was the RAF night raid that caused the most serious damage.

Flight Lieutenant Freddy Hulance was a pilot on the Dresden attacks with 227 Squadron, based at Balderton in Lincolnshire:

'As far as we were concerned it was another routine operation. There was no briefing about the industries in Dresden, about which all I knew was that that they made fine porcelain. It was a long trip, about 10 hours, but everything worked that night. The weather was very good, there was a real lack of fighter interference, the marking was magnificent, and frankly we were winning. I have to say I never felt any remorse at all about it afterwards, because it was always them or us.

The notoriety came along afterwards. Years later the BBC brought me in to pursue this agenda, but there I met a displaced person from Dresden who had survived the raid. He may have been Jewish but he was destined anyway the day after the raid to be shipped to a Nazi death camp. As the result of the bombing he was able to get away, and he wanted to shake me by the hand for giving him the rest of his life.'

There is no accurate figure on how many died; officially it is 35,000 but recent research showed it may be less than that. Dresden was dreadful, but war was dreadful. While some leaders at the time were uneasy about what happened, it is generally later generations that set out to allocate the blame. Their single scapegoat was Sir Arthur Harris.

We gave Churchill what he asked for in 1940, dominance of the skies over Germany. He turned around later and talked about 'terror bombing.'

In the last month of the war the pocket battleship Lützow was attacked on 16 April 1945 by 617 Squadron. Despite intense flak, 15 aircraft managed to bomb the target with Tallboys or with 1,000-pounders. One near-miss with a Tallboy tore a large hole in the bottom of the Lützow and she settled to the bottom in shallow water. One Lancaster was shot down, the Squadron's last loss in the war.

Grand Slam bombs were successfully used against the 30ft (9m) thick ceilings of the Huuge and Brest U-boat pens. On 14 March 1945 Bielefeld Viaduct, which had withstood so many attacks, was broken when Jock Calder flying a 617 Lancaster dropped the first 'Grand Slam' bomb from 6,000 ft (1,823m). More than 100 yards (91m) of the viaduct collapsed through the earthquake effect.

A day later two 617 Squadron Lancasters each carried a Grand Slam and 14 aircraft of 9 Squadron carried Tallboys to attack the railway viaduct. The viaduct was not cut but no aircraft were lost.

On 19 March 1945, 617 Squadron Lancasters hit the railway viaduct at Arnsberg using six Grand Slams and blew a 40ft (12m) gap in it. Last Witness Benny Goodman, a pilot with 617 Squadron dropped one of the Grand Slams:

'I never had any concern, carrying a Grand Slam bomb on take-off, that it wasn't going to get off the ground. It was a little bit sluggish, but anything they put on, a Lancaster was capable of handling. It was slow in climbing, but we got to bombing height and joined the others and got over the target. My recollection was that we didn't have to say "bomb gone" because the aircraft went up like a rocket. But my flight engineer Jock said, not only did the aeroplane climb quickly, but he heard a hell of a bang; it may have been the release mechanism. It never got to the point where the whole squadron had Grand Slams, we always had a mixture with Tallboys. There were no complaints about the flying characteristics, despite the huge load. Our target was the Arnsberg viaduct and we think we got it.

'We didn't know it, and they were bloody stupid, but the Germans put a whole school and the teachers under the arches of the bridge, and they were all suffocated. I found this out much later when I was invited to go and talk to the Germans in Arnsberg 40 years after the war. My real name is Laurence Goodman, but I am nick-named after the band-leader, so the headline in the local German paper was "Benny Goodman Kompt!".'

In Farge on 27 March 1945, 20 Lancasters of 617 Squadron attacked the Valentin submarine pens, a huge, nearly-ready structure with a concrete roof up to 23ft (7m) thick. Two Grand Slam bombs penetrated parts of the pen with a 15ft-thick roof, which made the shelter unusable. No aircraft were lost. A last word on Grand Slams rests with John Langston:

'Grand Slams were very difficult to make, they were one-offs, each individually hand-made. In order to pep up the workforce to produce more bombs, two aircrews were sent off to the English Steel Corporation in Sheffield to give a talk to these guys. We all put on our best blues, went to Sheffield and were met by company directors and given large whiskies, and went down to the casting furnace, the first place they took us. There, we were horrified to find that all the way around this huge vault were Russian flags and a large banner saying 'God Bless Uncle Joe' – Joe Stalin.

'We watched them pour the metal for the cast of the bomb, and then they took us into the next room where there was a bomb that was cooled and they were finishing it off. There was a huge bomb-casing and a chap with a flashlight looking through the back end of the hole, after the casting had been taken out. There were two little men, smaller than jockeys, with pneumatic hammers, and they were peering through the case with a flashlight. When they saw some piece of metal sticking out, one of these little men went in with his pneumatic hammer and had to hammer it out.

'He could only stand about 20 or 30 seconds of this and then they hauled him out by his legs, shaking. One of these little chaps came out and I gave him a cigarette and lit it, and he looked at me and he said, "What do you do?"

'I said, "I drop them."

'He asked, "What do they pay you?"

'I said, "Thirteen shillings and sixpence a day."

'"You're a fool," he said. "I get 10 quid a week for doing this!"

'God Bless Uncle Joe indeed!'

I was intimately involved in all three 617 Squadron attacks against the great German battleship the *Tirpitz* in the autumn and early winter of 1944. A number of questions hang over those attacks and surrounding events more than 60 years later.

One is the cold-blooded murder of my best friend, Drew Wyness, between the first and second attacks on the *Tirpitz*, which I only discovered more than 30 years later and which is still unavenged. A second question is how and why 617 Squadron was able to make a third attack on the *Tirpitz* – 'The Beast of the Atlantic' – with a crack Luftwaffe fighter squadron nearby, and none of us were shot down.

This was a target that had for years tied up at least three of the Royal Navy's battleships badly wanted elsewhere, and the *Tirpitz* had beaten off countless attacks over the previous four years.

How did we get her? We had been stripped of half our armament, with just enough fuel to get to Tromso and back, so had they caught us we were goners. Two German aces in 9.Staffel, a Luftwaffe squadron that included Heinrich Ehrler with 200 kills and Franz Doerr with 120 kills, would have made absolute mincemeat of our virtually defenceless Lancasters that day. Both men were court-martialed afterwards, one found guilty, the other acquitted.

One of our Last Witnesses who knew both men and was there that day has an explanation. Looking back at the 25-year-old youngster I was at the time – our Last Witness Kurt Schulze was two years younger – I feel I must deal more fully with the event.

CHAPTER EIGHTEEN

The Tirpitz — Two 617 Squadron Attacks

On 28 August 1944, we were playing football on the airfield at Woodhall Spa, and somebody arrived on the touchline and asked for our C.O., Willie Tait. He disappeared and came back a little later to say that we had a special job. Football was stopped. He didn't tell us what the target was, but we set off on a series of cross-country flights.

I did a consumption test that day with flow-meters fitted to our engines. The standard fuel-use was 50 gallons an hour per engine, so we set out to compile a very accurate report on what fuel we were using. My crew was in the air for 7½ hours. We flew at different altitudes and varied power to work out the most economic settings. Whatever it was we were going to hit, it was obviously going to be a very long flight.

Everyone on 617 knew that the *Tirpitz* was a prime potential target for us. Fifteen months earlier, when Guy Gibson first heard there was a special job on for a newly-formed special squadron – Cochrane had asked him to think about doing one more operation – he thought it would be the *Tirpitz*. Gibson did not know anything about the Dams at that time.

So, the most powerful of all German battleships had been hovering around us for a while.

On 1 September I flew a Lancaster III, P-Popsy, to Syerston and back. The same day I went up in a Mustang and flew from Woodhall Spa to Topcliffe to see my wife Christine, heavily pregnant with our first child.

I had asked Willie Tait for a couple of days off to see her, and Willie said, off you go, take the Mustang. It was a 35-minute flight. Christine lived in Topcliffe, near Thirsk in Yorkshire. I went up on a Friday and came back after the weekend, on 3 September. It was a Canadian base, 6-Group, and I was astonished as I taxied in to be waved into a hangar, and as I stopped the engine and climbed out, I got a salute. From a Canadian airman!

Then I saw Cheshire's wing commander pennant, still there on the side of the Mustang months after he had left the squadron, so I didn't take off my jacket and reveal the fact that I was a mere flight lieutenant.

We were only told on 11 September – my 25th birthday - what the target was, the *Tirpitz* at last, but that we were not going directly for it. At Alten Fjord it was too far away from any Scottish base. Instead, we were going to fly to a base in Russia and have a crack from there.

We set off at seven o'clock in the evening, out from Woodhall Spa across the sea, each of us routing individually. Our destination was Yagodnik somewhere near Archangel, well inside the Arctic Circle. We turned in over Norway and then into neutral Sweden and the Gulf of Bothnia, where we turned north. I saw lights on in a little town, which I discovered was Leuna, right at the top end of the Gulf. I had not seen lights on in a town from the air at night since Africa!

Suddenly flak came up, not at our height but directly in front of us, two or three bursts. I thought, aha, they don't want me to fly over their town. They were, in effect, saying come over this town and we'll have a real go at you.

As dawn broke there was 10/10ths cloud above us, and we were being forced down by cloud-base to 4,000ft (1,320m). All we could see was forest in every direction, and mist in the tops of the fir trees. We were flying on dead reckoning and had been told we would have radio aids – so that if we had problems and tapped out a certain code, we would get directions – but staff officer had forgotten there was a difference between the English and the Russian alphabet. The code was wrong, as far as the Russians were concerned. Nobody said a dicky-bird.

We could only fly on over endless tundra and try and discover where we were later.

Then we found what turned out to be the White Sea, and the little town of Onega; it was only later we discovered all this for certain. We were not sure where we were so we decided to make this town a start point for a search. There was a big field where I thought we could always come back to and land. We searched in a pattern, north-east, and then east, and then south-east looking for Yagodnik, always coming back to the safety of the field we had found.

In the end, quite low on fuel, I decided to land and touched down on what turned out to be a disused airfield.

As I taxied in, one of my crew said, 'Skip, there's another Lancaster coming in.' I was first in and the pilot of the other Lancaster was our American, Nicky Knilans, with Larry Curtis as the wireless operator.

We got out, they parked alongside us, Russians arrived; they were unshaven, wearing German greatcoats, carrying rifles and looking as if, for two roubles, they would have sorted us out. But they put us in the back of an open truck and we bounced our way to the town of Onega, and were taken to the town major's office. They had anticipated our arrival – there was an American hospital ship in the harbour, right on the White Sea – so a lady interpreter was there. Through her, I was asked from where we had come. They had a map on the wall, I pointed to Lincolnshire and they couldn't believe it.

Willie Tait arrived later in a little Russian aeroplane. He had been flown over in it, having reached Yagodnik. We had lost two aircraft in the tundra – Drew Wyness's was one – and there were four aircraft lost from 9 Squadron, so we left six Lancasters in Russia from that particular attack. The bulk of them had landed with their wheels up.

Willie knew where to go, and flew with me the 40 minutes from Onyega to Yagodnik – that is how close we were. Knilans, following me, had a difficult take-off because his flight engineer pulled the flaps up too quickly. One always took off with 15 degrees of flap on a Lancaster. There was a sinking feeling just after take-off and they hit the top of a tree and collected a large branch in the bomb-bay (that piece of wood is now in the bar at the Petwood Hotel, Woodhall Spa, unofficial headquarters of the Dambusters).

A day later I flew over to Kegastrov – with six Russians strap-hanging in the back – to get some stuff out of Drew Wyness's Lancaster. He had broken his undercarriage on landing, having hit a pole, so his aircraft was down on one wing. We landed alongside, Drew picked up what he wanted and we flew back, leaving his aircraft there. We never saw it again. The Russians later cannibalised two working Lancasters out of the wreckage.

They made us very welcome. After a day or two we asked for some entertainment. They laid on a cinema show, but they were all wartime newsreels. The camera moved to the front line, you saw Germans actually chucking stick bombs, and that was the entertainment.

There was a football match between our crews and the local garrison. They had a band, and whenever they had a penalty the commanding officer was brought on to take it. As they won 7-0, we got an awful lot of music; they played loudly at every one of their goals. Somebody said that their goalkeeper later played for Moscow Dynamo.

I played bridge with Guy Byam, a BBC reporter, he was there to fly with an Australian pilot and an aeroplane full of cameras. We had a Liberator with all our ground-crew, and were put up in an old paddle steamer – the airfield was on an island in the River Vena – and because we were late we didn't get a room. We slept in a lounge area in bunks, and woke in the night with the place crawling with bugs. For some extraordinary reason these bugs showed respect for rank, and Willie Tait was untouched by them. All our 'doc' had, a chap called Marshall, was Calomine lotion to soothe bites.

Every day a Mosquito aircraft flew out to do a recce over the *Tirpitz*, and came back and fired red lights. On 15 September he fired a green light, so we all clambered aboard our aircraft and set off on what is now called *First Tirpitz*. I had Drew Wyness with me, a particular friend, because he had no aircraft himself. He sat on a canvas 'dicky' seat normally used by the flight engineer. There was no job for Drew to do but despite the risk to his life, he wanted to do the trip.

We formed a loose gaggle as we climbed up and set off on track. The weather was good. The closer we got to the target, the more the gaggle tightened up. We were all given heights to fly at 250ft (76m) intervals, and set our altimeters to a common reading, operating from the same base. If I was at 15,000ft (4,950m), someone was at 15,250 and above him, someone at 15,500. It all worked out. We were experienced people.

I saw the *Tirpitz* over the nose of the Lancaster. We had seen a model of where she was, and knew that Alten Fjord was a north-south Fjord, and Kaa was a little fjord off the bottom end, running east to west. There was a 400ft (122m) cliff there, and the *Tirpitz* was sheltered by the cliff. There were torpedo nets and all around were hundreds of smoke generators.

As I identified the *Tirpitz* I saw all the smoke generators start up. They had picked us up on the radar. There were no fighters, but a lot of flak from the ship itself and from batteries around her. We went into the bombing run – with the SABS sight it took a long run, nearly 15 miles to get everything steady – then my bomb-aimer said, 'Skipper, I can't see a bloody thing.' We were not carrying 12,000lb Tallboy bombs but what were known as 'Johnny Walkers' (JWs) one of these funny wartime bombs that were supposed to fall into the fjord, reach the bottom and jump about in the hope that in one of their jumps they would strike the underside of the *Tirpitz*. We carried 12 JWs, each of 1,000lbs, while others carried Tallboys.

I cannot think of anything more stupid than the JWs we carried that day.

There was no point in taking them back. I said to Frank, if you can work out when we should bomb, let them go. We bombed on dead reckoning. One or two crews brought Tallboys back to Russia.

Willie Tait, leading us, got a sight of her before the smoke took effect. His bomb-aimer, Danny Daniels, was a boyish, curly-haired Canadian. Danny was a dead-eye dick, and was convinced he had struck the *Tirpitz*.

Tait was asked afterwards and replied in typical laconic form, claiming we 'gave her a bit of a nudge.'

We discovered long afterwards that Danny *had* hit her in the bow and a lot of water came in. From that moment, the *Tirpitz* was crippled. She would be very difficult to repair quickly, and useless as a sea-going menace. She had been damaged by two previous assaults in April and July by two of the task forces we had sent against her – 20 ships and more than 100 aircraft – but their little bombs were really not very effective. A number of people had been killed, and the damage done was repaired. Before our attack she could still have got out and annihilated our convoys. The Admiralty wanted her not just sunk, but to be seen without doubt to be sunk.

There was a political aspect that I learned later, that we had at least three of our battleships sitting in Scapa Flow, and all their attendant craft, in case the *Tirpitz* came out. The Admiralty wanted those ships in the Pacific, so that we could say to the Americans that we were making some contribution to the Pacific war, or the Americans would claim, with some justification, that they were doing it all themselves. So there were these considerations, and we didn't know until quite some time afterwards that the *Tirpitz* had been damaged to that degree.

No one was lost on the first the *Tirpitz* attack. There were no problems getting back to Yagodnik. The whole round flight was seven hours, by our standards not a long trip. It was the middle of September and we were two degrees north of the Arctic Circle, but it was not particularly cold. We had the fur-lined Irvine jackets, but they were grey days and no fighters chased us either going to the *Tirpitz*, or after we left her.

We flew back to England on 16 September with Drew Wyness on board and two of his crew. We laid a course direct from Yagodnik to Woodhall, and flew it at night, not bothering about the dog-legs used on the way out. It took nine hours. We were fired at first over the Finnish coast, flying individually, not with the main pack of the squadron, at about 15,000ft (4,572m). Somewhere over the coast of southern Sweden, we learned later it was Malmo, suddenly the cloud was full of flak as they had a go at us. They were neutral, we were at war and we were not supposed to fly over their country, so they felt justified in firing at us. We flew through it and then I handed the aircraft over to Drew, and he flew the second half of the journey over Denmark and the North Sea and home to Lincolnshire.

The other members of the squadron came back at the same time. Two of Drew Wyness's crew went with Flying Officer Frank Levy, a Rhodesian, and were killed when he crashed into mountains near Nesbyen. No one knew what happened to him. There were no survivors.

On 23 September we went back to the Dortmund-Ems Canal, scene of the worst losses in the squadron's short history. A number of veterans of the Dams Raids never came back from their original attack on the Canal. It was a night attack, they couldn't risk us during the day because of the heavy flak, and it was just one of those things.

Perhaps this time it was an attempt to answer the question, what the hell is 617 for? Let's give them something to do! The marking was by a chap called Rupert Oakley from 627 Mosquito Squadron on the same field as us. Rupert was a pre-war Halton boy who had made it. He had a wonderful big moustache and a DFC to add to a DFM he won in 1940, and he was to drop target indicators. We were supposed to bomb them. It was a crazy idea. Main Force was going to Munster, and we were tucked in with them before heading north to try to hit the Dortmund-Ems Canal.

We lost one of our aircraft, three engines shot away; some of the crew got out and evaded capture, but Flight Lieutenant Geoff Stout, the pilot, crashed in flames. I had been flying fighter affiliation with Geoff earlier in the day, in which I piloted a Mustang, and felt that he seemed preoccupied when we returned together to the mess for lunch, perhaps in a premonition of that night's events.

In a history of 617 Squadron after the Dams Raid, the author Alan Cooper claimed the Dortmund–Ems Canal attack was a success. He wrote that 10 miles of the Canal was drained, 23 barges were left stranded, and 4,000 workers were mustered to repair two miles of breeches. The Canal was out of action for six months, until just a few weeks before the end of the war.

There was no more flying for the rest of the month, and on 1 October there was a 90-minute flight – low-level, cross-country – the beginning of the training for the Kembs Barrage. We scooted around all the canals of Lincolnshire at nought feet.

Two days later we set off on a 2½-hour day-flight to Walcheren Island in Holland to support the British Army advancing through the Low Countries. Walcheren was a major island with a sea wall. The idea was to blow the dykes, the islands would flood and the Germans would have to leave their fortifications. When we got there, Main Force had been there before us and they had done the job, so we brought back our very expensive Tallboy bombs.

We went back to low-level practice on 4 October, another hour scooting around Lincolnshire canals, and the following day we did two practice flights, high-level bombing practice, flying in formation, as preparation for the *Tirpitz*.

Two days later we lost Drew Wyness, murdered in cold blood after attacking the Kembs Barrage.

Drew and I had had lunch that day, a Saturday, 7 October, with a young man called Chris Melville, Colonel of the King's Own Scottish Borderers, along with a couple of his officers. Afterwards, Chris drove us in his jeep from the Spa Hotel in Woodhall Spa and dropped Drew off at his aircraft, and me a bit further around the airfield. Drew and I had arranged to take Chris Melville out to dinner the same evening.

I remember Chris saying, 'Have a good trip, Drew, and, see you later.'

It was a day flight, a lovely day over France with cumulus clouds as we flew south. Eighteen aircraft were detailed from 617, 12 of us flying high-level at 12,000ft (3,657m) carrying Tallboys with 30-second fuses, six others going in at low level, 500-800ft (243m), in pairs, carrying Tallboys with 30-minute fuses.

The attack went in at five o'clock in the evening, just as dusk was coming on. We wanted to blow the Kembs Barrage because the Americans were coming up from the south of France and were making progress towards what was known as the Belfort Gap, which would have pushed them right up to the Rhine and into southern

Germany. The form was, at some stage the Germans would blow this barrage which would unleash an awful lot of water to flood the Americans. RAF Bomber Command decided that, while the Americans were well out of reach, we would do it for them, a pre-emptive strike, so the Germans wouldn't be able to use that particular tactic.

James Tait led us, as he always did in the six months he ran 617 Squadron, from the front. The low-level six were Tait and Phil Martin, then Johnny Cock-shott and James 'Cas' Castagnola, and the last two were Drew Wyness and Kit Howard. The first four went through their low-level raid without serious damage, but Drew was hit on the approach and was on fire. He dropped his bomb and then ditched in the Rhine. Kit went around again, though he was told by Willie Tait, 'Kit, abandon, abandon' but he tried again and, of course, the Germans had got the range and he was shot to pieces. He crashed somewhere on the German side of the Rhine.

Drew had put his Lancaster into the Rhine and most of his crew got out, including the two who flew back with me after the attempt on the *Tirpitz* from Russia. Williams was the navigator. I remember he had been in Coningsby the night before and had a bit of an altercation, and he had had a black eye. Two of Drew's crew jumped into the water and tried to swim to the French side, but they have never been seen or heard of since.

Drew Wyness and the surviving crew, including Williams, were picked up by the Germans and taken to a local village. There they were interrogated and then Drew and a chap called Bruce Hosie, his New Zealand wireless operator, were taken back to the riverbank.

They were shot and pushed into the river.

Their bodies were taken out of the water 50 miles downstream and buried in a place called Toul, west of Nancy, side by side. They still lie there.

I never found out what happened to the other crew members.

For years I had no idea that this dreadful fate had befallen Drew Wyness. I thought he had been killed in the crash. It was only 30 years later that I found out that the German who had murdered them was captured after the war, tried and sentenced to prison. He managed to escape and, as far as I know, he has never been heard of since.

We learned that half an hour after our attack the Germans were on the dam when one of our bombs with a delayed fuse blew up and the area was flooded at no danger to the advancing Americans.

That evening I met Chris Melville in the Spa Hotel, one of the haunts of our squadron in Woodhall Spa. I was on the stairs with him, and told him what I thought had happened. Until that time he had never been in action. His regiment had been in the Scottish Highlands for some years as part of a mountain division, preparing for a possible re-invasion of Norway. They were hard men, tough guys, and he just sat there, tears rolling down his face. Someone he had had lunch with, as far as we knew at the time, was dead and burnt, just a few hours later.

Chris Melville won a DSO a month later. It was a typical British Army tradition, in that you train a bunch of people for one particular purpose, as part of a mountain division, and Chris's regiment went into action actually on the island of Walcheren, up to their waists in water!

The difference between an air action and a land action – and a sea action – was that you didn't see your friend alongside you suddenly fall down in a heap, and he's dead. You didn't see his head blown off or see him dismembered. Or you're not on a ship when a shell arrives, takes four or five of a gun crew and converts them into meat. You don't see that in the air, unless it's someone in your own crew. If another aircraft is lost, well, it could be almost as if he had been posted away that day. Over a period of time you got used to it if someone in the squadron copped a packet.

Drew's death affected me more than anybody else because we were very close, but with others who were lost on 617, although I knew them, it wasn't the same. The feeling was, well, hard luck, poor bugger. Like everyone else, I knew it might be me tomorrow, but we found we couldn't have a memorial service every other day and stay in a fighting state. We had to get on with it. Everyone fought their own battles with their own feelings about going on an operation, knowing full well that the odds were against you.

Being in 617 I did feel part of an elite force. There was that extraordinary reputation, and the fact that we had this big bomb, 12,000lbs, when the original specification for the Lancaster laid down a limit of 8,000lbs. Only 854 Tallboy bombs were built, and we were to use 77 of them in the three attacks on the *Tirpitz*. We were the only squadron with the SABS bomb sight, and the only squadron doing these special ops on our own. We knew very well that much was expected of us, and we had to live up to the Squadron's reputation. As a unit, 617 was just over a year old when I joined it, but I was very proud to be there, and anxious not to do anything which might tarnish that reputation.

Drew had been a flight commander, a Squadron Leader, and almost immediately afterwards I was promoted to take his place.

For 13 days nothing happened, no training flights, no ops. F-Fox went in for a major service and was fitted with more powerful engines, Merlin T-24s, with paddle blades. It had the mid-upper turret removed. The front guns were taken out, as was the flare chute and armour-plating. A little extra fuel tank – 250 gallons – was put in. What flying I did was virtually jollies.

On 15 October the *Tirpitz* emerged slowly from Alten Fjord, escorted by at least five destroyers, and made her way south heading for Tromso. It was said she rarely reached three knots and frequently had to be towed, but the Germans made this dangerous move, bringing the great battleship 200 miles closer to Britain and in potential striking range of our Lancasters, because the Russians were advancing from the north. They had actually captured Kirkenes airfield, from which air cover had been provided for the *Tirpitz* at Alten, on 23 October. She was anchored over a flat seabed with 18ft clearance, instead of the 4ft (1.2m) clearance they had planned for, and rubble was later tipped into the sea to narrow the gap between keel and seabed. The Germans intended, even if the *Tirpitz* sank, to allow the grounded and damaged ship still to give the impression it was a going concern.

On 28 October we flew from Woodhall Spa to Milltown in Scotland, in preparation for a second attempt at the *Tirpitz*. We didn't use an airfield on the Shetland Islands because the runways there were not long enough for a heavily loaded 4-engined bomber. At 617 Squadron we used Milltown and Lossiemouth, while 9 Squadron used Kinloss; all three airfields were close together. Kinloss and Lossiemouth were permanent stations, while Milltown was a satellite. I was detailed to take off from Milltown.

I had a new pilot as 'second dicky' a chap called Flatman, a tall young man from Lancashire on his first operation. F-Fox was now equipped with a Tallboy. We had, thankfully, given up all those experiments with jumping 'Johnny Walker' mines. It was on this flight that I was so nearly killed and could have taken at least one other Lancaster crew with me.

For that flight the Merlin T-24s with paddle-blade props had a boost of plus 24lbs, just for take-off. You had to go 'through the gate' to get that boost. I would say, 'full power' and my engineer gave me that, so I could take off with both hands on the stick.

We would *not* normally go 'through the gate' – it could ruin an engine quickly – but we had to do it because of the load, up to 68,000lbs. But my port outer engine did not go to 24lbs and the engines on the right side of the Lancaster began to over-power the engines on the left! It happened so quickly, I couldn't control it. We were extremely lucky.

We always had to lead with the port throttle to compensate for the engine torque. Taffy, my flight engineer, just 20 years old but very bright, was watching the instruments as we rolled. He saw the imbalance in the boost – three engines boosting 24lbs, one boosting 18lbs – and pulled back the relevant throttle on the outer starboard engine. When I went through the gate, he had seen that we didn't get the expected boost from one engine. We were travelling at about 80mph, I didn't have time to push the rudder which only gave full control above that speed, and then I was off the runway and over the grass, just like that.

I centralised the controls in the air and I knew nothing of what Taffy was doing until he told me afterwards. It was his own initiative to give me equal power on each side. We got off the ground, streaking over the grass, heading for other 617

Lancasters lined up on the peri-track waiting to take off, one piloted by Benny Goodman. We had a 12,000lb Tallboy on board, as did they! Benny still has a vivid recollection of what happened:

'Lined up around the peri-track, a filthy night, low cloudbase, pissing down with rain. I had my head inside the cockpit doing checks, and suddenly Jock, my flight engineer, nudged me hard in the ribs and said, "Look!" I looked up and saw a bloody great undercarriage, it looked like it was coming straight through the cockpit. We had more than a full petrol load and an extra tank to go the distance. I confess I ducked. But Tony didn't hit us and we lined up and took off, nerves over, forget it.'

All I know is that I got the aircraft off the ground at the right climbing speed. I may have gone between two hangars, it was pitch black, two o'clock in the morning. We started breathing normally again around 2,000ft (609m).

I set the aircraft to climb steadily and slowly recovered. The near-miss was all part of the game in a period of intensive flying. Going off the airfield runway was just one of those things.

We flogged all the way up north to Tromso to arrive just after dawn, but there was cloud everywhere. The flight was long, 12 hours and 20 minutes round trip, and when we got there I was at 6,000ft (1,828m) trying to get a glimpse of the *Tirpitz*.

It was a case of, let's have a go, and I decided to bomb.

I could see some of my colleagues but thankfully, and possibly because of the very poor weather, there were no German fighters. I lined up at 15,500ft (4,724m) and made my run, dropped my Tallboy from that height at 07.50 hrs, and then turned around and went home again, landing at Milltown without any other incidents. We got back to Woodhall Spa the following day.

On 4 November, again in F-Fox, we set off for Milltown in preparation for yet another attack on the *Tirpitz,* but I was forced to land at Carnaby, near Bridlington *en route* because of a lack of brake pressure. F-Fox had been fine while we taxied around Woodhall ahead of taking off, and it was only when we got into the air that Taffy told me we had no air pressure.

With a Tallboy on board we could not have landed back at Woodhall because we would have run out of runway, and there was no way of stopping. Carnaby was one of three airfields in Britain – the other two were Manston and Woodbridge – where they had very long runways, three or four times wider than the normal runway. Their purpose was to allow damaged aircraft to land safely. I did a precautionary landing, with lots of power, nose-up, slow as we could, chopped the power as we went down the runway, with a fire engine on one side, an ambulance on the other and we gradually rolled to a stop.

There was a little valve point on the side of the aircraft where they applied a high pressure air system and filled us up. It took just a few minutes. I had no idea why it had bled away, nor why we could not have recharged it from inside the Lancaster. After taking off again there seemed to be no more loss of air pressure, and we joined the rest of the squadron.

We had psyched ourselves up for another *Tirpitz* attack, intending to leave for Tromso at two o'clock in the morning, but the weather was so bad the whole operation was scrubbed. Still carrying our Tallboy but with good brakes, we flew back to Woodhall.

A day later I flew with Jerry Fawke, my first flight on Mosquitoes which he was teaching me to fly, 40 minutes practicing attacks. Later that day I flew up to see Christine at Topcliffe, taking Flying Officer Flatman with me as 'dicky' pilot, giving him the experience of flying the Lancaster, which he took back to base the same day. I was only away overnight, with Christine so close to giving birth. Mark Flatman came back to pick me up the following day and flew me back to base.

Training was now intensive, with high-level bombing tests on 10 November in which we flew to Bassingham at 20,000ft (6,096m) and dropped practice bombs. My average strike rate was within 92 yards (84m) of the target from four miles up. That was the last test because next day we were sent back to Milltown on the real thing, our third attack on the *Tirpitz*.

CHAPTER NINETEEN

Sinking the Tirpitz

I had a second 'dicky' pilot with me on the third *Tirpitz* attack, Australian Flight Lieutenant H.V. Gavin, coming along for the experience The whole squadron was airborne by 3.25 am. We flew past the Orkneys and the Shetland Islands, and up to the Dead Reckoning point .

Jack said, 'Okay, Skipper, in five minutes, turn on to a course for Norway.' In five minutes he said, 'Turn now'. As we turned towards Norway there was a tiny crack of daylight, like a silver thread on the horizon. I saw a Lancaster silhouetted against it and pulled up alongside it. There in the rear turret was a warrant officer called Micky Vaughan making rude gestures at me. It was Tait's aircraft, and we flew together to the rendezvous, a lake in northern Sweden. We were first there and as we did a circuit, Lancasters came out of the black western sky and joined us. There were 18 aircraft from 617 Squadron, and 10 from 9 Squadron.

We had had trouble in Scotland because of hoar frost on the wings, and when we drove very early that morning to our aircraft, the ground crews had been spraying them. But for some strange reason 9 Squadron did not have sufficient facilities and eight or more of their aircraft couldn't get off the ground, including their CO, a wing commander called Bazin.

As aircraft joined us, Willie Tait fired a Very light, and we turned on track to start climbing to the north, still over Sweden. The day dawned, the sun came up, a most beautiful morning, clear sky, not a cloud to be seen.

We all thought, 'This is it!' Conditions could not be more ideal for our high-level bombing. Visibility was so clear.

Then, because we had been told about a new German fighter squadron moving near to Tromso, we thought, 'Christ, if it's okay for us it is also going to be equally perfect for the fighters!'

Where were they?

I became aware of, not flak, but a great unfolding golden cloud. The *Tirpitz* had fired her 15-inch guns at us at maximum range. These shells could travel 22 miles, they weighed 1,760lbs and were 2ft (60cm) across. The guns were at maximum elevation. They could time their shells to explode in the air, but they exploded below us. It was only a gesture because we were at 15,000ft (4,572), three miles high.

In what was later seen as a textbook attack, we climbed to bombing height, went through all the procedures – Jack Harrison passing figures to Frank Chance about wind speed, height and so on – to feed into the SABS bomb-aiming device. Then we went for the target.

Nine of our 617 aircraft bombed within 90 seconds. I was one of the first nine, and the other nine bombed within another 2½ minutes. The gaggle tightened up for the actual attack. Tait's bomb was released at 08.41. Five bombs were dropped at 08.42, and mine went at 08.42½. The first 9 Squadron aircraft bombed at the same time as the last 617 aircraft. Within 11 minutes of the first strike, which was Tait's with Deadeye Dick Daniels as his bomb-aimer, the *Tirpitz* had rolled over.

Then we pissed off.

We had done our job as well as we could and there were fighters within 40 miles. We had held the aircraft level and got the photograph, and our next thought was to get the hell out of it, turn and dive and get away.

We all made it back. So what had happened to the German fighters?

One of the senior German airmen on the airfield at Bardufoss that day, where the closest German fighters were based, was the adjutant of III Gruppe, *Oberleutnant* Kurt Schulze, one of our Last Witnesses. In 2009, by now a retired businessman in Southern California, Schulze told me a story he was unhappy to recount (my reaction was understandably different):

'It does not give me great pleasure to write about the failure of the German Luftwaffe to protect the *Tirpitz*.

'My report is based on my own experiences, often conflicting information accumulated from Luftwaffe participants, books and the once super-secret manuscript on the Luftwaffe court martial proceedings.

'Sixty-four years later, let me tell you about the Luftwaffe fighter Staffel (squadron) which was involved in the *Tirpitz* affair. The 9.Staffel was a part of III Gruppe of the Jagdeschwader 5 (Fighter Wing), the much talked-about "Eismeerjaeger". I was adjutant to the group commander of III Group. We flew Me109s. Some of our pilots had been stationed in northern Norway and Finland since the beginning of the war against Russia in 1941. We got the name "Eismeerjaeger" (Ice Ocean Fighters) because the Germans called the Barents Sea Eismeer. We were stationed next to the Barents Sea in Petsamo in Northern Finland, 300 miles north of the Arctic Circle and 65 miles west of the Soviet city of Murmansk. Being stationed "at the end of the world" we were a very close-knit unit of pilots and ground personnel. During the summer, with 24 hours of daylight, we often found ourselves flying in pyjamas or underwear. Finland left the alliance with Germany in September 1944, and in October joined the Russians in pushing us out of Finland.

'On 10 October we were chased out of Petsamo, then out of Kirkenes in Norway, and we finally wound up in Banak, approximately 75 miles south of the North Cape of Europe.

'At the end of October, flying out of Banak, my wingman shot down a Russian reconnaissance plane after my guns jammed. With daily flights, the Russians kept track of the German navy units stationed close to the North Cape. These navy units were a constant threat to the convoys going from England and the US to Murmansk – you may remember PQ17 and PQ19.

'On Wednesday 8 November – four days before the bombing of the Tirpitz – our 9.Staffel arrived in Bardufoss, about 50 miles south of Tromso.

'The orders given to the staffel commander were:

1. Convert the Staffel from Me109 to FW190
2. Protect the airfield where important torpedo-carrying aircraft were stationed.

'No orders were given regarding the Tirpitz!

'A total of 26 FW190s were available in Bardufoss for 9.Staffel and a small so-called "Commando Squadron" which was also a part of 9.Staffel. The "Commando Staffel" consisted of a few very experienced pilots who had previously flown the FW190.

'The Geschwader commander Major Heinrich Ehrler arrived in Bardufoss on Thursday 9 October to organise the conversion from one fighter aircraft to the other, and the formation of the "Commando Staffel." Although only a few pilots in Bardufoss had flown the FW190 before, Major Ehrler, in order to secure protection for the airfield, placed 9.Staffel on a 3-minute alert, which normally meant it would take three minutes to scramble.

'Together with the Group Commander, Captain Franz Doerr, I landed in Bardufoss in my Me109G6 on Friday 10 November. Before our flight we were told to stay out of the restricted zone around Tromso. After landing we heard that the Tirpitz was anchored in that general area, but we received no orders for the defence of the Tirpitz.

'In Tromso, officers of the Luftwaffe signal corps in charge of the area radar coverage and ground control had been in close contact with the Tirpitz for several days. They had assured Captain Lt Fassbender on the battleship that the main objective of the signal corps was to make sure that they would be in constant contact with their station at Bardufoss, which in turn would be in close touch with the "Eismeerjaeger" command post on the Bardufoss airfield.

'I will now try to describe what happened on our side on Sunday 12 November 1944.

'It was a beautiful cold morning with crystal clear air and a blue sky.

'Between 07.39 and 08.26, German radar detected and reported over-flights of enemy planes in the area of Bodoe, crossing into neutral Sweden. The assumption was, like often happened before, that they were on their way to Russia.

'A Luftwaffe soldier who had just been transferred to Bodoe and was not familiar with the area, nor the plotting system, made a mistake. He plotted the planes as entering Norway at Hammerfest – close to the North Cape of Europe – 400 miles north of Bodoe. Because two staffel of our III Gruppe were stationed in Alta and Banak, closer to Hammerfest than we were, Corporal Ulrich, in charge of our fighter command post, rightly took no action.

'Nobody in Bardufoss was notified.

'On the Tirpitz at 08.00 Captain Lt Fassbender was told about the over-flight of planes at Bodoe. It was his testimony that, at that time and again a little later, he had asked the

Luftwaffe signals corps command station in Tromso to secure fighter protection.

'The Luftwaffe signal corps officers testified to the subsequent court martial that they had not received such a request. After considering other testimony, the court martial sided with the Captain Lt.

'On the *Tirpitz* at 08.40 flak alarm was ordered, and at 08.50 air alert was ordered. At 09.14 their radar detected the bombers approximately 75 miles south of Tromso leaving Sweden and entering Norway. They immediately notified the signal corps command station in Tromso.

'Due to a bad telephone connection, the location of the bombers was lost and they were reported to Bardufoss as "location unknown." In the meantime, Captain Lt Fassberger inquired several times to ask if the fighter planes were ready to start.

'He was told twice by the signal corps officers, who had *not* checked with the fighter command post, that the fighters were ready.

'At 09.18, following orders, Geshwader commander Major Ehrler was ready to fly back to Alta when he heard the following report: "Airplane noise – location and altitude unknown."

'He asked for clarification about the location, and was given as "south of Bardufoss". He immediately ordered "alert start" for 9.Staffel and "Commando Staffel."

'Because of a mountain at the western end of the runway – right up to the edge of the runway – we could only take off in an easterly direction. This delayed the alert start from three minutes to nine minutes. Because of the existing layout of the airfield, all our aircraft were located at the easterly end of the runway, opposite the take-off threshold.

'In addition, when the first fighter aircraft were ready to take off, the control tower allowed a Ju-52 transport plane to land first. This delayed the fighter take-off by an additional five minutes.

'With his radio not working, Major Ehrler had got into the air at 09.25. When he reached a height of 6,000ft (1,828m) he saw that the FW190s had their propellers rotating but were still on the ground. When he reached 18,000ft (5,486m) he still could not see any bombers, and decided as ordered to fly to Alta. Then, all of a sudden, he saw a white mushroom cloud and flak. Arriving near Tromso he saw that the *Tirpitz* was lost and the Lancasters gone.

'After the first planes of 9.Staffel were in the air, one of the telephones at the fighter command post was ringing. The very excited flak officer of the *Tirpitz* asked if the fighters had taken off. Our corporal Ulrich told him that a few fighters were in the air and the rest were in the process of starting.

'Driving with the group commander from our quarters, we arrived at the airfield at about 09.30. We started with the command squadron at 09.36. After getting into my aircraft in front of our command post, I was in the air at approximately 09.39. Soon after my take-off I heard over the radio: "Flak over Tromso."

'When I arrived there the *Tirpitz* had already capsized – 9.Staffel had also been too late.

'Returning to the airfield, Staffel Commander Leutnant Werner Gyko detected and got close to a 4-engined bomber flying towards Sweden. Close proximity to the Swedish border, and a gun jam, ended that encounter. He had to be very careful not to get into Swedish air-space, because his wingman had shot down a Swedish plane trying to shoot down Gyko at the Finnish-Swedish border. That had created a lot of diplomatic trouble. With Germany losing the war, the Swedes evidently did not take the long-time British violation of their air space too seriously.

'After returning to the command post, we prepared for the celebration of Major Ehrler's 200th victory. He had left the airfield with 199 victories to his credit. We were very disappointed when it finally sank in that the *Tirpitz* was lost, and that all of us had been too late to stop the attack.

'Right away some of our ground personnel, equipped with blow-torches, left the airfield to help save the lives of some of the trapped sailors by cutting holes in the upturned hull.

'From the beginning it was evident that the staff officers in Oslo who had neglected to organise a defence for the *Tirpitz*, were desperate to find a scapegoat. It did not take long for them to decide that we were to be selected for this role.

'I found it difficult to get Heinrich Ehrler and Franz Doerr to sit down with me, as Ehrler's adjutant, to write a report while the facts were still fresh in our minds. The two great aces, with a total of 320 victories between them, felt very insulted by the many accusations.

'"Look, Kurt, if they don't like it let them come up here and hang their asses over the icy waters of northern Norway."

'"Kiss my ass" were the final words of a telephone conversation Heinrich Ehrler had with one of the generals in Oslo.

'This did not create a good climate for the court martial, which started in Oslo on 17 December. It was impossible to prove that we had received any orders for a co-ordinated protection of the *Tirpitz*. Finally – in desperation – it was alleged that Major Ehrler had not followed one of Reichmarshall Goering's many orders, in that he had not placed an officer – as opposed to a corporal – in charge of the airfield command post. When Ehrler had arrived in Bardufoss the only officer on the airfield was the staffel commander, Gyko.

'During the court martial the question was asked why I, Kurt Schulze, was not ordered into that position? I was certainly lucky that I had not been directly involved in that mess. Major Ehrler had always insisted that the few pilot officers in Petsamo flew with him in combat. Regardless, he was convicted and sentenced to three years in prison, also with demotion.

'Our gruppen commander Captain Franz Doerr, who knew all along that Ehrler was innocent, fell asleep during the court martial and was found not guilty.

'On 3 March 1945 – two months before the end of the war – Adolf Hitler reduced Ehrler's sentence to three months confinement in a fortress, no loss of rank and he was granted a "front probation." Major Ehrler immediately started flying the Me262 jet fighter in the defence of Germany. His wing commander in JG-7 was his old friend from Petsamo, Major Theodor Weissenberger, who had 208 victories.

'On 6 April 1945, after shooting down two B-17 Flying Fortresses, Heinrich Ehrler said goodbye to his friend over the radio: "Theo, I am out of ammunition and now I will ram an enemy bomber. Auf Wiedersehen in Valhalla!"

'And that is what he did.

'In my opinion, among the reasons why we were too late for the defence of the *Tirpitz* were:

1. No orders were given to us for the defence of the *Tirpitz*.
2. There was wrong plotting from the beginning.
3. We had a disorganised system of communications.
4. We were in the middle of a conversion course from Me109s to FW190s.
5. Bardufoss Airfield was not suitable for a quick alert start.
6. There was no radar coverage towards Sweden.
7. The skilled use of neutral air space by the British bombers.

'I almost forgot to mention that the main reason for the loss of the *Tirpitz* was the meticulously planned and executed attack by RAF Bomber Command and 617 Squadron, the Dambusters.'

It seems to me there were only seconds between us leaving the scene, and the first German fighter turning up. Without a mid-upper gunner or any armour plating, we would have been cut to pieces, especially if we had been caught by two of the best fighter pilots in the Luftwaffe, Ehrler and Doerr.

I am extremely grateful for all that went wrong on Bardufoss that day. Aside from losing Frank Levy's crew on the return flight from Russia on *First Tirpitz*, the only casualty we suffered in all three attacks on the *Tirpitz* was one aircraft, Easy-Elsie, which was shot up and had to land in Sweden. Easy-Elsie was a brand new Lancaster, and her nose-art depicted a comely young lady, a half-crown and a red light. Bits and pieces of her were still there in Sweden 60 years later, in the bog where she landed.

After we flew back to Scotland I was diverted and landed at Fraserborough, I don't know why. At that time we were all a bit tired, and if someone said divert, we did so. Fraserborough was where I had been based in northern Scotland. There was a company called the Consolidated Pneumatic Tool Company which had been evacuated from Fulham to Scotland, and I knew the managing director, so when we landed at Fraserborough at two o'clock in the afternoon, I rang him up. He came and got us and gave us a party, and we stayed overnight. Next morning we flew back to Woodhall Spa.

In fact, Willie Tait had wanted me to go to London with him, because he was flown there for a BBC Radio press conference, but I missed that because of landing at Fraserborough.

There is an existing photograph of Wing Commander Tait, saying his piece. Next to him is a squadron leader called Williams who led the 10 aircraft of 9 Squadron, he was their senior pilot actually on the attack.

I am told that AVM the Hon Sir Ralph Cochrane, commander of 5 Group, decreed that neither squadron was to see the other squadron's bomb plots. 9 Squadron didn't have SABS, the bomb-sight that we had. They had a Mark XIV bomb-sight, okay for a city but not an individual target like the *Tirpitz*.

Another difficulty for them was that, coming along after nine Tallboys had gone off on or close to the *Tirpitz*, throwing up muck and smoke, they had nothing specific to aim at beyond looking down into an inferno. The first nine of us had a sight of the ship, although it looked like a Dinky toy, but we could actually see it. But when 18 617 aircraft had bombed, what chance did 9 Squadron have?

CHAPTER TWENTY

Lancasters at War's End

When war in Europe ended on 8 May 1945, Lancaster bombers continued to pour off the production lines. Contracts had been agreed, and Japan needed to be beaten. There were plans by Sir Alan Cobham, the air-refuelling pioneer, to produce 600 Lincoln tankers to send out to the Pacific theatre, together with 600 Lancaster bombers, to add to the American island-hopping campaign. But when Okinawa, just 340 miles from the Japanese mainland, was taken on 21 June, there was no need of tankers as Lancaster bombers could get to Japan from Okinawa without mid-air refuelling. Then, when Japan surrendered on 15 August 1945, there was no more need for Lancaster bombers either.

In between, Lancasters did four jobs; they brought food to a starving Holland while still under the guns of occupying German forces; they brought back thousands of British prisoners of war; they took their ground crews on Baedecker journeys to show them just what they had done to Germany at such cost; and they tried and failed to blitz Adolf Hitler's 'Eagle's Nest' in Berchtesgaden in the Bavarian Alps.

Manna

The winter of 1944/5, known as the 'Hongerwinter' to the Dutch, was particularly harsh. Half of Holland had been liberated, but after the failure of 'a bridge too far' at Arnhem in September, the Dutch authorities called a railway strike, and in retaliation the Germans blocked supplies to the populace. A lot of fighting was going on anyway, and the retreating German army destroyed locks and bridges to flood the Dutch countryside. This limited the growth of food because much of the flooded land was agricultural, and was a final destructive blow to the transport of existing food stocks. Reports came through to London that a thousand Dutch people a day were dying of starvation.

At the end of April 1945, after tense negotiations between the occupying Germans and the Dutch authorities, the RAF set up 'Operation Manna.' The Americans organised a smaller effort called 'Chowhound.' Between them they dropped 11,000 tons of supplies to relieve the Dutch famine. The war went on all the time these operations were carried out.

The RAF devised the Manna system whereby food could be air-dropped by bombers, using panniers called 'blocks', four of which could be fitted to a standard Lancaster bomb bay. Each block held 71 sacks (with a total weight of 1,254lbs per block) variously containing sugar, dried egg powder, margarine, salt, cheese, tinned meat, flour, dried milk, coffee, cereals, tea, high vitamin chocolate, potatoes, all supplied from the Ministry of Food's reserve stockpiles.

The first of the two RAF Lancasters chosen for the test flight on the morning of 29 April 1945, was nicknamed 'Bad Penny', as in 'a bad penny always turns up.' This bomber, piloted by Robert Upcott, a Canadian from 460 RAAF Squadron, took off in bad weather to Holland without a ceasefire agreement by the Nazis. He left this account:

'Early in the morning of the 28 April my crew and I were briefed together with another crew with an Australian pilot. We were informed that our bombers had been filled with food to be dropped over Holland. The ground personnel simply stacked the food on the bomb doors.

'We were very excited about the drops. The Germans were still occupying Holland when the drops began. We had to fly low to the targets to be able to drop the food without damaging it, and were told to carry no ammunition for our guns.

'We were not only excited about the food drops, we were also scared. We had been flying over Holland at altitudes of 15,000 to 20,000ft on our way to targets in Germany and all of a sudden we were asked to fly at 400ft. German soldiers were still manning the flak guns near the corridor we had to fly through. If our mission was a success and we could drop our food without being shot at, Operation Manna would be launched.

'The weather was really bad, and we were not able to get airborne until the morning of 29 April. We flew the Channel on instruments and then the weather cleared and we could see where we were.

'Crossing the Dutch coast anti-aircraft guns were pointing directly at our planes. German flags flew on many buildings as we approached the target for the drop, and German soldiers stood guard at railroad bridges over canals. We arrived at the target area at less than 400ft and could see people on the ground quite clearly. For the drop we lowered flaps and wheels to slow down. The target was open ground just outside of Utrecht. There were no parachutes attached to the load, just free-falling boxes.

'We saw tanks trying to keep us in their sights, and we were looking right down a number of barrels. We were very lucky that they observed the truce and held their fire.

'There were very few people on this first mission. Nobody knew that we were coming. Then we saw our drop zone for the day, the Racetrack Duindigt, and could fly in directly, without circling. The Australian pilot flew echelon on my port side. I dropped first when we were over the racetrack, while the Australian dropped almost the same moment. I had waited a little bit too long with the drop, partly overshooting the drop zone. We had to follow the corridor back and as soon as we were over the

North Sea, our radio operator transmitted the message to our base that the mission had been successful.

'To see the people waving at us, to see "Thanks Boys" and "Many Thanks" spelled out with flowers gives you a warm glow and brought tears to my eyes, and I'm not ashamed of it, either! To think that today we did good instead of blowing towns and people to hell makes me realise that there is still some good left in this world.'

At noon that day the BBC broadcast the news about Operation Manna, and 240 Lancasters set off that afternoon to deliver the food. They flew at very low altitude, typically 500ft or less, and at very slow speed.

Last Witness David Fellowes ran the subsequent Manna Association until 2005:

'I did three Manna trips. In the first there was no truce with the Germans. Prince Bernard and RAF Air Commodore Geddes arranged with the Germans for us to drop this food in certain places.

'Of course, the war was still on, and this part of Holland was all cut off. They were very nice flights because we could go low-flying, rather a thrill.

'We carried food in the bomb bay, held in by sacking – tins of bacon, tins of milk, tins of egg powder, mostly tinned stuff wrapped up in individual sacks. We went to Rotterdam three times, a place called Tebrecht, we ran in, opened the bomb doors, the stuff fell out. There were lots of Dutch people there ready to pick up the food.'

One Canadian pilot recalled 'flying by a windmill and people waved at us from its balcony and we had to look up to wave back!' Rear gunner Sgt. Ken Wood:

'People were everywhere - on the streets, on the roofs, leaning out of windows. They all had something to wave, a handkerchief, a sheet – it was incredible.'

Flight Sergeant S Gibson:

'I will always remember seeing "Thank you, Tommy" written on one of the roofs'.

There were reports that some German soldiers took first pick of the supplies.

During the operation, in which many lives were saved, Bomber Command delivered 7,030 tons of food, and the USAAF 4,156 tons. A secondary effect was that it gave the Dutch hope and the feeling that the war would soon be over, which it was on 8 May, the last day of the Manna operations. Three RAF Lancasters were lost, two in a collision and one due to engine fire.

The Eagle's Nest

There was one raid at the end of the war that many RAF aircrew would have forgone leave for, and it heaved with volunteers. On 25 April 1945, 359 Lancasters and 16 Mosquitoes of 1, 5 and 8 Groups visited Berchtesgaden in an attack against Adolf Hitler's 'Eagle's Nest' chalet and the local SS guard barracks. Between them they carried a thousand tons of bombs, which they dropped on the homes and offices of high-ranking Nazi officials, military barracks and security police head-quarters. Among the force were 16 Lancasters of No 617 Squadron dropping their last Tallboys. There was some mist and the presence of snow on the ground also made it difficult to identify targets, and while the barracks were destroyed, the Eagle's Nest – the Berghof – survived to become a tourist attraction.

On one hand it was a satisfying two-finger gesture from RAF Bomber Command to the man who had started the war. On the other hand, two Lancasters were lost making that gesture.

Repatriation

Lancasters were involved even before the war ended in bringing PoWs home. In *Operation Exodus* which began on 2 May, Lancasters were converted to carry up to 25 passengers, and the first flight back home with PoWs was from Brussels two days later. Soon receiving camps were established in England and dealing with 1,000 PoWs a day. Last Witness John Langston, a navigator with 617 Squadron:

> 'On VE Day we flew into Rhineart in Germany and picked up 20 ex-PoWs from 1940, very early prisoners. We were in a queue of aeroplanes to pick up chaps, and flew them back to various holding centres, in our case Dunsford. Some were groggy, but they were all elated. We came back in daylight over the white cliffs of Dover, and these chaps were taking it in turns to visit the cockpit and have a look at England for the first time in five years. They started crying, and we were crying. We made two trips like that.
>
> 'We did the first trip into Dunsfold and that evening flew back to Woodhall Spa, changed into ordinary uniform, and all went to the Spa Hotel, the drinking place for 617 in those days. In the back of the hotel they had a wooden Horsa glider where the Army used to practice their ground rolls. They set it on fire to celebrate the end of the war.'

Thirty days after the end of the fighting, some 3,000 round trips had been made bringing home 74,178 PoWs. Lancasters were used in *Operation Dodge* to bring home the British Eighth Army from Italy and the Central Mediterranean. It was September before all the troops were brought back. Preparations had already been made for the post-war world.

Lancasters battle on

The first Lancaster to reach a Civil Register was on 11 Nov 1943. It was registered to BOAC as G-AGJI and evaluated for airline use, which led to the development of the Lancastrian, a 9-12 seat airliner. The prototype Lancastrian flew on 17 Jan 1945 with test pilot Jimmy Orrell. Designated G-AGLF, it was delivered from Woodford to BOAC at Croydon on 18 Feb 1945. BOAC used Lancastrians on long-range routes until Sept 1950. I was one of the airline captains flying them, with none of the comforts of a modern traveller. It was not unusual to see passengers on the long rackety routes to Australia staggering off at the journey's end and needing days to recover afterwards.

The last Lancaster produced was TW910 from Armstrong Whitworth on 2 February 1946. It served with 207 and 115 Squadrons and was SOC on 6 March 1950.

In Canada, RCAF Lancasters were in front line service until 1965. Victory Aircraft built 430 Lancaster Mark Xs, powered by the Packard-Merlin, from 1943-45 at the rate of four per week. They were supplied to 6 Group (RCAF), with 105 being lost in action by the four squadrons operating them. A total of 288 Mark Xs returned to Canada at the end of the war.

Apart from Canada, other air forces using Lancasters included France, Egypt and Argentina. The French Navy operated 54 Lancs in the Mediterranean, North Africa and the South Pacific. A further five were used by the French Government in a civilian rescue capacity.

The Royal Egyptian Air Force took delivery of nine Lancasters in June 1950. They were flown to Egypt, little used, and disappeared without trace.

Argentina received 15 Lancasters between May 1948 and January 1949. They saw service in the revolutionary period in the 1950s, including border patrols and reconnaissance.

The Russians used two Lancasters made airworthy by cobbling together spares from the six aircraft from 617 and 9 Squadrons which had force-landed in Russia during the Sept 1944 attack on the *Tirpitz*.

The Royal Swedish Air Force used a Lancaster as an engine test bed.

Production of Lancasters was difficult to stop when the fighting was over. The last-ever batch of 11 Lancaster IIIs was built by Avro's satellite factory at Yeadon in West Yorkshire after the end of the war. The first of this batch was built in September, four months after VE Day, and a month after VJ-Day, and the last delivered in October 1945. The statistics tell a sad story. None of them saw any action, most were used for ASR (Air/Sea Rescue) or for GR (General Reconnaissance) and a high proportion crashed, as if those flying them were more careless with peace-time life than on operations.

TX263 ASR No 38 Sqn SOC 3.8.50

TX 264 ASR GR. No 120 Sqn. Crashed at night near Ross & Cromarty 14.3.51

TX265 ASR GR No 236 OCU. Crash landed at St Eval 22.12.53

TX266 ASR 3 No 236 OCU SOC 30.8.48

TX267 ASR GR No 37 Sqn, 38 Sqn. SOC 6.9.56

TX268 ASR GR No 236 OCU SOC 18.10.56

TX269 ASR No 38 Sqn. Crashed off Italy 3.9.48

TX270 ASR GR No 37 Sqn, 38 Sqn. Collided with a Vickers Valetta, crashed 15.1.53

TX271 ASR GR No 236 OCU. Suffered fire on ground at Kinloss, not repaired.

TX272 ASR GR No 38 Sqn. SOC 11.4.53

TX273 ASR GR No 38 Sqn Sold for scrap 6.9.56

(SOC – Struck Off Charge)

The Berlin Air Lift

In 1948, two Lancasters operated by Flight Refuelling Ltd, run by the famous pioneer Sir Alan Cobham, ferried a great deal of petrol to the German capital during the Berlin Air Lift. Ten other Lancastrians were also sent in by FRL as part of the air operation to thwart Soviet leader Joe Stalin who was trying to starve Berlin in East Germany into surrender by cutting off land links with British- and American-occupied areas of West Germany.

The Berlin Air Lift lasted from 24 June 1948 to 11 May, 1949, and during the winter delivered 6,000 tons of coal and petrol a day to the beleaguered city as well as 1,500 tons of food. Avro Lancasters and the Lancaster variants Lancastrians, Yorks and Tudors were among the British aircraft involved.

Last Witness John Curtiss made 263 flights on that rescue mission to Berlin, as a flight lieutenant with RAF Transport Command:

'We were flying Avro Yorks, which were Lancasters with a different body. I flew from Wunsdorf, an airfield near Hanover, into RAF Gatow in Berlin, starting in June 1948, whenever we had a load to deliver. We made five return trips a day, 40 minutes there, 40 back. I saw no interference from Soviets. It soon became well-organised, airline stuff, we went on to nights as well, restricted to three sorties a day/night. In good weather, every 90 seconds an aircraft was landing, like Heathrow is now but with primitive equipment.

'Providing we had four serviceable engines and a radio, we flew. There was none of this health and safety stuff. Our cargoes were mainly coal and flour. We used to carry 19,000lbs of whatever we had. It did get incredibly dirty, but every four or five weeks the aircraft would return to the UK for deep servicing. They used to find corn growing through the floor-boards, from the mixture of coal and flour.

'Going back to the UK gave us five or six days leave every six to seven weeks. We flew with the same crew, but took whatever aeroplane came up. It became routine, a bit like driving a bus.

'Most of us were ex-bomber aircrew who had gone on afterwards to fly to and from the Far East, which had been rather a lonely business and there were few occasions when one socialised. Suddenly we were all together in Wunsdorf, old mates with a shared history, so we did a lot of getting together and drinking. We were no longer expecting to die the next time we took to the air, no attacks to and from Berlin.'

In fact there were 101 deaths attributed to the Berlin Air Lift, including 39 British and 31 Americans, mostly due to aircraft crashes, of which 17 were American and eight British. The cost of the Air Lift was $224 million, $2 billion in inflation-adjusted 2009 dollars.

Some Lancaster Mk1s were converted to photo reconnaissance, known as PRMk1, first operated by 541 Squadron, then reformed as 82 Squadron on 1 October 1946, and 683 Squadron in Africa and the Middle East in the fading days of the empire. Last Witness Flight Lieutenant Michael Beetham was flight commander, 82 Squadron in 1949:

'We flew Lancasters on photographic surveys for the Colonial Office out in Africa, based in Nairobi for seven months of the year in East Africa, and five months in West Africa. We were replacing the maps in the Colonial Office that Stanley and Livingstone had used.

'Most of Kenya had been done by the time I reached the squadron. We did Tanganyika, Northern Rhodesia, and went down to South Africa to do Bechuanaland, Swaziland, and Basutoland, based in Pretoria. Then we went to West Africa to Takoradi on the Gold Coast and did Sierra Leone from Kano, Nigeria. We were there for about five months operating from Accra, Takoradi and Lagos.

'What other aircraft could be better than Lancasters to do this? We would do eight to 10 hours each sortie, taking thousands of photos. Then we were ordered up to Abadir in Iraq because a Mr Moussadec was giving trouble in Iran, and back home they realised that they didn't have any up-to-date maps of Iraq. I took a detachment of three Lancasters and we were given six weeks to survey the whole of Iraq, which we did.'

The last Lancasters to serve overseas were MRs (Maritime Reconnaissance) of 38 Squadron out of Luqa, Malta. Its last Lancaster, RF 273, returned to England in February 1954, three years after the Avro Shackleton went into service. The Shackleton was a grandson of the Lancaster through the Avro Lincoln, its direct father, and employed on maritime reconnaissance. A total of 185 Shackletons were built and served with the RAF and South African Air Force. The last RAF Shackleton retired in 1990.

A farewell RAF ceremony took place in St Mawgan in Cornwall on Monday, 15 Oct 1956, when Lancaster RF325 from the School of Maritime Reconnaissance was retired and flown away to Wroughton in Wiltshire to be scrapped.

A total of 7,377 Lancasters were produced, of which 36 completed more than 100 operations apiece.

The Lancaster with the longest combat life, surviving an astonishing 147 operations, is judged to have been ED888, an Avro-built Mark III from the fourth production batch of 620 aircraft built by A.V. Roe at Newton Heath, Manchester. The first Lancaster in this batch was delivered in November 1942, the last in June 1943, with production averaging 24 per week.

ED888 arrived at 103 Squadron in 1 Group in April 1943. Coded PM-M (M-Mother), it did its first 55 operations under two non-commissioned skippers, Sgt D.W. Rudge and Flt Sgt H. Campbell, who took it through the whole Battle of the Ruhr and Hamburg, surviving seven trips against the worst of all targets, Berlin. ED888 was transferred to the newly-formed 576 Squadron at the end of November 1943, and went on to make eight more trips to Berlin, for a total of 72 operations before a major service. That meant it missed the 'Night of the Long Knives', the loss of 69 Lancasters among 95 RAF bombers over Nuremburg on 30 March 1944.

ED888, with four new engines and recoded UL-V2, was skippered for most of the next 40 ops by F/O J.E. Bell, who kicked off on 24 March 1944 by attacking Karlsruhe, but mainly flew against targets in France, covering the Allied invasion of Normandy. ED888 ended its 123rd operation on 10 September 1944 against Le Havre. For the next 14 operations (of which eight were against tough German targets) ED888 remained with 576 Squadron, before reverting to 103 Squadron on 31 October 1944 after attacking Cologne.

The lucky skipper for the last 9 trips made by ED888 was a Canadian, F/O S.L. Saxe, who flew the veteran Lancaster's last operation, again against Cologne on Christmas Day, 1944. There was no sentiment, though, when it came to disposing of the old girl – ED888 was scrapped and SOC on 8 January 1947.

There is no record for the shortest-lived Lancaster, but plenty of unintentional competition for that title.

Although they were hardly the ideal aircraft for athletic aerobatic displays, Lancasters were barrel-rolled and looped, and still attracted 'can-do' spirits such as Last Witness Captain Eric Brown, RN:

'We did improve the Lancaster in 1947, after the war, by putting power controls on. Power controls were unknown in the war except for the Germans, and the Americans with the Superfortress. The Germans were first in the European war. Putting on power controls turned the Lancaster into a four-engined Spitfire. In basic terms, it relieved the pilot of 60 per cent of the manual forces he had to deal with. You could do 30° a second on all three controls. It had the capability of putting the Lancaster up to 45° a second, but we decided we had better go easy, otherwise we would bend the aircraft. Indeed, it was so skittish that we had to put in a G-load restricter on the aeroplane, so we didn't bend its elevators so viciously that you could actually snap the fuselage.

'We did a barrel-roll in this hydraulic-controlled Lancaster, with ten people on board. I knew this roll could be done because test pilot Alex Henshaw famously barrel-rolled a Lancaster before me. While we were testing this aircraft with the hydraulic power, one of the things we had to do was test it over quite a large range of centres of gravity, which meant changing the ballast, and this could have meant coming down each time and then moving weights around. We decided instead, long before this health and safety nonsense, "Let's get ten or twelve people in there, and we'll draw up a chart up and distribute them where they have all got to stand."

'The special technique required that you keep the aircraft under G-force all the time, so you're not just inverting it or all the ballast guys would have fallen on the roof of the aircraft. But if you put enough G on you're not just rolling, it's like going around a barrel, and it can be done but very carefully. I have to take my hat off to Alex Henshaw because he did it with a Lancaster with normal controls, without power controls. The rate of roll on the Lancaster I was flying was so much higher than he had.

'I did say to my ballast boys, "Are you up for this, barrel-rolling a Lancaster?" There were some not too happy but it worked out fine. In the event, none of them fell down. But we had one lady whom I shall not name, 22 years old and very comely, a daughter of the manse and still alive and still comely. There was always some skylarking guy among this lot, and distributing the "ballast" around the Lancaster this girl was given the Elsan toilet to sit on. She had been among the majority in voting for the barrel roll.

'Of course, the Elsan had got no lid on it, and when I put the G-force on, she disappeared into the seat. She went into the Elsan all right, but could we get her out?

We had quite a delicate situation when we landed. To save her any embarrassment we decided to bring the fire brigade in. They proposed to hacksaw the seat off her. We put a screen all around and allowed one fireman to do the job. We didn't get any photographs, we could have, but we didn't. And of course there were suggestions of that old song, "Oh, dear what can the matter be..."'

The death toll of the young men of RAF Bomber Command, calculated from September 1939 to September 1945, which includes the end of the war in Japan as well as in Europe, was terrible.

The sister service, RAF Fighter Command, rightly lionised for its defence of these islands during the Battle of Britain, lost 3,690 killed throughout the whole war. They had 1,215 wounded and 601 were made prisoners of war. In all, 4,790 fighter aircraft were lost. For 'Bomber Boys' the price was much steeper.

Fifteen bomber crewmen were lost for every fighter aircrew.

RAF Bomber Command deaths, Sept to Sept:

1939-40	1,906
1940-41	4,330
1941-42	8,018
1942-43	14,163
1943-44	18,948
1944-May 1945	8,376

Total: 55,741 (we accept that this aggregate total disagrees with the figure of 55,573 given by the RAF Historical Branch).

Many of the Luftwaffe 'Old Hands' who, when they got into the RAF bomber streams, were able to inflict such damage and kill so many, survived the war with 'kill scores' nearly 10 times higher than their RAF and UISAAF opponents.

Last Witness Captain Eric Brown, RN:

'I know a lot of people are sceptical about the high scores of the German aces, but most of the scores were against Russian pilots. I had a long chat with Erich Hartmann, who died in 1993, who was credited with 1,404 combats and was the all-time top-scoring German fighter pilot with 352 kills, 260 against fighters. Hartmann said the tactical naivety of the Russians made it simple.

'You would get aircraft like the Illushyin 2, many of them flown by women pilots, doing exactly what the B-17s did, flying in straight lines in massive formations. Unlike the B-17 they didn't have any firepower, they had one peashooter at their back. He told me he used to wait until the Russian aircraft filled his windscreen before he fired. He only had to fire a few shots before he moved on to the next one, fire a few shots, move on to the next one and so on. He said he could knock down six in one sortie.

'He rated the Lancaster very highly. The Luftwaffe found it a difficult aircraft to attack at night because it did not really have an obvious blind spot, except the under-belly. They said that there was no effective way of attacking at night until the Schräge Musik was introduced, then the problems began for the Lancaster. On the first night's sortie in anger by the Heinkel 219, Hartmann said it shot down six Lancasters.'

According to Max Hastings in his 1980 book, *Bomber Command*, one seventh of all deaths suffered by the British in the war was incurred by Bomber Command.

RAF: 38,462 (69.2%)
RCAF: 9,919 (17.8%)
RAAF: 4,050 (7.3%)
RNZAF: 1,679 (3%)
Others: 1,463 (2.7%)
PoW: 9,784.

War Record

In October 1945, the following statistics were recorded:

- Total tonnage of high explosive bombs dropped by Lancasters on primary targets came to 608,612. Packed together, the bombs could fill a goods train 345 miles long.
- Lancasters accounted for two thirds of the total tonnage dropped by the whole of Bomber Command from March 1942 to May 1945.
- Average of four tons per bomber, means 150,000 sorties, using a total of 228 million imperial gallons of fuel.
- Total incendiaries dropped by Lancs, 51,513,106.
- In comparing the bomb tonnage dropped with aircraft lost, Stirling amounted to 41 tons, Halifax to 51 tons, Lancaster to 132 tons.

On 12 March 1949 I was at the Albert Hall for a meeting of 7,000 aircrew from RAF Bomber Command. I was between two men who served in 617 Dambuster Squadron and counted among the greatest bomber pilots of the war. One was Leonard Cheshire VC, DSO** DFC*, the other Mick Martin DSO*, DFC*, AFC, Guy Gibson's low-flying expert.

Cheshire went on in later life to set up the Cheshire Homes and was awarded a life peerage.

Martin had recently won the *Britannia Trophy*, the highest award in the gift of the Royal Aero Club. He became an Air Marshal and was knighted.

All three of us at the time, like the overwhelming majority of the men there that night, were at or under 30 years of age. My generation had been the cutting edge of the bomber campaign, doing our duty, fighting and making sacrifices for the greater good of our country, pawns pushed out on to the chessboard battlefield by the grand master.

Air Chief Marshal Sir Arthur Harris, also known as 'Butch' Harris within Bomber Command, was not present at the Albert Hall, having retreated to South Africa not long after the war ended without the kind of honour or peerage given to lesser men and having been rebuffed in his efforts to secure RAF Bomber

Command personnel a campaign medal from Clement Attlee's Labour Government. It should be recorded that Attlee was *not* lobbied on this deeply-felt issue
by Winston Churchill, and Gordon Brown's current 'New' Labour Government
feels the same way in 2009.

Bomber Command's leader that year was Air Marshal Sir Aubrey Ellwood, who
was in the hall that night, and stepped forward to address the gathering of young
men. As fighting men, we had never heard of him.

There arose from the hall a chant – 'We want Butch! We want Butch!' – which
grew in volume and in fervour and which I am sure was started by the more rowdy
elements amongst us. However cerebral the rest of us were, the chanting spread
quickly and showed no signs at all of dying away. Hardly any of us had ever met
Harris personally, and he remained an unseen Olympian figure whose word came
down from the summit, 'Cologne Tonight, Maximum Effort!'

We wanted our Chief and at that moment it was not Ellwood.

It was nothing personal.

It was tribal.

CHAPTER TWENTY-ONE

The Lancaster vs the Halifax

(and a nod to the Stirling)

There is no real comparison between the Short Stirling, first flown on 14 May 1939, and the Lancaster – as a Manchester III – with its first flight on 9 January 1941. The Halifax came in between, at a time when all war-plane makers were on a steep learning curve, having to clear their minds of the accumulated junk of thinking from the locust years.

The production line for Stirlings ran to 2,374, including 618 built by Austin Motors, of which 1,631 had been built as heavy bombers. They were starting to be withdrawn from Main Force bombing in 1943, although the Stirling's last raid was actually in September 1944. They were switched to glider-towing for the Normandy invasion on D-Day, and the 'Bridge Too Far' at Arnhem. They were also used for 'gardening', the RAF euphemism for mine-laying.

Even as late as July 1944, Stirling flight engineer Peter Rowland heard he was converting to Lancasters and in his diary he was upset at the prospect:

'Lancasters were regarded with suspicion and apprehension as being somewhat tinny and a bit of a bone-shaker compared to our smooth, massive, mighty Stirlings.'

Last Witness Flight Lieutenant Benny Goodman, a pilot with 617 Squadron:

'I flew the Stirling quite a lot, and I did a bit of flying on the Halifax. The Lanc was far and away above the others, because of its handling. You felt secure. You knew you could do anything with the Lanc, within reason. I flew a Halifax on a Baedecker tour. It wasn't a bad aeroplane to fly, but once you have flown a Lancaster you are terribly biased.

'But the Stirling does not deserve the criticism it attracted. It was difficult to get off the ground, and you never knew whether the electrics would work for you or against you when you got in the Stirling. You had to press a button which read positive or negative. If it was positive you were all right but if it was negative it wasn't all right and you all got out, and never got near the controls.

'If it showed negative, you knew it was the wet winters in East Anglia. Things used to go wrong because of the electrics. I have heard stories about people trying to retract the undercarriage and instead they have feathered an engine.

'I know Stirlings went through the Alps with a full fuel load and – okay, not exactly a full bomb load – to bomb Milan. At 12,000ft to 14,000ft they were not a bad aeroplane, and I flew them a lot.

'The Stirling did suffer from being chopped about because they hadn't got the engines, and they had shorter wings because they couldn't fit into the hangars. They did modify it, but they suffered from being under-powered.'

The Halifax, main competitor within the RAF to the Lancaster, entered service with 35 Squadron at RAF Linton-on-Ouse in November 1940 and its first operational raid was against Le Havre in France on the night of 11 March 1941. This was a year before the Lancaster went to war. Bomber Command Halifaxes flew 82,773 operations in total, dropped 224,207 tons of bombs and suffered 1,833 lost aircraft.

The first batch of 50 Mk I Halifaxes had a serious flaw in the design of the tail units that caused it to go into a steep, uncontrollable spin if the aeroplane lost engine power from two engines on the same wing, or if it was flung about vigorously. This fault undoubtedly caused a number of fatal crashes.

These were followed by 25 of the Mark 1 series II Halifaxes with increased gross weight to 60,000lbs, but with the maximum landing weight unchanged at 50,000lbs.

A total of 6,178 Halifaxes were built of all marks, of which the most numerous were the Halifax B Mark III, with 2,091 built. The Mark III first appeared in 1943 with the Merlin engine replaced by the more powerful Bristol Hercules XVI radial engine, and with rounded wing-tips and de Havilland Hydromatic propellers.

But that fatal first flaw in the early Halifaxes haunted it throughout its service life and even in early 1942 the Halifax was being investigated because its loss rate was 50 per cent higher than the Stirling, except on lightly defended targets. The report concluded that two factors contributed to this failure:

Its engines' exhausts were too highly visible at night.
Some pilots were afraid to throw it around, especially in a 'corkscrew'.

It is worth examining a detailed description of what a 'corkscrew' is, the technique used to evade enemy fighters:

The Corkscrew Manoeuvre was violent evasive action with dives and turns to the right and left, flying through the air like a corkscrew, in order for a bomber to shake off an attacker.

It is the standard action against a night-fighter, but very tough on the pilot. When a gunner spots a fighter on the left side and calls 'Corkscrew port – Go!' the pilot begins a steep dive and turn to the left, toward the attacker, diving approximately 1,000ft (305m), and then begins a climb. The Lancaster is still in a left turn, but after 500ft (152m), and still climbing, the pilot changes direction and makes a sharp turn to the right, which will reduce speed and hopefully make the fighter pilot miscalculate the Lancaster's speed and distance, and over-shoot. When the Lancaster is back up on its original altitude, the pilot dives 500ft (152m) to the right, and then turns left. By now the fighter will have been shaken off, but if it is still there, the pilot will have to Corkscrew again.

As RAF losses rose anyway because the German night-fighter tactics improved, the Halifax was seen to be better than the Stirling, but that was not enough of a recommendation and modifications were made. The Halifax III saw its weight reduced and changes were made to the rudder, making it square with more surface area. The Merlin engine replacement by the radial Hercules XVI greatly improved the performance. But the higher-than-average loss rate of the earlier Halifaxes – 1,977 Halifax I's were built – continued to be poor.

Harris complained loudly about the inadequacies of some aircraft, especially the Stirling and the Halifax, and characteristically minced few words. He wrote to the Air Member, Sir Archibald Sinclair on 30 December 1942, 'The manager of Short is an incompetent drunk' and recommended that 'Handley-Page and his gang be kicked out, lock, stock and barrel.'

If Harris could have converted all the 'heavies' in Bomber Command into Lancasters, he would have. It was considered in March 1944, that Handley-Page *would* stop building Halifaxes and convert their production lines to Lancasters – Chadwick and Dobson must have chuckled – but it was decided the hassle was not worth it. By contrast, some Halifax aircrew, especially those flying the Mark III, liked their aircraft, and very few of them would have opted to swap them for Lancasters.

Yet another report in June 1943 stated that the Halifax had acquired a bad reputation for instability during hard manoeuvres. The report said:

'There is no reasonable doubt that pilots on their first two operations have a casualty rate well above the average. Those who have survived 20 sorties had a rate well below the average. This must be aircraft-related as the Lancaster does not have the same problem.'

Last Witness Tony Hiscock, a pilot with 156 Pathfinder Squadron:

'The move from Halifaxes to Lancasters was a big improvement. The Halifaxes we were flying were the early ones, and they had a bit of trouble with them. They were not supposed to handle very well in an emergency. I didn't like the Halifax throttle arrangement, four straight throttle sticks, my hands were not big enough to do the job. On the Lancaster the throttle arrangement was different, and we were more easily able to cope. Normally we would open the throttles, push them right up and then the flight engineer would handle them.

'We were also not impressed, just training and on cross-countries, at losing a Halifax. It crashed on finals, something to do with problems which were identified later, its fins and controlling the aircraft. They put big fins on the later models. Halifaxes could spin-in on approach, and apparently it had been a fairly regular occurrence.

'There was some suggestion of a rudder-stall. The Halifax was not reliable in a "cork-screw", a vital means of escape when stalked by night-fighters. At the extreme of a cork-screw, either getting up or pulling over the top, you could lose it, and you couldn't correct it. Just flying the Lancaster, I preferred it. I am not analytical about this, it just "felt better" than anything else I had flown.'

Another Last Witness and supreme test pilot Eric Brown DSC, RN did exhaustive tests on the Halifax to find out what was wrong:

'What we were trying to do was to see the effect of one engine being knocked out in the course of a corkscrew. We decided not to use a second pilot, just had an engineer there, and he could pull any one of the engines back in the middle of a corkscrew. To make it realistic we did it at night, and we had searchlights coned on us.

'We were told that a representative of Bomber Command would come with us. And, we couldn't believe it, because it was Cheshire! We were astonished, to say the least, but to his ever-lasting credit he never commented at all. He raised his eyebrows at what we were doing – this was before he got his VC but he was still a famous bomber pilot – as he sat in the second pilot's seat, and I said, "Don't touch!"

'We cut the engines, and we had a bit of a problem getting out of the corkscrew. You get tremendous yaw, and the immediate effect is that it takes you by surprise. It was vital that it was not pre-arranged, you don't know which engine is going to go wrong. What the boffins had told the engineer was, cut the outer engine on the top wing, and when it went off we went into a spiral dive.

'The forces on us were tremendous, and we got out of it just by experience, I suppose, having practiced it so often, that I was prepared for it. You needed height, of course, and we had that. The solution was to try and get the aircraft into symmetry, the same forces working on both wings.

'The Lancaster did not tend to go into a spiral dive in similar conditions because of the position of the engines on the wings, clustered as close to the fuselage as possible. That gave the Lancaster a much more docile reaction than the Halifax.

'The Lancaster was a legend; we all thought the world of it. People used to tell us, "It's an in-line liquid-cooled engine. You've only got to be hit and you've had it," but you could come back on three engines. It was no bother. They said, "It's no good, you want a radial engine. If you get hit there's no liquid glycol to come out, and you don't lose an engine immediately."

'They were wrong. We got hit, everybody got hit, and had near escapes.'

This was a comparison at the end of 1943:

	Halifax	Lancaster
Number of sorties dispatched	12,382	19,338
Number of sorties attacking	11,080	17,923
Tons of bombs dropped	27,844	72,751
Number of aircraft missing	657	681
% of a/c attacking to sorties dispatched	89.5%	92.2%
% of a/c missing to sorties dispatched	5.3%	3.65%
Weight of bombs per attacking aircraft (lbs)	5,635	9,070
Tons of bombs dropped for every a/c missing	42.58	102.05
Average sorties/month per 20 aircraft	96	112

The most important of these statistics was the tonnage dropped, the Lancaster having nearly twice the performance of the Halifax.

The higher ceiling of the Lancaster also gave them an advantage. Halifaxes aborted more missions than Lancasters, often because of wing icing.

As the Lancaster flew higher than the Halifax, which in turn flew higher than the Stirling, these statistics showed up in the loss rate. It was easier for night-fighters to attack lower targets.

Oddly, when the bombing force was Lancasters only, losses tended to be higher than with a mixed force of Lancasters and Halifaxes. The reason may have been the Germans went after the 'easier' Halifaxes rather than the 'tougher' Lancasters.

Operational Squadrons

	Halifax	Lancaster
Sept 1942	10	10
Feb 1943	11	17
Aug 1943	15	23
Feb 1944	21	35 ½
June 1944	26	41
Dec 1944	27	58
May 1945	17	66

Lettice Curtis was one of the first eight women taken on by the ATA – Air Transport Auxiliary – delivering aircraft to working squadrons, and she was the first to deliver a Lancaster. Many a bomber pilot, feeling gung-ho because he was flying Lancasters, was somewhat cut down to size when, after watching a brand new Lancaster make a smooth touch-down and taxi in, he saw a neat, diminutive blonde climb out, followed only by a flight engineer. Later, Lettice wrote:

'Lancasters, the Anson of the four-engined class were so easy to fly that pilots were not even required to do a "stooge" preliminary trip. They had little tendency to swing on take-off, had a simple and well-designed cockpit layout, were no heavier on the control than, say, a Wellington and most of all were very easy to land because, unlike the Halifax or Stirling, they flew and landed without a significant change of attitude.

'In fact, given the handling notes, virtually any twin-engined pilot could have handled the Lancaster safely without a special course. In this connection it is worth recalling that, under ferrying conditions, the stalling speed with flaps and undercarriage down was as low as 85mph. Even a simple engine failure at the weights we flew them caused little inconvenience; it was possible to maintain height at climbing power with two engines out on one side.'

The Lancaster's greatest fault

From the point of view of a great test pilot like Captain Eric Brown, the Lancaster was 'viceless', but that is not quite true. There was one disturbing aspect to Lancasters when things went wrong that one boffin claims cost the lives of several thousand RAF aircrew. The escape hatch was too small.

While the estimate of 'several thousand' is a scarcely credible claim, the figure being so high that the numbers do not add up, the claim that any aircrew were lost due to such a fault is still a serious allegation.

There is no argument that in all three of our heavy bombers which flew at night, aircrew faced the terrifying difficulty of finding escape hatches in the dark.

Operational research statistics showed that about 50 per cent of Americans on daylight attacks successfully bailed out of damaged aircraft. By contrast, only about 25 per cent of British airmen made it safely out of either Halifaxes and Stirlings.

With a mere 15 per cent escape rate, the Lancaster was worst of all.

The reason is said to be the width of the front escape hatch. On a Lancaster the front escape hatch measured 22in (56cm) wide by 26½in (67cm) long, and that width is 2in (5cm) narrower than either the Halifax or the Stirling. The allegation is that this difference in size made a difference between one man in four getting away, and one man in seven.

The charge is made by Freeman Dyson, a British scientist who has achieved great fame in the USA since the war as an expert on space travel, quantum electrodynamics, and the 'greening of the galaxy.' But in 1943 Dyson was a brilliant 19-year-old 'teenager' – the word was not invented then – when he joined Harris's RAF Bomber Command Headquarters near High Wycombe in Buckinghamshire. He was hired as an analyst to document the flaws and failures of the bomber campaign.

It is Dyson's view – he is alive at the time of writing - that 'several thousand' Lancaster aircrew died because Bomber Command allegedly did not 'care' about their welfare. The authorities were, he says, not interested in finding out why the survival rate from downed Lancasters was so much poorer than from other British bombers.

Officially, the word was that airmen had an excellent chance of survival if the aircraft was shot down. They would simply jump through the escape hatch, pull the rip cord on their parachutes and float down to earth. Mike O'Loughlin, one of Dyson's colleagues in RAF Operations Research, spent two years fighting what he claims was totally unresponsive management to get the hatch enlarged, and he succeeded only as the war was ending in widening the hatch to 24in (60cm).

I can think of one famous RAF airman, Group Captain Evans-Evans DFC, station commander at RAF Coningsby – whom I knew well – who would never have been able to get through a 22in (56cm) hatch. Evans-Evans was a big man, and at 43 he was too old and too senior to be flying on operations anyway. But as men do, on 21 February 1945 he went out on a Lancaster III operation with 83 Squadron, one of the two Pathfinder squadrons in 5 Group. His was a very experienced crew, four were decorated, but they were caught and shot down by a night-fighter while heading to 'mark' the Mittelland Canal. All the crew were killed.

I have no idea why Freeman Dyson and Mike O'Loughlin failed to convince Harris of their case, except they may have been too young to count.

Through another part of his research, Dyson also discovered that experienced bomber crews no longer had any survival advantage over fresh ones; they had done better earlier in the war, but later this advantage disappeared. Something had changed; the Germans had developed an attack method that gave even experienced crews no chance to defend themselves.

Dyson's surmise, later proved correct, was that the Germans were fitting their fighters with upward-firing guns – the infamous Schräge Musik – and attacking the bombers from their blind spot, underneath.

Dyson and O'Loughlin went on to suggest deleting the 'useless' defensive guns altogether, making the bombers lighter and substantially faster, and also reducing the number of skilled crewmen needed. At the very least, they claim, with all the impatience of young men looking at their elders mucking things up, it could have been tried as an experiment.

Citing statistics, Dyson said gunners could not defend the bombers against night-fighters, which most often attacked from the gunner's blind spot, below the aircraft. 'Privately, I had another reason for wanting to rip out the turrets,' Dyson wrote later. 'Even if the change did not result in saving a single bomber, it would at least save the lives of the gunners.'

Bomber Command vetoed the idea, because, the radical young scientists thought, to remove the gun turrets flew in the face of the romantic image of the gunner riding shotgun for his crewmates. The armour went, the ammunition was cut back, but the turrets and gunners stayed.

In a dispatch on war operations in 1945, Sir Arthur Harris wrote:

'The Lancaster, coming into operation for the first time in March 1942, soon proved immensely superior to all other types in the Command. The advantages it enjoyed in speed, height and range enabled it to attack with success targets that other types could attempt only with serious risk or even certainty of heavy casualties. Suffice it to say that the Lancaster, in no matter what terms, was incomparably the most efficient of our bombers. In range, bomb-carrying capacity, ease of handling, freedom from accident and particularly in (low) casualty rate, it far surpassed the other heavy types.'

CHAPTER TWENTY-TWO

That Shining Sword

'The Lancaster surpassed all other types of heavy bomber. Not only could it take heavier bomb loads, not only was it easier to handle, not only were there fewer accidents with this than any other type throughout the war, the casualty rate was also considerably below other types. I used the Lancaster alone for those attacks which involved the deepest penetration into Germany and were, consequently, the most dangerous. I would say this to those that placed that shining sword in our hands – without your genius and efforts we could not have prevailed, for I believe that the Lancaster was the greatest single factor in winning the war.'

Air Chief Marshal Sir Arthur Harris
in a letter to Sir Roy Dobson,
6 Dec 1945

Captain Eric Brown RN:

'I always say there were three great aircraft in the Second World War on the British side, and our three were the Lancaster, the Mosquito and the Spitfire. There was only one, in my mind, as soon as you got into it as a pilot, you knew it was a great aircraft. That was the Lancaster. You got in and you said, "This is a pilot's aeroplane. It looks right, it feels right."

'You looked around it, the view is great, it just sits right on the ground. It's one of these aircraft. Much the same can be said of the Mosquito and the Spitfire, but they look a bit more lethal to the pilot. They remain great aeroplanes. And, of course, all three were blessed with having the Merlin engines which were incredibly reliable.'

Roy Chadwick, designer of the Lancaster, was honoured in 1943 with the CBE after the Dambusters Raid. After the war, he designed Britain's first pressurised airliner, the 60-passenger Avro Tudor, based around the Lancaster derivative the Avro Lincoln, though few were built. The Tudor played an honourable role in the 1948 Berlin Airlift carrying food and fuel.

Chadwick began to focus on jet flight, and the Air Ministry called for a long-range bomber capable of carrying an atomic weapon. In the winter of 1946/47 he designed a delta-winged craft, envisaging an airliner based on the same shape.

In Avro's subsequent brochure it was styled as the Avro Atlantic, fore-shadowing the Avro Vulcan.

Chadwick died on 23 August 1947 during a crash on take-off of the prototype Avro Tudor 2, *G-AGSU* from Woodford airfield. The accident was due to an error in an overnight servicing in which the aileron cables were inadvertently crossed. There was a widespread belief that he was overdue a knighthood. He is commemorated by a blue plaque on the surviving office building of the Avro factory at Greengate.

Lest We Forget

Victoria Crosses are the rarest and most valued of all decorations for courage in the British Armed Forces, and only 22 were awarded to RAF Bomber Command during the Second World War. Ten of these were awarded to Lancaster pilots, and one was awarded to the pilot of a Manchester, the Lancaster's blighted predecessor. It is unusual for a VC winner to survive winning the award and as previously mentioned, Pathfinder's Chief Air Vice Marshal Don Bennett swore there would be 'no living VCs in Pathfinder Force.' The Pathfinders did ultimately have three dead VCs. Of the 11 Lancaster VCs, the following died winning their awards:

Flying Officer Leslie Manser, a 20-year-old pilot of a 50 Squadron Manchester that was shot to pieces over Cologne on 30 May 1942 in Arthur Harris's first 'thousand bomber raid.' With one engine shot away and the other failing, Manser held his crippled aircraft steady so his crew could bail out successfully. He was not able to escape himself.

Canadian Pilot Officer Andrew Mynarski, 27, was mid-upper gunner with 419 RCAF Squadron attacking Cambrai on 12 June 1944 when a night-fighter set his Lancaster on fire and the captain ordered a bailout. Mynarski suffered severe burns attempting to release the rear gunner, and only left – saluting the rear gunner – when all efforts failed. Mynarski jumped with his clothes and parachute on fire. The rear gunner survived the crash and told of Mynarski's courage, winning him a posthumous VC.

Acting Squadron Leader Ian Bazalgette, 25, Master Bomber from 635 Pathfinder Squadron, attacking Trossy-St-Maximum on 4 August 1944, continued his bombing run after two engines were shot away and the aircraft was on fire. He held his burning aircraft steady while four of his crew bailed out, and instead of bailing out himself, crash-landed to avoid a French village to try and save two wounded crewmen still on board, but the Lancaster blew up.

Acting Squadron Leader Robert Palmer, 24, Master Bomber of 109 PFF Squadron, having completed 110 operations, attacked marshalling yards in Cologne in daylight on 23 December 1944. Ignoring two engines and his bomb bay set on fire, he continued his bombing run to accurately set markers for the rest of the force before falling in flames. Such was the strength of the opposition that more than half his formation failed to return.

Flight Sergeant George Thompson, 24, wireless operator in a 9 Squadron Lancaster attacking the Dortmund-Ems Canal on 1 January 1945, suffered terrible burns in rescuing two crewman from flames, and beat out other flames with his bare hands until the aircraft successfully crash-landed in Holland, where he died of his injuries. One of the injured crewmen he rescued lived.

Captain Edwin Swales, 29, SAAF Master Bomber from 582 Squadron, attacking Pforzheim on 23 February 1945, ignored repeated fighter attacks and the loss of two engines to ensure his force accurately pressed home the raid, then held his Lancaster steady while all his crew baled out before the aircraft crashed. He was found dead at the controls.

John Deering Nettleton, a 24-year-old acting squadron leader with 44 Rhodesia Squadron led the low-level Augsburg Raid of 12 Lancasters on 17 April 1942. Seven of the Lancasters were shot down, but the U-Boat engine factory was successfully bombed and Nettleton survived. The press called him the 'Roof-Top VC.'

Nettleton married WAAF officer Betty Havelock before the year was out, and, having made a triumphal public relations tour of the USA, was posted back on operations. On 12 July 1943, his 44 Squadron Lancaster, returning from a raid on Turin, was posted missing. He and his crew have no known graves and are commemorated on the Runnymede Memorial. A delayed announcement of his death was made on 23 February 1944, the day the birth was announced of his son, also called John Deering Nettleton.

Guy Gibson, 24, formed and led 19 Lancasters of 617 Squadron into the attack on three great German Dams on 17 May 1943, successfully breaching two of them, the Mohne and the Eder despite the loss of eight aircraft. He won his VC for this single action, and his is the pilot's name most associated by the general public with the Lancaster bomber. He did not survive the war, but his demise was, ironically, not in a Lancaster.

This is Robert Owen's tale, official historian of 617 Squadron, about how Gibson died:

'Guy Gibson, who held a VC, DSO* DFC*, was taken off ops after the Dams Raid and sent on a tour of North America. When he returned he was sent on a staff course, then posted back into 5 Group as a base operations officer in Coningsby. After 175 ops, Bomber Command did not want to risk him again. Paperwork and administration to Gibson was oil and water. They did not mix.

'People may have felt that putting him back in an operational environment would have been kind, but I think he found it even more frustrating. He was surrounded by people who were operating, and he was tied to a desk and planning.

'In Sept 1944 he managed to scrounge a number of sorties flying in aircraft shepherding the Main Force. He did one in a Lightning and one in a Lancaster; they were relatively easy-peasy sorties, and they were unofficial. But in Sept 1944 he found himself in a position where the station commander was off-base and Gibson was running the show, and he put himself on the battle order. He picked up a spare navigator and said, right, we are going to fly a Mosquito and become the controller for this target tonight. He took off from Woodhall Spa, because he was flying a 627 Squadron Mosquito.

'The target was initially Bremen but it was switched to Munchengludbach. It was a difficult target, and Gibson had hardly any experience as a controller, aside from his own pioneering role over the Dams. He was taking on two aiming points that night, and marshalling two marker forces as well. Though various marker aircraft had problems, the target was relatively successfully marked, and Gibson marshalled a moderately success-ful attack.

'He was heard to say, "Nice work chaps, right, now beat it home." He then set off back to base in the Mosquito he was flying. There is a lot of controversy about what happened next.

'He had maintained before he left that he intended to return at low level, even though the official briefing laid down not to return that way. It looks as though he stuck with what he wanted to do. His aircraft was heard by the inhabitants of the Dutch town of Steenberg to be approaching. Witnesses say it sounded as if it was running rough, other witnesses say it circled the town. There's one report where the crew could be seen silhouetted against the cockpit, but for whatever reason, the aircraft was certainly running rough. There was a sudden spluttering, a jet of flame, and the aircraft was seen to dive into the ground and explode.

'What caused that is open to conjecture.

'One theory that seems most viable was that Gibson was inexperienced at flying the Mosquito, as was his navigator. With the Mosquito, the navigator was responsible for fuel management. There is a possibility in the heat of battle that the navigator had not switched tanks, or that Gibson had not asked the navigator to switch tanks. The engines could have suddenly started to run dry, they switched tanks but in doing so got a rich mixture into the carburettor which caused the gout of flame, and if one engine picked up

before the other – especially with the Mosquito – it was likely to flick. There is a possibility
that one engine did pick up, and Gibson was not able to catch it and it went in like that.

'There was not much left of the aircraft. The destruction was such that the people who
recovered the crew believed that they were dealing with one body, and it was only before
interment that someone came up with a third hand, and they realised that two men had
died.'

Barnes Wallis said of Gibson:

'For some men of great courage and adventure, inactivity was a slow death. Would a
man like Gibson ever have adjusted back to peacetime life? One can imagine it would
have been a somewhat empty existence after all he had been through. Facing death
had become his drug. He had seen countless friends and comrades perish in the great
crusade. Perhaps something in him even welcomed the inevitability he had always felt
that before the war ended he would join them in their Bomber Command Valhalla. He
had pushed his luck beyond all limits and he knew it. But that was the kind of man
he was... a man of great courage, inspiration and leadership. A man born for war...
but born to fall in war.'

Three Lancaster winners of the Victoria Cross did survive the war.

Bill Reid, 22, was an acting flight lieutenant pilot with 61 Squadron on 3 November 1943 when, shot-up twice and losing blood from a number of wounds, with
a dead and a dying crewman on board, decided nevertheless to fly 200 miles to
his target in Dusseldorf. He bombed successfully, and after prolonged periods of
unconsciousness, landed safely back in England.

Reid left the RAF in 1946 and resumed his studies at Glasgow University, where
he met his future wife, Violet. They were to marry in 1952 and Violet, still alive as
we write, had this to say about her husband:

'I met Bill in 1948 where he was in his last year at Glasgow University, studying to be a
farmer. There were dances at the university and students lodged in the hall, where they
could eat and they had a wee dance place. I went to one of the dances with a friend in her
first year.

'Bill touched me on the shoulder and asked me to dance with him. And that was it. For
me it was love at first sight.

'My father was a journalist in Glasgow with the *Daily Record*. He was the sports editor
there for years. He came in one night and said, "Do you know who you are going out
with?"

'I said "I am going out with Bill Reid."

'"Do you know he's got a Victoria Cross?"

'I had been going out with him for a whole year and he hadn't said a word about it.

'Bill was a very quiet, shy person. He was not one of these people that told everybody about it. I met a few VCs and most of them were like Bill. They were all the same, quiet and shy.'

After graduating in 1949, he went on a travelling scholarship for six months, studying agriculture in India, Australia, New Zealand, America and Canada. In 1950, he became an agricultural adviser to the MacRobert Trust, Douneside. From 1959 to his retirement in 1981, he was adviser to a firm of animal feed manufacturers. Bill Reid died at the age of 79 on 28 November 2001.

Wing Commander Leonard Cheshire, 27, won his VC in October 1944 after completing 100 missions in four years of fighting against the bitterest opposition, maintaining a record of outstanding personal achievement, invariably in the forefront of the battle. What he did in a single Munich operation in 1944, diving to 1,000ft (305m) to ensure accurate marking, and staying under withering fire for 12 minutes, was typical of the brilliant flying which made his reputation second to none in Bomber Command.

Group Captain Leonard Cheshire VC, DSO** DFC* was official British observer when the atomic bomb was dropped on Nagasaki in 1945. He was quoted as saying afterwards: 'I for one hold little brief for the future of civilization.'

He left the RAF in 1946, converted to Catholicism in 1948 and set up Leonard Cheshire Disability, now one of the top 30 charities in Britain. He dedicated the rest of his life to supporting disabled people. Cheshire had a short-lived marriage with American actress, Constance Binney, in 1941 and in April 1959 in Bombay he married Sue Ryder, also the founder of a charity. They had two children, Jeremy and Elizabeth Cheshire, and lived in Suffolk.

In 1981, he was given the Order of Merit, and in 1991 a life peerage as Baron Cheshire of Woodhall (unofficial 617 HQ) and sat as a cross-bencher in the House of Lords. He died in 1992 of motor neurone disease. The Queen paid personal tribute to him in her Christmas message. Voted 31 in a BBC poll in 2002 to find the 100 Greatest Britons, his VC is in the Imperial War Museum.

Sergeant Norman Cyril Jackson, 24, a flight engineer with 106 Squadron, was on a mission to Schweinfurt on 24 April 1944 when his Lancaster was attacked by a fighter and set on fire at 22,000ft (6,705m). Jackson climbed out on the wing in a 200mph slipstream to try to extinguish the flames, but eventually was pulled off the aircraft by his burning parachute. He survived the fall.

He had been promoted to Warrant Officer when his VC was gazetted on 26 October 1945, after the war ended, following his escape from a PoW camp and the authorities learning of his extraordinary story.

When he went to Buckingham Palace to receive the VC from King George VI, he was accompanied by Leonard Cheshire, also receiving his VC, the only two that day. Cheshire insisted that, despite the difference in ranks, group captain and warrant officer, they should approach the King together

'I can't remember what the King said to him,' Jackson said later, 'but Cheshire said: "This chap stuck his neck out more than I did – he should have the VC first!"'

'Of course the King had to keep to protocol, but I will never forget what Cheshire said.'

Jackson went on to have four sons and three daughters with his wife, Alma. He died at the age of 74 at his home in Hampton Hill, Middlesex in March, 1994. After Alma's death in 2004, his VC and other medals sold at auction for £235,250, the highest price paid at that time for a Victoria Cross, against a pre-auction estimate of £130,000. His family was upset because the VC went to a private bidder – thought to be Lord Ashcroft, who has more than 100 VCs – rather than to the RAF Museum at Hendon. They had planned to give their father's medals to the museum but found they could not do so under the terms of Mrs Jackson's will, and the museum was out-bid.

Last Witnesses

There are not many left of the Last Witnesses to the force and power of the Lancaster bomber, and those that are left survived by skill and – as they will say themselves – they had luck, too. We all lived into the second half of the first decade of the twenty-first century, to look back on a youth dominated by our association with the greatest British bomber of the Second World War. Without the Lancaster, our lives would have been very different, and because of the random way chance works, some of us alive today would not have made it through to 2009. This is what happened to the others.

Bob Horsley, the Wireless/Op who grew up with me in Yorkshire, and who bailed out of the Manchester piloted by 20-year-old Leslie Manser VC during the first 'thousand bomber' raid on Cologne in 1942, succeeded in evading capture and got back to England.

He was awarded a DFC for the Cologne Raid, went to Canada as an instructor and then converted to pilot. He returned to England and distinguished himself as a pilot on 617 Dambuster Squadron. After the war he became an RAF jet flying instructor and an instrument rating examiner, earning a King's Commendation and an AFC – Air Force Cross. Horsley did two tours of the Middle East as an Air Attache, one tour of four years in Iraq, the other of two years in Saudi Arabia.

After retiring he did five years Special Duties for the Foreign Office in Beirut before emigrating to Australia.

Rupert Noye, rear gunner to Last Witness Tony Hiscock on 156 Pathfinder Squadron, won a DFC after 72 ops as a rear gunner, outliving the average life of a Bomber Command crewman by more than a factor of three: 'I stayed in the air force after the war for three years, then left and joined the Southern Gas Board. I found a wife then, and we've been married 55 years. Maybe I was spared for that.'

Laurence 'Benny' Goodman, pilot with 617 Squadron flew 30 ops and dropped a Grand Slam bomb on Belefeldt. After the war he flew Hastings aircraft with 51 Squadron, bringing back PoWs who had suffered under the Japanese. He had a brief role in the Berlin Air Lift, and went on to fly Canberra PR7s, leaving the RAF in 1964 as a squadron leader. Benny joined his father, who owned the advertising rights to cinema curtains and later made films. This business had very good clients, enough that Goodman senior could travel around in a Rolls Royce.

Benny continued with his father's business, including three years in Ghana, for the rest of his working life. In 2008 he was still flying his own Comanche 250 private plane.

Reg Barker, the 22-year-old Pathfinder Squadron pilot who survived a Schräge Musik attack which cut his Lancaster in two and left him and four of his crew PoWs for nine months, was offered a permanent commission after the war in RAF Transport Command. Instead, he married his beloved Joan, a WAAF Intelligence officer commissioned eight days before Hitler's death: 'We're sure he despaired at this news and blew his head off.'

Barker went into his father-in-law's jewellery business, had two children and four grandchildren and took up a passion for sailing. He goes to all the 635 Squadron reunions, and one grandson is now a doctor at RAF Waddington.

Flight Sergeant Stan Bradford, mid-upper gunner with 57 Squadron who shot down six Luftwaffe night-fighters and won the DFM: 'I went to Abingdon as a gunnery instructor, and when the war ended I was detailed to get our returned PoWs into an Air Force way of thinking. It wasn't an easy task, as most of them were due to leave the RAF immediately. On the camp we had 200 German PoWs and 200 Italian PoWs, and tried to keep that lot apart. They would have fought if they had had the chance.

'One day I got lost on my way to Oxford and popped into a pub for a pint. I married the landlord's daughter. We've been married 62 years. I became a landlord myself.'

John Langston had gone to Wadham College, Oxford, trained in Canada as a navigator, and did a tour of 25 ops as a navigator with 189 Squadron. In 1945 he did a second tour with 617 Squadron, including 9 Tallboy raids and 3 Grand Slam raids as lead navigator in the attack on the Bielefeldt Viaduct.

After the war he was awarded a full-time commission, commanding 49 Squadron flying Valiants, each carrying two atomic bombs. He went to Staff College, to central planning, on to Northern Ireland as the Air Commander at the start of 'The Troubles', finishing as Air Commander Gibraltar with the rank of Air Commodore and a CBE. In Gibraltar he always kept two Hawker Hunters with pilots on 10 minutes notice in case of harassment by the Spanish.

Jim Norris CGM never went back on operations, and finished the war working as a flight engineer at St Athans in Wales, fitting new equipment and being sent up to flight-test it on Lancasters, Halifaxes and Stirlings. His view on the Lancaster was that it was unbeatable.

> 'I flew Halifaxes but I didn't like them. I suppose it was their design and the noise they made. The Lancaster was so sweet if you tuned the engines properly, and I tuned the engines. There was nothing to touch the Lancaster. On that night over Düsseldorf when we were shot up, I don't think there was any other aircraft that would have stood up to it, the damage that was done, and to fly like it did.'

After the war, at the age of 25, he came out of the RAF and worked on the railways, later ran a General Stores for 22 years, then he was area sales manager for a bakery.

John Curtiss had a tour on Halifaxes, then stayed in the RAF after the war. Initially he flew to and from the Far East in Stirlings '... a bloody awful aircraft, designed for bombing and not passengers. Then we moved to Yorks, a very gentlemanly aeroplane, a Lancaster with a different body. We flew to Singapore in five days, flying only by day, and occasionally flew to Southern Rhodesia.'

In 1948 he flew in the Berlin Air Lift making 263 return journeys. When the Korean War started in 1950 he went to Hamble to train national service aircrew. He had 41 years' of RAF service and was Air Commander for the Falklands operations in 1982. Made KBE and later KCB, as Sir John Curtiss he reached Air Marshal, the first navigator to reach that rank.

David Fellowes was an air gunner on 460 Squadron RAAF, flying Lancasters. He did 33 ops, a tour and a bit:

> 'Our crew kept in contact after the war, and my pilot, Art, got a DFC and went to civil airlines as a pilot. I also went to airlines as a loadmaster/steward flying Lancastrians on

BOAC. I went on to fly Yorks, Dakotas, Lancastrians as a steward, on to Argonauts, then flying boats, and a Lockheed Constellation.

'I got back into the RAF in 1952, and served as an air gunner on Shackletons. I did a radar course, came out of the RAF in 1957, and went back into civilian airlines as a steward. I went on to start a school teaching safety procedures.'

John Bell started as an airman, became operational and was commissioned in 1944 when he was with 619 Squadron:

'I was bomb aimer for Bobby Knights and did 27 trips with 619 and 23 with 617, then went to an OTU to instruct on bomb-aiming. At the end of the war I had acquired a family and decided it was better to stay in the RAF rather than travel up to London every day for a career in the City.

The RAF took notice that I had been an accountant before joining up, so I was sent on an accounts course and became an Accounts Officer at Tangmere and then at Gatow during the Berlin Air Lift.

'I got out of that by volunteering for photographic interpretation, which I did for the next 20 years. Ended my career as a wing commander with an MBE and DFC.'

Canadian 'Doc' Sutherland, front gunner to Les Knight on the Dams Raid, survived being shot down after bailing out on 617's worst night, attacking the Dortmund-Ems Canal later that year, when Knight died. Sutherland evaded capture, got to Gibraltar and was flown back to England. After de-briefing he was posted back to Canada – undecorated - and proposed to a local girl:

'I had to ask my father's permission because I was not yet 21. This has always been a family joke. I was not going to stay in the air force, and Margaret and I were married in January 1944. We decided to go to Vancouver. She went to work and I had some high school work to pick up on so it took us a while, but I could not have gone to UBC – University of British Columbia – in Vancouver, or finished the degree in Forestry where I made my career, without her help.'

Their 65th wedding anniversary was in January, 2009.

Kurt Schulze, adjutant of Luftwaffe 9.Staffel who might have decimated 617 Squadron's third attack on the *Tirpitz*, was 23 at the end of the war and a squadron commander in Norway:

'I became a prisoner of war of the Americans. At that time the US turned over 700,000 German PoWs to France for slave labour. For two years I was one of them. I came home in 1947 and found my wife, Annerose, in the then American sector of Berlin. She had been there with all the pleasures of the Russian occupation and refused to talk about it at all. Because I had been an officer on active service, in socialist, communistic Berlin I was not allowed to vote and not allowed to go to college, so I got a job as an apprentice for $12.50 per month.

'Fortunately I was in the American sector. My wife had worked for the Americans cleaning houses and then as a typist until our son was born in 1948. I became a real estate broker in Berlin and an uncle who had emigrated to America in the 1920s said, "Why don't you sell your real estate business, we will sponsor you, and come here?"

'In 1953 we emigrated to California where we lived in Inglewood and I spent the rest of my life as a businessman. I am now a member of an association for "old, bold pilots" of every nationality. Every Wednesday I am there with 50 to 60 pilots. Annerose, who passed away five years ago, always refused to talk about the Russian occupation. She couldn't understand that we were still talking about the terrible war.'

Patrick Dorehill, won a DFC for his part as co-pilot to John Nettleton's VC-winning attack on Augsburg with 44 Squadron. Later in the war he won a bar to his DFC, and then a DSO, completing 54 ops.

On one raid into Germany he survived cannon shells shot through his starboard fuel tank without an explosion. His bomb bay wouldn't close after that raid and when he tried to land he had no flaps and only one wheel went down. But he and his crew got away with it.

Sir Arthur Harris wrote to congratulate him on his DSO. Dorehill wrote back asking for a transfer to Transport Command. This transfer came through and he spent his career as an airline pilot, first with BOAC, then with BEA, retiring at 55. He once met a German Luftwaffe fighter pilot who had shot down two of the seven Lancasters lost on the Augsburg raid, but they were in a hurry and the promise to meet and talk it over was never fulfilled.

Les Munro, last surviving Dambuster pilot, one of the founders of 617 Squadron:

'I arrived back in New Zealand at the end of October 1945 on the SS *Andes*. There were a lot of prisoners of war returning to Australia and New Zealand. It was a fast ship, broke all records from England to Melbourne. We headed on for New Zealand and then the ship was reduced to half-speed. The ruddy wharfies in New Zealand wouldn't disembark us because we were going to land on Labour weekend, and they didn't want to work that weekend. There was a rebellion on the ship but it didn't matter what we said, the ship maintained half speed. When Fred Jones, the Minister for Defence came out on the Lighter to welcome the troops back, he was pelted with eggs and anything else we could throw at him. That was quite a sight.

'I went on to civvie street, did a course at Massey College and a refresher in sheep farming, and then went on to land valuation and settlement of ex-servicemen. I worked on that for 14 years, settling ex-servicemen on farms, and then farmed on my own account from 1961. I also got involved in local politics and in 1965 I became a county councillor and later Mayor of Waitomo for 17 years, the sheep-shearing capital of the world. Decorations: CNZM (the NZ equivalent of a knighthood), DSO, QSO (Companion of the Queen's Service Order), DFC.'

Tony Hiscock, Pathfinder pilot with 156 Squadron, ended the war with two DFCs which he alleges were 'for just ploughing on' through to 68 ops, more than three times the average life of an RAF bomber pilot.

He applied to join the airline BEA, but there was a delay of three weeks and then they sent him an application form which asked: 'What does your father do?' Hiscock felt this was a damned cheek and applied to join a new airline set up by Pathfinder Chief Don Bennett, British South American Airways. He was accepted immediately.

Hiscock married and had two children, and in his career survived the merger with BOAC and later the merger to form British Airways, retiring at the age of 54. 'I am one of the reasons pension schemes have problems because I am coming up to my thirty-second year in retirement.'

Rolf Ebhardt, a 21-year-old Luftwaffe night-fighter when he shot down four Lancasters and four Halifaxes in the last year of the war, went to South Africa in the late 1940s and trained as a dentist, a profession he practised for the rest of his life back in Hamburg in Germany. To this day he admires the Lancaster:

'In a certain way it was a mystery for me, because we never saw it in the daytime, we only saw the blackness of it. We never saw the airmen. I think she was a very good plane. After the war I have read that flying her was a pleasure, that she could be very fast, especially when the bombs were gone and they dived to gain speed. Sometimes we could not follow, we were not fast enough. The nicest thing I could expect to do is to fly a Lancaster, but that remains a dream for ever.'

Don Briggs, flight engineer in 156 Pathfinder Squadron:

'I managed to get through 62 ops, all on the same squadron, all on Lancasters, and was commissioned after my first tour, without a break except for two week's leave between tours.

'Awarded DFC. Made a career in the RAF, qualified as pilot in 1952 on Canberra jet bombers, became flight commander with 10 Squadron at RAF Scampton. The grave of Guy Gibson's dog, Nigger, was right outside my office window.

'I flew all three V-bombers, Valiant, Victor and Vulcan, including a two-and-a-half-year tour on Valiants helping to drop a Christmas Island H-Bomb. We dropped *a weapon called Purple Granite, roughly 300,000 tons, an air burst, so it didn't suck up sand and sea. The highlight of my career was as a flying instructor on the Vulcan B2 bomber.'*

Ray Grayston, flight engineer to Les Knights and Dambuster veteran, baled out on the Dortmund-Ems attack before Knights crashed and died:

> 'The goons were all over the place looking for us, determined to capture us. I was on the move for about three or four days, no more than that. I was invited in to go to a house where somebody could speak English. Unfortunately, the Germans were watching the house.
>
> 'I went to the front door. A charming lady opened it and said, in English, "Oh my God! What are you doing here?" The Germans came along and picked me up. They tried to get me to get her hung but I took them on. Told them they were a bunch of bloody idiots, typically British at that time. You get very brave when you have no options.
>
> 'I was a PoW for the rest of the war. I did not find it hard. Immediately afterwards I left the RAF and joined Hawker Siddeley and stayed with them for 30-plus years as a technician.'

Group Captain James Tait, DSO*** DFC* remained in the RAF after the war, initially reverting to the rank of squadron leader. He served in South East Asia, India, the Middle East and Singapore, commanded RAF Coningsby, was promoted to group captain in 1953, appointed ADC to the Queen in 1959, and retired from the RAF in 1964.

He retrained as a computer programmer, and joined ICL working in Eastern Europe. After a period with a haulage company and as an investment adviser with Scottish Widows, he retired in 1981.

He married Betty Plummer, a WAAF officer, in 1945. They had a son and two daughters. Betty died in 1990. Tait himself died in August 2007.

Captain Eric 'Winkle' Brown, RN is the most highly decorated officer in the Fleet Air Arm. He went on to command the Enemy Aircraft Flight, test-flying captured German aircraft. Brown flight-tested 53 German aircraft, including the Me163 rocket plane and the Me262 jet plane.

Fluent in German, he helped interview Werner Von Braun, Hermann Goering, Heinrich Himmler, Willie Messerschmitt and Dr Ernst Heinkel after the war.

'Winkle' Brown was responsible for the first carrier landing using an aircraft equipped with a tricycle undercarriage (Bell Airacobra Mk 1) on HMS *Pretoria Castle* on 4 April 1945. He also made the world's first landing of a jet aircraft on an aircraft carrier in the DH Sea Vampire on the HMS *Ocean* on 3 December 1945.

He holds the world record for the most carrier landings, 2,407. He is listed in *Guinness World Records* as holding the record – 487 types – for flying the greatest number of different aircraft. He doesn't think that this record will ever be beaten. In his ninetieth year, he is official advisor to the Royal Navy on Britain's two new aircraft carriers… if they ever get built.

Heinz Orlowski, who nearly did for me over Bergen that January day in 1945, could not go back to his home town of Loetzen when the war was over. It was in Communist East Germany and he would not have been very welcome. In Hanover at the age of 23:

> 'I sought and found employment in my trained profession as a timber merchant. I worked in Hanover, then in Hamburg – marrying in 1951 – and then in 1956 I moved to Berlin where I continued my profession until I retired. I did a certain amount of glider flying but we were all very busy for years after the war, just making a living. I have two children, and two grand-children.'

George Hart, ground crew with 83 Squadron at Scampton:

> 'I was an LAC and I didn't want to get any sergeant stripes because I wanted a sensible finish to the war. I wanted to get back to the City and my previous job in Cornhill Insurance; they had to keep the job open for you when you were called up.
>
> 'I wrote to them as soon as I knew I was leaving the RAF and had a return letter which said, "Would you please come up to have an interview? We'd like you to start almost immediately." I had hoped that I would have a fortnight or three weeks leave, but I went back and I did 50 years, 6 months and 14 days at Cornhill, as they told me at my retirement party, but that was including my pre-war service. I have been retired 30 years now.

Desmond Selley was shot down by a Schräge Musik fighter east of Cologne as a 21-year-old Pathfinder pilot on 13 February 1945:

> 'From then on it was another story until the end of the war, about being a PoW. I made a complete diary of my time as a PoW on the back of cigarette packets. Eventually I ended up as a PoW in Nuremburg, and as the Russians got close, the Germans moved us out of that camp and walked us for two weeks down to Ruisberg, just outside Munich. There the Americans released us.
>
> 'I demobilised in 1946 as a flight lieutenant, having been awarded a DFC and was offered a very good job in the City with a firm called William France Fennick, owners of 24 ships. My whole career has been in shipping, at later stages in Marine insurance.'

Michael Beetham completed a tour of 30 operations and won a DFC as a 21-year-old pilot with 50 Squadron on Lancasters, including 10 raids on Berlin and surviving the 'Knight of the Long Knives' over Nuremburg in March 1944. After the war he was sent on a splendid 'Jolly' to the USA to show the Americans how big the Lancaster's bomb bay was – at least five times the capacity of a B-17 – and displaying impeccable timing turning up to all the air displays to which they were invited.

He also completed tours of Africa and the Middle East in the later 1940s, taking thousands of aerial photos to replace the maps used by Dr Livingstone and other pioneers, and amassing more than 2,000 hours on Lancasters. Beetham went on to command a Valiant squadron, became an expert on mid-air re-fuelling, and later as RAF Chief of the Air Staff, planned the RAF Vulcan attack on Port Stanley during the Falklands War in 1982. He is now Sir Michael Beetham GCB CBE DFC AFC, the most senior Marshal of the Royal Air Force.

Lancaster Music

The Lancaster has its own piece of music. Wing Commander Rob Wiffin, a previous Director of Music, conducted the Central Band of the RAF on occasions where the last Lancaster would end the solemn Sunset Ceremony of "Beating the Retreat" with a flypast. This was a dramatic and poignant moment for many in the crowds. These memories came to mind in planning the music for the Service of Commemoration for Bomber Command in St Paul's Cathedral on 24 April, 2002. A special piece of music was needed to accompany the parade of the Queen's Colour of the RAF from the west door of St Paul's to the altar. Inspired by Harris's description of the Lancaster as our "Shining Sword", Rob Wiffin composed a fanfare with that title as his tribute to lost bomber aircrew. It is played at many Bomber Command events.

Long Distance Lancasters

In February 1943, RAAF Headquarters in London decided to send a Lancaster to Australia. A brand new Mark III, ED 930 with Merlin 28 engines, was built at Avro's works in Manchester. The upper turret was removed, a spare tank installed, and it was given the letter 'Q' and called "Q for Queenie VI". Flight Lieutenant Peter Isaacson, DFC, DFM, an Australian Pathfinder pilot with two tours of operations under his belt, was selected as captain. But his boss, Don Bennett, also an Australian, insisted Isaacson completed his full second tour of ops by bombing Berlin on the night of 29 March 1943. His crew, all Australians, were chosen from 156 Squadron.

They left RAF Lyneham in Wiltshire on 21 May, heading west via Prestwick in Scotland, and a long Atlantic flight to Montreal – 15½ hours – and then Toronto, San Francisco and Honolulu. Heading south to Canton Island they were struck by a violent tropical storm in which all four engines were lost and they dropped two miles before flight engineer Don Delaney got the engines started again. They landed on the nearest island, Palmyra Atoll, to repair and check the damage, then flew on via Fiji to reach Australia near Brisbane and landed at Sydney that evening. There they were met by "Ministers, Brass Hats, the Press and speeches" as Peter Isaacson puts it.

Q-Queenie VI was sent to show off around New Zealand, and then all over Australia. Isaacson gave short flights to the Prime Minister and the Governor-General, and to thousands of schoolchildren – often 40 at a time – and anyone who bought £250 of war bonds. Famously, during one exhibition flight over Sydney in October 1943, Isaacson flew Q-Queenie VI under the Sydney Harbour Bridge. He could have been court-martialled, instead the RAAF awarded him the Air Force Cross.

Sent for maintenance on a too-short runway, Q-Queenie VI swung off into a swamp, damaging undercarriage, engines, wings and tail unit. Don Delaney refused to accept his favourite Lancaster was beyond repair, and by April 1944 she was taxied out of the swamp as good as new. By the end of tour 2,300 customers had been carried and over £250,000 accumulated!

The Lancaster was handed over to an Operational Training Unit at Tocumwal, New South Wales, in August 1945 after 765 landings and having been flown by 52 different pilots, and later put into storage before being 'SOC' in 1948 – an air force term for 'scrapped'.

The only other Lancaster in the country, G-George, which arrived in Australia in November 1944, met a better fate. It now stands in the Australian War Memorials Hall in Canberra. In restoring G-George to proper condition, many of Q-Queenie's component parts were used, so part of her lives on!

Wing Commander Peter Isaacson, AM, DFC, AFC, DFM, was born in London on 31 July 1920, another Lancaster brat. His father was an Australian soldier who met Peter's mother in England just after World War One. They moved to Melbourne in 1926 and Peter joined the RAAF in 1940. After retiring from the RAAF in 1946 he bought a local newspaper; his company grew to employ 370 staff in Australia and New Zealand, publishing 60 titles. He still lives in Melbourne.

The Last Lancasters

Physically, there are few Lancasters left, but it has become an iconic subject for artists, ensuring that the aircraft's image will be remembered by future generations. One of the most distinguished of these artists is Gerald Coulson, a founder of the Guild of Aviation Artists. In 1969 Coulson was commissioned by Rolls-Royce Aero Engines to produce a painting of the attack on the *Tirpitz*. His adviser was Group Captain J B Tait, DSO***, DFC*, Commanding Officer of 617 Squadron, whose 5-ton Tallboy bomb scored a direct hit on the 56,000 ton warship. The painting, one of the best-known by Coulson, hangs at the foot of the main staircase of RAF College, Cranwell.

> 'It is an aircraft that is easy on the eye, a most attractive aircraft. It wasn't meant to be attractive, after all it was a war machine, it just turned out to be! It is nicely balanced, sits nicely in the air and on the ground. In my mind what I had to see on the painting was three things, the Lancaster, the bomb, and the *Tirpitz*. That's how I came to that composition, three-quarters behind so all three would be illustrated. I placed all three somewhere on the canvas, in a relationship with each other, and the rest followed.'

It was sheer chance that Coulson chose the code for the main Lancaster in the picture, my own F-Fox.

The only Lancaster still flying in Europe belongs to the Battle of Britain Memorial Flight, a unit of the Royal Air Force based at Coningsby in Lincolnshire. Today the BBMF has one of the world's best-known collections of historic aircraft, maintaining in airworthy condition five Spitfires, two Hurricanes, a Dakota, two Chipmunks and the Lancaster. It was formed in 1973 from the RAF's Historic Aircraft Flight which began life at Biggin Hill, Kent in 1957.

The only full-time serving RAF officer is the Commanding Officer, currently Squadron Leader Al Pinner, MBE, BSc. All other aircrew are volunteers from other flying duties, supported by four administrative staff and 25 full-time ground crew personnel.

The Flight receives far more requests than it can handle, but in 2008 it was tasked with 944 independent appearances at 529 separate events which included 127 air displays and 402 fly-pasts at venues in the UK, Northern Europe, Berlin and Poland. Its arcraft appeared before more than seven million people! For that audience the sight and sound of its historic machines is a tangible demonstration of the nation's respect and gratitude to those who designed, built, flew and maintained these aircraft during the Second World War. It enables them to pay their tribute to all those who died in the service of their country in the air.

Lancaster PA474 is one of only two airworthy Lancasters left in the world out of the 7,377 built; the other is in Canada. Built at Vickers Armstrong's works in Chester in 1945, PA474 was assigned to photgraphic duties with 82 Squadron in East Africa for several months.

After a period with Sir Alan Cobham's Flight Refuelling company at Tarrant Eushton, Dorset, as an experimental tanker aircraft refuelling Meteor jets, it was later used for trials of the Handley Page Laminar Flow Wing which was mounted vertically on the rear upper fuselage.

In 1964 it was taken over by the RAF Historical Branch for display at the RAF Museum, Hendon, London and was featured in two major films, *Crossbow* and *The Guns of Navarone*. In 1965, 44 Squadron (the first to get Lancasters in 1942) asked to have it at its base at RAF Waddington in Lincolnshire. Restoration work was begun and continued for several years until, being structurally sound and in flying condition, it was transferred to the Battle of Britain Memorial Flight at Coningsby in November 1973.

Every year since then it has been a major attraction at hundreds of air shows and flypasts all over the UK and Europe. Usually restricted to about 100 flying hours per year, it receives the most detailed servicing and maintenance and during the winter of 2006/7 it underwent a major overhaul during which it was completely taken to pieces with every part being meticulously examined and replaced if necessary. When it was returned for service it was pronounced good for another 50 years !

At present the BBMF Lancaster carries two wartime Squadron markings – on the port side it is EE 139 and HR-W, an aircraft which flew 30 operations with 100 Squadron; and on the starboard side it is PA 474 and BQ-B which flew 91 operations with 550 Squadron.

The BBMF, and in particular the Lancaster, is supported by the Lincolnshire Lancaster Society, a registered charity formed in 1973 and now with more than 5,000 members worldwide. The Society has provided generous and practical support over the years with equipment and items for that aircraft and the other machines of the Flight.

The BBMF attracts thousands of visitors annually to its base at RAF Coningsby where experienced guides offer conducted tours of the hangar in which these historic aircraft are housed.

The other airworthy Lancaster is operated by Canadian Warplane Heritage, a Canadian-built Lancaster X. It carries the number KB726, from 419 RCAF Squadron, the colours of the Lancaster VR-A in which Andrew Mynarski won his VC and which was shot down near Cambrai, France on 12 June 1944.

Originally it was FM213, part of a batch of 130 Lancaster Xs produced by Victory Aircraft Ltd, Malton, Ontario, Canada, most of which were shipped to Britain between March and May 1945. Some of these served with RCAF squadrons, and most were flown back in August 1945. FM213 was stored in Canada, then modified to Mark 10MR (Maritime Reconnaissance), serving with 107 Rescue Unit, RCAF. It was returned to storage around1958 and SOC in 1964 before being rescued by Canadian Warplane Heritage.

There is a fully-restored, but not air-worthy Lancaster R5868 code PO-S, in 467 Squadron RAAF colours at the RAF Museum in Hendon, North London. It is actually one of the most distinguished of all Lancasters, in that it flew 137 operations against some of the toughest targets in Germany... and survived. It is on Static Display (SD).

Built by Metropolitan Vickers at Trafford Park, Manchester, Lancaster R5868 was passed ready for service and joined 83 Squadron at RAF Scampton, Lincs on 29 June 1942.

The first 68 operations were with 83 Squadron, RAF as OL-Q (known as 'Q-Queenie'), between June 1942 and September 1943, including 51 as a Pathfinder. The next 69 ops were with 467 Squadron, RAAF as PO-S ('S-Sugar'), between September 1943 and April 1945. That was a total of over 800 hours operational flying in 34 months in Squadron service.

It was involved in all the major battles of Bomber Command over Germany and its targets included Berlin (9 attacks), the Ruhr industrial region (21), Cologne, Frankfurt, Hamburg, Munich, Leipzig, Stuttgart, Danzig, Wilhelmshaven, targets in Czechoslovakia and the Italian cities of Genoa, Milan and Turin (five return visits over the Alps in November 1942). In total, R5868 dropped more than 500 tons of bombs.

As S-Sugar it had its adventures, surviving frequent flak damage, a collision over Berlin with another Lancaster (both returned safely) and a fight over Belgium in May 1944 on its 100th sortie, which lasted over 10 very long minutes and ranged from 16,000ft (4,876m) to 9000ft (2,743m) before the two Junkers 88 night-fighters were driven off.

After the war it became the gate guardian at RAF Scampton where it had started its wartime career. Following a major refurbishment it moved to the RAF Museum on 12 March 1972 where it stands today, a reminder to present generations of the achievements and sacrifices of RAF Bomber Command in the Second World War.

The Royal Air Force Museum is situated on the former RAF aerodrome at Hendon, North London. It is open daily and admission is free. Four Lancasters are known to be currently undergoing restoration, although not necessarily to flying condition. Three are in Canada, one is in France.

Lancaster V.VII (NX664) is being restored by Ailes Anciennes, in Le Bourget, formerly Paris's premier airport where Charles Lindbergh landed in 1927 after his non-stop flight from New York.

Lancaster B.X FM104 Toronto Aerospace Museum, Toronto, Canada. Used to be displayed at the Canadian National Exhibition grounds in Toronto, but has been moved to the site of the Toronto Aerospace Museum.

Lancaster B.X FM 136 Calgary Aerospace Museum, Alberta, Canada.

Lancaster B.X FM159 Lancaster Society Museum, Nanton, Alberta, Canada. After years of exposure to the weather, it was re-sited at a dedicated display building in 1992 thanks to fund-raising efforts by the Nanton Lancaster Society.

Other Lancaster survivors or bits of survivors:

Lancaster B.1. W4964 – Newark Air Museum, UK – Fuselage only.

Lancaster B.1 W4783 – Australian War Museum, Canberra, Australia (SD)

Lancaster B.1. DV372 – Imperial War Museum, London – nose section.

Lancaster B.VII NX622 – Aviation Heritage Museum, Perth, Australia. (SD)

Lancaster B.VII NC665 – Museum of Trans & Tech, Auckland, NZ (SD)

Lancaster B.X FM212 – City of Windsor, Ontario, Canada (SD)

Lancaster B.X KB839 – Canadian Forces Base, Greenwood, Canada (SD)

Lancaster B.X KB882 – St Jacques Airport, Edmonton, Canada (SD)

Lancaster B.X KB889 – Imperial War Museum, Duxford, UK (SD).

Lancaster B.X KB944 – National Aviation Museum, Rockcliffe, Canada (SD)

Lancaster B.X KB976 – Weeks Air Museum, Florida, USA (stored)

Colin Hudson from Aces High in Wendover sells memorabilia about wartime aviation:

> 'The Lancaster is in the top three icons, which are the Spitfire, the Lancaster and the Me-109. I think the Lancaster's major attraction is from films like *The Dambusters*. We sell more pictures on that subject than absolutely anything else, even more so than the Battle of Britain. I think people like the romance of the whole event. It was such an historic time. There were hundreds, thousands of raids made by Bomber Command, but the Dams Raid is the one everyone seems to know about. Anything with the 617 theme is popular.'

Just Jane

Lancaster B.VII NX611 is based at the Lincolnshire Aviation Heritage Centre, East Kirkby. Now called *Just Jane*, it is owned by two farmers, Fred and Harold Panton, and they acquired it after a story worthy of the mythical 'Wandering Jew.'

Built in Longbridge near Birmingham by Austin Motors in April 1945, and registered NX611, it was destined for *Tiger Force* against the Japanese. But when the second atomic bomb ended that war in August, NX611 was sent for storage to the RAF Maintenance Unit at Llandow in Wales. In 1952, NX611 was one of a number of Lancasters sold to the French Government for Maritime Reconnaissance, working for 10 years as a L'Aeronavale aircraft from Lann-Bihoue in Brittany and Agadir in Morocco.

NX611 had a major overhaul in 1962 and was then sent on a 23-day journey over 60 flying hours to New Caledonia, a French island a thousand miles east of Australia. There she did Air/Sea Rescue patrols over the Pacific. By 1964 NX611 was proving expensive to service and run, and was given – free – to HAPS (Historic Aircraft Preservation Society) by the French, so long as HAPS picked it up from either New Zealand or Australia. After arriving at Bankstown Airport near Sydney in August 1964, and a major overhaul, NX611 set off on ANZAC Day, 25 April 1965, to fly 12,000 miles home again.

NX611 appeared in displays and exhibitions until 1972, but by then was very expensive to keep airworthy. She was sent for auction in April 1972 looking, according to Fred Panton, 'desolate, weather-damaged and like an unwanted orphan.' He was unable to buy her, failing to meet her reserve price.

After a difficult period, including 10 years as 'gate guardian' at RAF Scampton – from where Gibson had led his Lancasters out on the Dams Raid – the tenacious Panton Brothers finally acquired NX611. She was dismantled and, over a period of 13 weeks, brought in pieces to East Kirkby to be reassembled, 16 years after Fred Panton had first cast eyes on her.

Just Jane is not airworthy, it would cost millions of pounds for her to pass airworthiness tests, but she does taxiing runs and is the centre of a thriving museum dedicated to the Lancaster's role in World War Two.

The Pantons were inspired to buy 'Just Jane' because they had lost their uncle, Chris Panton, a 19-year-old flight engineer in 419 Squadron, RCAF flying in a Lancaster crew including 5 Canadians and an American. Chris died on Bomber Command's worst night, 30 March 1944, in the notorious attack on Nuremburg in which 95 RAF bombers were lost of the 795 sent on the attack. Three of his fellow crew members got out in time before Chris's aircraft blew up. He had five ops left to complete his tour.

But this is not the way to end the story of the greatest RAF bomber of the Second World War. The Lancaster should not be thought of nowadays as simply a charity case, something to be rescued after years deteriorating on the scrap heap. In her prime she could do anything required of a heavy bomber, the unique sound of her Merlin engines providing reassurance for her crew in the way that no other aircraft could. Hundreds of surviving Lancaster aircrew would say they would rather be in a Lancaster than any other aircraft. This was especially so for me as a young bomber pilot on 25 January 1945, over Bergen...

CHAPTER TWENTY-THREE

The Bergen Incident (continued)

12 January 1945

We were on our own, just the four of us, missing our wireless operator Alan Tittle, our mid-upper gunner Leslie Smith – just along for the ride – and our rear gunner Ted Wass. We knew they had taken to their parachutes when M-Mike had been shot half to pieces, but not what had happened to them or if they had survived. With me was navigator Jack Harrison, flight engineer Taffy Phillips, and bomb-aimer Frank Chance. We were separated from the surviving aircraft of 617 and 9 Squadrons, heading into the prevailing westerly wind and facing up to two hours' flying.

I remember asking the others to keep an eye on the fin, rudder and elevator which was flapping constantly on the port side. If they had said, 'It's had it, Skipper,' what could I have done?

The big hole in the port fin made us concerned in case it broke off. If it had, we would have gone straight into the sea. It is odd that you don't think of abandoning an aircraft if it has even the least possible chance of staying in the air. If anything had gone wrong we would not have had time to get out, because the other three were all up front with me, and it is one of the characteristics of the Lancaster that there's a bit of an obstacle getting to the back of the aircraft and the open door there. The bomb aimer's compartment had a hatch up front which could be jettisoned, and that's how he was to get out, if it came to it. The rest of us would be expected to follow him. If the aircraft had gone out of control, which is what the threat was, we would have had great difficulty.

I remember Jack saying at one time, 'It's going to take us another hour before we get there.' One lives minute-to-minute in such situations. None of us had any illusions about what could go wrong. We were in it together.

I brooded about those Polish fighter pilots in Mustangs who were assigned to us as protection, and wondered if they would face a reprimand. They had turned up but spent their time shooting at the flak positions down below rather than

the German fighters around us. I don't know if they got into combat with the
Focke-Wulfs.

It was a great relief to me that training just took over after we were damaged.
I didn't say, 'Oh, Christ, let's get out of here.' I was correct in telling my crew to
stand-by to abandon the aircraft, because if that fire in the wing had really got
going we would have had to get out – the wing would have come off. We were very
lucky that did not happen. I had automatically gone through the drills with my
young flight engineer, Desmond Phillips, and they worked, and we then worked
on stabilising the controls, and just flew it. It may sound rather routine, but it
really was.

If we had delayed in any way going through the fire drill it would not have
worked. I think we did it so quickly and automatically, because we were well-
trained. I had been a flying instructor, I knew my drills, I knew how important
they were. Dinghy drills give you something to do when you were not on operations. You're told to go out to that heap of an aeroplane out there and practice
your dinghy drills. We had to know, automatically, the routine of abandoning an
aircraft, especially if you were destined to put it in the sea. Each member of the
crew had a position to take up for ditching, knew exactly which exit he would
take, and each crew member knew he had to take something with him, like the
dinghy radio.

Some crews may have sauntered out and gone through the motions, but I
didn't. I was serious about it. I thought, if this happens on a filthy January night
in the middle of the North Sea, we are organised and trained and do it, and we
might survive. If you were not prepared, you had no chance. Being an instructor
had been very good for me. I know I was training others, but that was when I
really learned to fly.

After what seemed an age we raised Sumburgh on the radio, told them our condition and checked to add up all the damage that would affect our landing.

We discovered that the hydraulics had gone, also shot away, so while we could
blow the undercarriage down, once we did that it was locked down. That obviously would affect the flying performance, an added factor affecting the damaged
tail, so we did not want to do it too early.

You cannot measure 340 individual miles over the featureless sea, you can
only endure it. The relief at seeing the misty islands of Shetland appearing on the
horizon was palpable. We headed for the south end, still apprehensive, still looking
at the burnt-out port inner engine and the tatty wing and wondering how much
structural damage the Focke-Wulf's cannon shells had done.

I do not remember being fearful. I think in some way, though we were very
young, we were professionals. Aviation was our business; a bomber was our

business; we had flown a lot of hours together on Lancasters. As we knew to our cost, losing friends on previous attacks, we could get the chop as easily as anyone else. It had always been my opinion that it didn't matter whether you were on your second tour, twentieth trip, or first trip, you could be knocked down by a fighter.

But if you were in a situation where you had the opportunity, through experience and flying skills, to try to make it back, that was where your experience really counted.

As long as M-Mike was in the air, we felt she was okay. We kept on flying. I don't remember discussing anything about our fears. We went through whatever it took to get from Bergen to the Shetlands.

The runways at Sumburgh appeared. Not noted for their great length, this was not an operational airfield for bombers, just for aircraft like ours that had no other choice. The longest, on 33/15, was about 1,500 yards (1,371m).

I took the aircraft into the left-hand circuit for 33 and lined up for finals, undercarriage locked down, just minutes from what I hoped was safety.

Suddenly a Spitfire cut in front of us! Its propeller was stationary. Dead stick! The control tower told me to go around again.

Obviously the Spitfire had priority. I think our language may have got fruity. We had to nurse the stricken Lancaster gingerly into a long slow go-around circuit, careful not to put any added strain on to the damaged wing. We knew we were steering into our own dead engine, but a left-hand circuit was what the rules demanded, as well as being the natural thing to do.

We were all quite detached by then. Either we were going to make it, or we weren't.

I lined up again on long finals. The Spitfire had got down safely and been pushed straight off the runway. I had a clear run in and I did not want to go around a third time. M-Mike behaved beautifully, landed and ran off the runway to the left; one tyre shot through, a natural consequence of being housed underneath the shot-up inner port engine.

We got out.

It was about then that we started to shake a bit.

Within a couple of minutes an official RAF photographer captured us in black and white, next to the tattered port fin. I looked at the damage. It was considered Category E, not-repairable. As far as I know, M-Mike stayed there.

I know we never got it back.

Flight Lieutenant Ray Harris's 'Willing Winnie', in the same situation as I was, was attacked no less than 15 times, suffering severe damage. With the hydraulics out and the trim tab controls shot out, it took two men to pull it out of the final dive that had turned the German fighters away. Harris and his crew eventually managed to nurse their stricken Lancaster back across the unforgiving North Sea to make an excellent wheels-down landing at their base. It never flew another operational mission again, but it is a testimony to the Lancaster's toughness that it was repaired and served with 103 and 57 Squadrons before being finally broken up two years after the war.

Shortly after we landed, a Dakota touched down, which we discovered was bringing a concert party to Sumburgh. We went to the concert that evening, and in the Officer's Mess beforehand I met some of the performers who asked me where I was from.

I said, 'York.'

Someone said, 'Who's here from York?' It turned out that the conjurer was, and he knew my father! I said, 'When you go back, if you see him, please tell him I'm all right.' To meet a conjurer on the Shetland Islands, from my home town, who knew my father… now there is some luck.

I did later learn that Ted Wass finished up in the snow on the side of a mountain, and was soon captured by the Germans and taken to Oslo. He met Tittle a day later, also captured, and subsequently we found that Leslie Smith had survived and was also a prisoner of war. They survived the war.

'Commanding Officer's citation: SQUADRON LEADER T.C. IVESON

'Squadron leader Iveson has completed one tour of operations as a fighter pilot, and 18 sorties of his second tour as a heavy bomber captain. He has attacked Brest, Lorient, Le Pallice and Kembs Barrage. He has taken part in three attacks against the 'Tirpitz' including the one resulting in the sinking of the Battleship. On 12th January 1945, this officer was detailed to attack the U-Boat pens at Bergen in Norway. Whilst over the target area, his aircraft was attacked by two FW190s. The first burst of fire from the enemy aircraft struck the tail plane, rudder and elevator. At the same time, the port inner engine was set on fire, and the rear turret put out of action. Although not ordered to do so, the wireless operator and both gunners baled out, and the aircraft was defenceless when the next attack materialised. When the fighters eventually broke off their attack, the flak defences engaged the crippled machine. The aircraft by this time had become so tail-heavy as a result of damage that it was physically impossible to maintain level flight. S/Ldr Iveson therefore ordered his flight engineer to tie the central column in such a way as to ease the strain. Under these very trying conditions, Squadron Leader Iveson made a successful landing in the Shetland Isles.

'This officer has always displayed the highest standard of devotion to duty. On this particular sortie his courage and resolution in an emergency undoubtedly resulted in the safe return of his aircraft.

'I recommend him for the immediate award of the Distinguished Flying Cross.'

My favourite Lancaster, F-Fox came up next day, flown by Arthur Keller, the Australian, and took us back to Woodhall. He wouldn't let me fly it, so I just sat there and we got back safely. I had been de-briefed in Sumburgh. That was my only night on Shetland. I never went back.

It turned out to be my last flight with 617. Not long after that that I was posted to RAF Ossington, where they were training Lancaster pilots to be airline pilots and that was my career for a while. It may have saved my life. At the time I did not see it as a favour, but there was a different atmosphere in 617 now that Willie Tait had gone and a few others such as Bobby Knights and Paddy Gingles also left around the same time as myself.

I felt that, at last there was a horizon. I could see the end of the war and a young man's life still ahead of me. I was still only 25 years old.

And what of F-Fox, my faithful Lancaster ME554?

When I left the squadron, I gave it to Bob Horsley and he and it survived the war. My younger brother Peter was the last known person to see it when he spotted it in what he described as a 'graveyard of Lancasters.'

Peter Iveson:

'It was 1946, I was 18 years old in June that year, and in July I had joined the 30th Infantry Leader Training Battalion, an Officer Cadet School, stationed at Elgin in Scotland.

'We went on a route march over Morayshire one hot afternoon, on the route through to Lossiemouth. I was on the left of the column, and we were being shouted at by a tough sergeant named McGawin. We came across a graveyard of Lancasters, dozens and dozens of them, standing around waiting to be broken up. Still facing the front and marching, but with my eye on the Lancasters, I suddenly recognised one of them, not by its code KC-F Fox on the side, but because it had a distinctive work of art below the cockpit on the pilot side. It featured Captain ReillyFoul, a cartoon character from the Daily Mirror.

Captain ReillyFoul was a wicked squire-type bloke with a soft hat, a moustache and a monocle. He had a servant called Jake, who wore a horizontally striped jersey, such as in those days criminals were supposed to wear. On one side of the panel – the side depicting bombing trips – Jake was holding a bomb in his arms like a baby, and Captain ReillyFoul was looking at him (his favourite expression was Stap Me!), a cheroot in his mouth. Jake was saying 'Now?'

Like all the Lancasters ever built, F-Fox had cost the country £58,974. Now its scrap value was £250. S.O.C. 15-1-47.

Peter Iveson again:

'I couldn't help it....That's my brother's Lancaster! See, there! Sergeant McGavin was not impressed. "'Keep f*****g marching!" he bellowed.'

Sergeant McGavin could have been speaking for the whole new post-war world.

You can't believe how young
We were back then;
One thing's for sure, we'll never be
That young again;
We were daring young men
With hearts of gold,
And most of us never got old.

John Gray
'Billy Bishop Goes To War'

The Avro Lancaster

Type: Heavy bomber
Power plant: four 1,640 hp Rolls Royce Merlin 24
Performance: Max speed at sea level 245mph (374kph)
Maximum range: 2,530 miles (4,070kms)
Service ceiling: 22,000ft (6,706m)
Empty weight: 37,000lbs (16,780kgs)
Normal weight: 65,000lbs (29,480 kgs)

Dimensions:
Wing span: 102ft (31.09m)
Length: 69ft 6in (21.18m)
Height: 20ft (6.10m)
Wing area: 1,297sq ft (120.49 sq mtrs)

Armament:
Two .303 calibre Browning machines guns each in nose and dorsal turrets
Four .303 calibre Browning machine guns in tail turret.
Max bomb load: 18,000lbs (8,165kgs)

Crew: 7

In service: Great Britain, Australia, Canada.

Variants (with number built):

Prototype: Manchester III with1,130hp Merlin X engines (2)

Lancaster 1: Avro-built, with 243 completed under Manchester contract (896)
Lancaster 1: Metropolitan-Vickers-built, with 57 completed under Manchester contract (944)
Lancaster 1: Vickers-Armstrong-built (535)
Lancaster 1: Austin Motors-built (150)
Lancaster 1: Armstrong-Whitworth-built (919)

Lancaster B1 (special): Converted Mark 1s; extended bomb bay (without doors) to carry 22,000lb (9,979 kg) Grand Slam bomb (33).

Lancaster 1 (Far East): Tropicalised, intended for Far Eastern service.
Lancaster PR1: Post-War conversions for photographic reconnaissance duties.

Lancaster Mark II prototypes: improved Mark 1; Bristol Hercules XI or XVI (2)
Lancaster II production model: Armstrong-Whitworth built (300).

Lancaster Mark III: Prototype, converted Mark 1, Packard-built Merlin engines (2)
Lancaster III: Major production model; Avro-built (2,774).
Lancaster III: Metropolitan-Vickers-built (136)
Lancaster III: Armstrong-Whitworth-built (110)

Lancaster Mark IV: Renamed Lincoln 1 before first flight

Lancaster Mark V: Renamed Lincoln II before first flight

Lancaster Mark VI: Converted Mark 1 (2) and Mark II (7) airframes with Merlin 85s and 87s (9)

Lancaster Mark VII: Austin Motors-built, Martin dorsal turret; final production model (180)

Lancaster Mark X: Canadian production of basic Mark III by Victory Aircraft Ltd (430)

Total production: 7,378

Bibliography

Allen, Warner – *Lucy Houston DBE*

Brickhill, Paul – *The Dambusters*

Brown, Capt Eric 'Winkle' – *Wings on my Sleeve*

Catford, Jack – *View from a Birdcage*

Clark, Alan – *The Donkeys*

Clegg, Peter – *Avro Test-Pilots since 1907*

Cooper, Alan W – *Beyond the Dams to Tirpitz*

Corrigan, Gordon – *Mud, Blood and Poppycock*

Cruddas, Colin – *In Cobham's Company*

Darlow, Steve – *Five of the Many*

Flower, Stephen – *A Hell of a Bomb*

Glancey, Jonathan – *Spitfire, The Biography*

Gunston, Bill – *Chronicle of Aviation*

Hastings, Max – *Bomber Command*

Holmes, Harry – *Avro Lancaster, Combat Legend*

Mason, Francis K – *Aircraft of World War II*

Mason, Francis K – *The Avro Lancaster*

Overy, Richard – *Bomber Command 1939-45*

Probert, Henry – *Bomber Harris, His Life and Times*

Raymond, Robert S – *A Yank in Bomber Command*

Richards, Denis – *The Hardest Victory*

Sweetman, John – *Tirpitz, Hunting the Beast*

Taylor, Frederick – *Dresden*

Toliver, Raymond F – *Fighter Aces of the Luftwaffe*

Turner, John Frayn – *VCs of the Air*

Walton, Jenny – *Just Jane, Two Farmers & a Lancaster*

Weal, Elke – *Combat Aircraft of World War II*

Wells, Mark K – *Courage and Air Warfare*

White, Stanley (Exec Ed) – *The Means of Victory*

Wood, DC – *Avro Lancaster 50th Anniversary*

Index

Picture Credits

All photographs are reproduced courtesy of the RAF Museum apart from Tony Iveson (the author's own photograph); A V Roe, courtesy of Eric Verdon Roe; the Battle of Britain Memorial Flight over Buckingham Palace courtesy of RAF News; Gerald Coulson courtesy of Gerald Coulson; Lancaster preparing for 'Gardening' mission courtesy of Popperfoto/Getty Images; 44 Squadron Lancasters in flight courtesy of the Imperial War Museum; Loading the 'cookie' courtesy of Hulton Archive/Getty Images.

The cutaway drawing of the Lancaster on pp.2-3 is reproduced courtesy of *The Aeroplane*.